THE CHANCES OF DEATH

Pip

THE CHANCES OF DEATH

A Diary of
the Spanish Civil War

———

PRISCILLA SCOTT-ELLIS

Edited by Raymond Carr

Today the deliberate increase in the chances of death,
The conscious acceptance of guilt in the necessary murder . . .

W. H. AUDEN 'Spain 1937'

MICHAEL RUSSELL

First published in Great Britain 1995
by Michael Russell (Publishing) Ltd
Wilby Hall, Wilby, Norwich NR16 2SP

Typeset in Sabon by The Typesetting Bureau
Allen House, East Borough, Wimborne, Dorset
Printed and bound in Great Britain
by Biddles Ltd, Guildford and King's Lynn

Contents

Foreword

My sister, Esyllt Priscilla Scott-Ellis, was born on 15 November 1916. She claimed that she was born during an air raid on London, more to explain a liking for drama and excitement than from any basis in fact so far as I know. At the time of her birth the family consisted of a twin brother and sister, John and Bronwen, born in 1912, and another sister, Elizabeth (sometimes referred to in the family as Ebits), born whilst our father was fighting in France. He was the 8th Lord Howard de Walden and Seaford, the first title being one which descends through the female line. He often used to say he was not only descended from a line of heiresses, but even his racehorses constantly produced fillies. My own advent in June 1919, and finally that of Rosemary in 1922, proved the point.

For the first few years of her life my sister used her Welsh name of Esyllt, but as this was constantly turned into Ethel she changed very early to Priscilla, and soon became, and remained to the end of her life, universally known to her friends of all ages and nationalities as Pip.

She was a very pretty little girl with golden curls and blue eyes, and bitterly resented the disappearance of the curls and her entry into the comparative drabness of schoolroom life. Our homes were Seaford House, Belgrave Square, now the Royal College of Defence Studies, which my father had taken on a long lease when he inherited, and Chirk Castle in North Wales, leased from the Myddelton family not long before he and my mother became engaged. My mother was born Margherita (always called Margot) Van Raalte and lived with her brother and sister on Brownsea Island in Poole Harbour. Her parents had become friendly with the Infante Alfonso d'Orleans Bourbon, a first cousin of the King of Spain, and his family, and Prince Ali, as we called him, became a great and lasting personal friend. After his marriage to Princess Beatrice (Princess Bee) and the birth of his three sons, Alvaro, Alonso and Ataulfo, the whole family stayed frequently at Brownsea, and we spent many summer holidays staying with them. After the abdication of the King of Spain in 1931 they came to England and lived there much of the time; and Pip, who came out in 1934, became close friends with Alonso and Ataulfo. When the Spanish Civil War broke out, the family returned to Spain and Prince Ali and all three of the sons flew. Alonso was killed in 1936, and Pip, having become bored with the London season, determined to go out to Spain as a nurse. Our parents insisted she should first learn Spanish as well as some basic nursing, so she did a first aid course and a charming bilingual girl, Evelina Calvert, was found to teach her Spanish. Ours was a completely non-political family; Pip's views were a simple expression of support for her friends, and therefore pro-monarchy and anti-Communist. Prince Ali told our mother they had absolute proof that a Communist take-over was imminent.

As to Pip's character, and the reasons for her taking such an adventurous course in life, I am struck by how little likely such a course would have seemed. As children we went to day school in London at first, then when we were nine and seven began to live almost entirely at Chirk, with two governesses at a time to teach us. There we lived to a large extent a highly imaginative life of make-believe, involving roles as knights and fairies and dragons, largely inspired by Elizabeth, and helped by the fact that we lived in an old castle full of armour and ghosts and could ride all over the countryside on our ponies, subject only to enforced subjection to giants in the form of governesses. Pip was always a participant in these games, but gave a somewhat mundane turn to them by describing in endless detail what she was wearing, her horse etc. I think she was by nature more of a practical person, resembling her mother in many ways. Our mother had run a hospital in Egypt in the First World War with her friend Mary Herbert. Curiously enough, Mary Herbert's daughter Gabriel was the only other English girl to go and nurse in Spain on the Franco side. Although we saw quite a lot of each other as children, Gabriel was several years older than Pip and they knew each other only slightly. Possibly both were inspired by their mothers' example.

When our sisters grew up, Pip's wish to go to boarding school was granted and she and I went to Benenden when we were fifteen and twelve. She only stayed a year or so, but greatly enjoyed it. She then went to a finishing school in Paris, full of English and American girls, so that although we had been brought up with a French maid and a French governess, and spoke a sort of Franglais, she appeared on her return to know less rather than more French. She then went to stay with the Harrach family in Munich, whose daughter Nucci subsequently married our brother. Here too she seemed to learn little German. Yet when she wanted to learn, her excellent musical ear stood her in good stead: she became virtually trilingual in English, French and Spanish, and learned fluent Polish as well as being able to manage adequately in Portuguese, Italian and Russian.

Pip, as a child, had a frightening riding accident, being dragged quite a distance in Rotten Row with her foot jammed in a stirrup. This made her nervous for a while. She also had the disadvantage of a very bad circulation that could make her turn blue with cold. Yet she grew up to become an extremely brave horsewoman, and to show courage in all sorts of difficult and dangerous situations. When she was about thirteen we had a governess much given to casting horoscopes, who foretold our futures. Bronwen was to marry a Scot, which she did, Elizabeth a Russian, which she did, I was to be a widow with a double-barrelled name, which I did indeed become, but Pip was to marry a foxhunting squire who would become an MP, while she wore toothpaste pink and furs and opened bazaars. I have often thought that had her life taken a very slightly different turn she might have been happy at least for a while, leading an intensely energetic country life with perhaps intervals of skiing and beach life in the south of France.

When Pip was ten, my father, who had farms in Kenya and went out there every year, took her with him. She was thought to be big enough not to be taken by a leopard, and was I suppose safe enough, though she described the terror of the walk in the dark to the outside loo at night. Later on he took her on sailing holidays and to America with John and to the West Indies with me. She remained a great traveller all her life till the last few years.

When the diary ends and she returned to England, Pip told me years later how completely lost she felt. I suppose it must have been rather like returning from France in the First World War. Life continued exactly as before, nobody was much interested in Spain. We had always been very close and confidential, but I had become engaged and seemed to have grown up and away from her. It was most reluctantly that she edited the diary, which was accepted for publication. She was not much of a reader or interested in writing, and the editing was merely to ensure that nothing was said about Prince Ali and Princess Bee and their family that could in any way embarrass them. When war broke out in September 1939 the publishers naturally withdrew, and the diary was put away. Pip told me towards the end of her life that for many years she could not bear to look at it, though shortly before she died she had agreed to go through it with me.

I think she was glad to return to war and nursing in 1939. She joined the Hatfield/Spears ambulance outfit and went to France, escaping through Bordeaux when France fell. The ship in which she returned to England carried a great many Polish soldiers who were going to Scotland and who told her they had no hospital. I do not know the details of how she managed it, but she did in fact set up and run a hospital for Poles in Scotland, becoming a colonel in the Polish Army and learning fluent Polish. At this point her bad circulation, which made life a misery in the Scottish winters, was diagnosed as Raynaud's disease, and she was told she must live in a warm climate. She therefore left the hospital and obtained a job at the Consulate in Barcelona. Whatever this might or might not have led to, she met, almost immediately, José Luis de Vilallonga, the dazzlingly good-looking and attractive son of the Marques de Castellvell, whose home was on the outskirts of Barcelona. Their romance caused enough talk to concern Princess Bea and Prince Ali who swept Pip once again under their wing, insisting on a strict Spanish-style engagement whereby the couple were never to meet alone again until their marriage at Sanlucar de Barrameda in 1945.

None of Pip's family could travel to Spain at that time, and Pip eventually arrived in England, heavily pregnant, on the way to start a new life in Argentina. The honeymoon was spent in Portugal, where Pip relied, not for the first or last time, on a system she had been shown for roulette. On this occasion the system failed and resulted in her pawning her evening dresses to get to England. Our father at that time owned a small shipping line – the South America Saint Line – and he was able to arrange their passage and ensure that a nurse and a doctor (though I believe he was a specialist in some quite other branch and had not dealt with a birth since his student days) were fellow passengers. My own daughter was fairly newborn, and I remember the confidence with which Pip inquired for a detail or two to enable her to manage the whole thing herself if necessary. In fact her son was born with very great difficulty and some danger before the ship reached the Canary Islands.

At that time no money could be sent out of England until one had established oneself as a British resident abroad. Pip had very little money, and José Luis, whose family were not pleased by his marriage, had none either, so that their survival in the Argentine was extremely difficult. Pip ran a dress shop and they both had a riding school, but debts mounted and the marriage suffered considerable strain. Their daughter, Susanna Carmen, was born in the Argentine and they managed somehow for another two or three years; then the children came home to stay with me while Pip and her husband established themselves in Paris.

For several years Paris remained their base, but eventually a villa with a bit of land and two workmen's cottages knocked into one were acquired at Auribeau, near Cannes. José Luis became a successful novelist and actor, Pip moved between England and France. The children were at school in England to begin with, spending their holidays sometimes with us in Somerset, sometimes in fairly glamorous surroundings such as Schloss Mittersil or St Moritz. Their father's life was sufficiently irregular for Pip to keep them out of the way and as they grew up they took over the cottage at Auribeau. Eventually José Luis separated from Pip, and her money having almost completely run out, she returned to live in England. During these years she had often been extremely unhappy and the very close, confidential relationship we had as sisters, which had lapsed slightly during our separation in the war, was resumed.

With characteristic courage Pip set about earning her living with few paper qualifications, imperfect health and about enough money to keep herself and the children for a year. She worked at the Inland Revenue for a while, then in the British Tourist Office in St James's, where she was in charge of a number of employees. Her lack of paper qualifications prevented her rising there, so she became a courier, escorting parties of National Trust members. Although this was not very financially rewarding, she was a brilliant success. Her languages, practical gifts, and liking for all kinds of people proved exactly what was needed. Eventually she went further afield, taking a party to India, where nothing but her strength and determination got some of the passengers home safely in spite of heart attacks. On a visit to

Russia the Intourist guide fell ill, and she was able to carry on where I think few people would have managed. She took two further tours to the Seychelles and all round South America before deciding that it was becoming too exhausting and that, with the children now grown up, she would start a new life in a better climate. During her London years she had been living in a houseboat on the Thames off Cheyne Walk, Chelsea, and this became a centre of fun to many people of all ages, including a gifted young singer, Ian Hanson.

Ian went on tour to America and invited Pip to join him out there. She went off, with as usual the highest hopes of starting a business and making a success now that José Luis had turned the separation into a French divorce. After looking round she and Ian finally settled in Los Angeles, and eventually married there. They lived in West Hollywood in half a Spanish-type house, full of all sorts of bits and pieces charmingly arranged. The money Pip had received from the sale of the villa and land would have kept her in reasonable comfort, but that was not her style and she embarked on a characteristically optimistic and disastrous investment involving a tract of land in the hills on the outskirts of Los Angeles, near Topeka Canyon. The land was indeed beautiful, with huge trees and a wonderful view to the Pacific, but it was close to the national park, not zoned for development and there were legal problems about access and water which rapidly led to lawsuits with neighbours. Pip absolutely refused to recognize the obvious difficulties, and would talk with confidence about the house she would build, the money she would make from selling off lots, where her swimming pool or riding stable would be, whilst almost simultaneously admitting that it was far too dangerous to live there with anything less than a retired policemen and guard dogs. Charles Manson and his gang had been caught around this time, and had been based in Topeka. But Pip needed her dream to keep her going. She had always had immense energy and had depended on being able to stay up all night and deal with whatever came along. She did not find it easy to accept old age. Her interests were never intellectual, and although she tried painting and various hobbies, and did her best to promote Ian's musical career, the considerable gap in their ages and her own increasing ill health made the present discouragingly bleak and a dream future increasingly essential.

Pip lived to see Ian give a successful concert in New Mexico and to hope that this was the beginning of a better life. But her health became much worse, and eventually cancer of the lung was diagnosed. Her children were able to visit her, coming from France and New Zealand, and Ian remained devoted, until she died of a long illness in 1983.

Throughout her life Pip gave love, encouragement and friendship to all kinds of people, often those down on their luck. Her own indomitable optimism saw many friends through bad patches in their lives, and until her final illness she continued to work at Sotheby's Los Angeles, despite the fact that, through physical disability, it took her two hours to get up and dressed. On my last visit, when she was obviously desperately ill, she talked of her Spanish diary, and planned for us to go over it together when she was better. She still hoped for a magical renewal of life and to overcome all difficulties and achieve some recognition and success on her own. Our brother would have helped, and did take over once her illness required hospitalization, but she always wanted to do it on her own. She was cremated in Los Angeles and Ian and I brought her ashes back to England and scattered them high in the hills above Chirk, where we had walked and ridden and played all those years ago. Ian survived her by less than two years.

GAENOR HEATHCOAT AMORY

Biographical Note

THE ORLEANS FAMILY

The Infante, Alfonso Maria (b. 1886), commanded approximately half of the Nationalist Air Force. Given his relationship with his cousin King Alfonso XIII he was an enthusiastic monarchist who fell out with Franco on his refusal to restore the monarchy after the Civil War. In 1909 he married **Princess Beatrice of Coburg** (b. 1884 in England). Pip was a devoted admirer of the Infanta whom she usually calls Princess Bee. The Princess ran Frentes y Hospitales, the organization which looked after women and children after towns had been taken by the Nationalist armies.

Prince Alvaro (b. 1910) first joined the Foreign Legion and transferred to the Italian Air Force serving in Spain. He flew Savoia 39s, the three-engined bombers.

Prince Ataulfo joined the German Condor Legion as a navigator. He was trained as an engineer. Pip's closest friend, he is sometimes called 'Touffles' from a childhood nickname.

General Kindelán was commander of the Nationalist Air Force and was mainly responsible for creating Franco head of the Spanish State. Like his friend, the Infante Alfonso, General Kindelán was a committed monarchist who fell out with Franco on his refusal to restore the monarchy. Pip became friends with the Kindelán family.

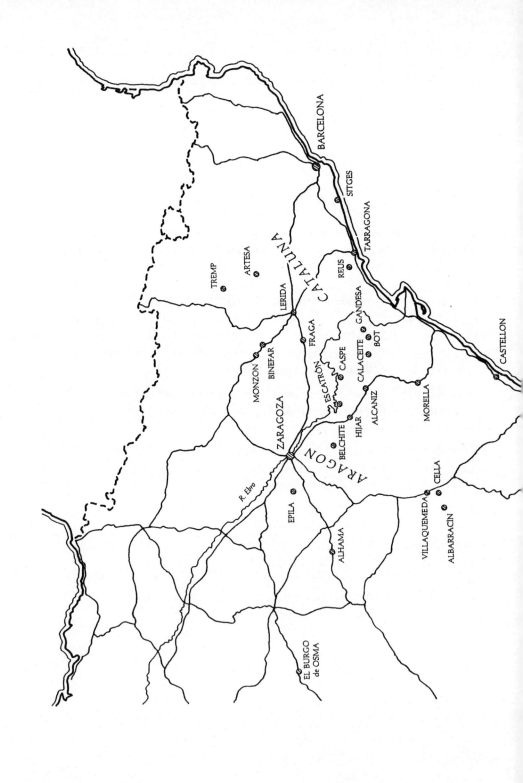

Introduction

On 18 July 1936 a group of Spanish officers rose against the Republican government, the legal government of Spain, formed as a result of the victory of the Popular Front in elections of the preceding February. The Civil War that ensued and which was to last to the spring of 1939 was, as Gerald Brenan wrote, the explosion of a powder magazine that had been slowly accumulating in Spain itself. But it was seen in Europe less as a Spanish affair than as part of the struggle between a triumphant Fascism and a threatened Democracy. The left in general sympathized with the Republic, the right with the Nationalists whose undisputed leader was General Franco.

Whereas many on the left volunteered to serve in Spain, for example in the International Brigades, few conservatives ventured beyond strident vocal support for Franco. Among the few who did volunteer were Peter Kemp, Gabriel Herbert and Priscilla Scott-Ellis, known as Pip. Peter Kemp, who came down from Cambridge with a poor degree and no firm prospects, formed the Carlist Requetés and later transferred to the Foreign Legion.[1] He became a friend of Pip. Gabriel Herbert, whom Pip met briefly in Salamanca, became an ambulance driver. Both had strong convictions. Kemp was a right-wing conservative; Gabriel Herbert a militant Catholic to whom the war was a crusade to save Christian civilization.[2]

Pip had no strong convictions either political or religious. To keep up appearances she attended Mass with her friends, all of whom shared the belief in the war as a crusade against the atheists, masons and Communists of the Republic. Her political convictions were

1 Peter Kemp's account of his time in Spain (*Mine Were of Trouble*, 1957) is essential reading to understand the atmosphere of Nationalist Spain.
2 Her family had been converted by Hilaire Belloc. To the end of her life Gabriel believed the Francoist myth that Guernica had been burned by anarchists rather than bombed by the Condor Legion, the air force unit sent to Franco's Spain by Hitler. She left no account of her experiences except her remarkable poetry (privately printed). Like Pip, she was a brave woman who revelled in danger; she was an intrepid mountaineer.

naïve in the extreme and she swallowed uncritically the Francoist propaganda and shared the monarchist convictions of her friends; the Republicans were 'Reds' and barbarians who used dum dum bullets and burnt churches.

Apart from sharing the political prejudices of her Spanish friends which reinforced her diffuse conviction that the Republicans were bent on destroying the Spanish values she had come to admire, her motives for coming to Spain were personal: a desire to find some purpose in life other than the enjoyment of society; and an insatiable thirst for the excitements of adventure. 'It is really funny', she wrote in February 1938, 'that my two childish passions were Spain and aeroplanes and my ambition to be a surgeon, and here I am in Spain being a surgical nurse.' Most important of all was her friendship with the family of the Infante Alfonso de Orleans, cousin of the deposed king, Alfonso XIII, whose representative in Spain he was to become. She was particularly fond of the Infanta Beatrice (Princess Bee in her diary) and of her son Ataulfo (Touffles in the diary). Ataulfo was a navigator attached to the Condor Legion, the German unit serving with the Nationalist forces. Through Ataulfo and his father she met other aviators – including the Germans of the Condor Legion and the Kindelán family. General Kindelán commanded Franco's air force and his children became her close friends.

When Pip arrived in Spain the war had been going on for just over a year. During that time Franco – Pip describes him as a 'weeny little man' – had been elevated by his fellow generals to supreme power as *generalissimo*, Head of State and head of the government, a concentration of powers enjoyed only by Napoleon.[3] After training as a nurse in Jerez, Pip was sent to an *equipo* (a clearing station) in Aragon. Her first casualties came from the final combats in the Battle of Teruel in January 1938; her heaviest work came with the Aragon offensive that followed in the spring. She convalesced in England during the July and August of 1938 and arrived back in September during the last stages of the Battle of the Ebro which had begun in July and was to end in November. She then followed the Nationalist advance into Catalonia and entered Barcelona with the victors. She

3 General Kindelán had been the orchestrator of Franco's ascent on the assumption that he would install the monarchy after the war. When the Caudillo clung to power, Kindelán broke with him and became his bitterest opponent. Together with the Infante Alfonso, he became the leader of the Spanish monarchists.

ended the war working with the Infanta in Madrid hospitals and canteens.

To follow her progress the diary which she wrote up almost every day – sometimes at great length – has been divided into sections. Each section contains a brief account of the battles which provided her *equipos* with the casualties she cared for.[4]

Apart from its interest as a human document revealing the secret life of a truly extraordinary woman and as a historical document that gives both a picture of life in the Nationalist zone and a vivid, and at times terrifying description of the state of the Nationalist hospital services, the fascination of the diary lies in the contrast between the dirt and squalor of life in the hospitals in which she served, and what she calls 'the other life' that centred round the Infantes and their children and their aristocratic friends. The 'other life' consisted of visits to these friends, often travelling vast distances over awful roads on her leaves to visit them. It was a leisured life spent in comfortable houses with hot water and good food, the time passed in picnics, card games, practical jokes, and gossiping while Ataulfo played the piano. During her exhausting hospital work on the Aragon front she stayed, in her free time, with the Orleans family at Epila, near Zaragoza. In spite of official 'one course meals' she found the restaurants of Zaragoza were crammed, serving large and varied dishes. There were nightclubs, cinemas – showing German, Italian and American films – shopping expeditions, drinks at the Grand Hotel. It was the same in Andalusia, most of which had been easily occupied by the Nationalists in the first months of the war. The normality and abundance (apart from cigarettes) of conditions in the Nationalist zone described in the diaries contrasts with the scarcities in the Republican zone, where the population was living on lentils – 'Dr Negrín's resistance pills'.

Even more striking is the contrast the diaries reveal between life behind the lines in Nationalist Spain and life at the front; strawberries and cream, smart clothes and hot baths in one; semi-starvation, filthy bloodstained uniforms and freezing cold in the other. Pip's resilience astounds. When depressed and ill, she talks of 'all the petty illusions of heroism and justice with which I came to this stinking

4 For a detailed account of the battles, consult Hugh Thomas, *The Spanish Civil War* (Pelican Books, 1968). Raymond Carr, *The Civil War in Spain* (1986) is a more general analysis.

country'. Next day, after twelve hours in the operating theatre, she dances and drinks until the small hours. Next to her car, her gramophone was her most treasured possession.

It was the capacity to bounce back that enabled her to write her diary every night – often by candlelight on a packing case – after an exhausting day in the wards. The diary is over half a million words long. It has been drastically shortened and many accounts of her vivid social life have had to be omitted, interesting though they are as comments on conditions in the Nationalist zone. I have included a few passages on her 'other life' but the main interest of her diaries must lie in the descriptions of her work in the *equipos*, not least of the feuds which made Pip's life a torment. By the end of the war, at the prospect of a European conflict which might force her to choose between loyalty to her Spanish friends and to her country, she was broken in body and – at least temporarily – in spirit.

I

Waiting for Action

*Pip left England with the Infanta Beatrice. On 9 October 1937 she
arrived at Sanlucar de Barrameda where the Orleans family had
their family house which Pip was to visit frequently. She stayed
some of her time with the Duchess of Montemar whose daughter,
Consuelo, was to be her companion and friend throughout her stay
in Spain. They both took a course in nearby Jerez to qualify
as nurses. Although she thoroughly enjoyed the company of the
Andalusian aristocracy, untroubled by the war and plentifully
provided with the good things of life, she soon tired of this
relatively idle existence. On 22 November she writes, 'I do wish I
could hurry up and go to the front. I am tired of waiting and doing
nothing much. I want action.' On 2 November she collected the car
her father had sent her to Gibraltar. It was to make all the difference
to her life, giving her the means to visit the Orleans family during
her periods off duty. She drove hundreds of miles over terrible
roads.*

Monday, 18 October. This morning at 11, I went to the hospital to
start my course. There were about 30 of us there. First of all the
Commandante [*Major*] Huertas made us a speech at the end of which
he said that there was one English girl amongst us, and he hoped
everyone would help me as I did not know much Spanish. All the girls
turned round and stared, and I felt like sinking through the floor
with acute embarrassment and blushed purple. Then we all trooped
off with the doctor who allotted five or six of us to each ward.
My lot stayed with the doctor in the operating theatre to watch the
dressings. It was very interesting and quite horrible. There were five

[5]

Moors to be treated.[1] The first one had a wound in the calf of his leg which had shattered the bone and was so big one could have put both one's fists into it; the second had one in his heel and had to have his heel bone removed, and had a wound about five inches deep that went right in behind the bone; the third was almost cured, but had had his whole arm blown up and only had a semi-paralysed pulpy mess left; the fourth had two awful wounds in his knee where one could see all the veins and everything on one side and the bone of the other; the last was almost cured except for a huge raw patch on his knee and a hole the size of a ping-pong ball in his thigh. It was horrible watching as the wounds were packed with gauze, and as it was pulled out or stuffed in, the poor men, who are incredibly brave, would moan and shout and struggle and sometimes even scream. But how they stood it all I don't know. I did not feel sick at all, but afterwards when I had left the hospital I kept seeing wounds all the time and hearing the screams of agony as they were being dressed. Never having seen a wound before in my life I could hardly believe my eyes when I saw the size of them, and so it is only natural that they should impress themselves on me at first. Also I believe all this is absolutely nothing to what I shall see at the front. When I think of those wounds this morning and how small they are compared to what I will have to see, I almost wish I had stayed at home, but not really as I will get used to it. Consuelo says that one very soon gets quite hardened to it. I understand now why nurses are so often hard and inhuman. They can't be anything else or they could not stand being a nurse. But it is madly interesting.

Tuesday, 19 October. I was at the hospital at 9.30 this morning and went along to my ward. Then we started to do the dressings, and at first I got into an awful muddle with the forceps as it is difficult not to be able to touch anything with one's fingers. Of course we only had to do the very small wounds; they were pretty well healed, but it was very interesting. When they were all done we washed up and tidied everything away, and then went and cut up gauze for some time and got it ready to be sterilized. The doctor told us all about sterilization,

1 Most of the wounded were Moors. i.e. natives of the Spanish Protectorate in Morocco commanded by Spanish officers. They had been brought from Morocco in the autumn of 1936 in the first air-lift in history and later by sea, and played an important role in the march on Nationalist Madrid.

antiseptics and anaesthetics. I could understand very little of it which was a pity, as I know nothing about anaesthetics and the routine of operations. I got home at about 1.30 and had a bath and changed. Some friends came to lunch and afterwards we all went to see the Arab stud at Cartuja.

Thursday, 21 October. Work at the hospital this morning was more interesting as after doing the usual dressings and tidying and giving my first injection, which I did very badly, we watched the doctor inspecting various wounds and he showed us the X-rays and explained how they had been cured. Then he explained the various instruments to us, all of which had impossible names. Just as we were finishing, all the bells began to ring to show that Gijón had fallen.[2] Everyone was hilarious with delight, and directly we were able to go we all rushed out into the streets and went and joined everyone else in a café where we celebrated with a drink or two. I had to walk home in the pouring rain and got quite soaked. It is wonderful that Gijón has fallen, as that finishes off the North completely. Everyone is now feeling very optimistic. Carmen Abrantes's two eldest daughters, Miriam and Carmen, came to lunch and we spent the whole afternoon discussing religion. We had an enormous tea and then went to a rotten film. After that, at about ten, we went to the club at the polo ground where everyone was forgathering to celebrate. We stayed there until 5 o'clock in the morning. There were lots of people there, some of whom I know and some I don't. The girls who are in my ward and dozens of men. At first no one talked to me but then things got better. At dinner I sat between two very nice men, neither of whom could talk English. One of them was quite sweet but ordinary, the other, already tiddly, called Gonzalo Segovia, was absolutely typical of the English idea of a Spaniard. Tall, dark, rather handsome, always making incredible compliments and very difficult to cope with, and a *torero* into the bargain. He talked such atrocious Andalusian that I could not understand a word he said. It was terribly funny as everyone listened in, and he kept saying silly things about how beautiful I was and how much he loved me and

2 The main port in Asturias. Its capture meant the end of the war in the North, and Franco could transfer the Navarrese and Italian divisions for a renewed offensive against Madrid which he had failed to take and which now, according to the Germans and Italians in Spain, had become his 'obsession'.

what lovely eyes I had, etc., which they understood but I very seldom did. After dinner at about midnight we put on the gramophone which was very bad and danced. We all stayed talking and dancing and flirting until 5 o'clock in the morning, by which time there were only us three and six men left. By the end Gonzalo Segovia was absolutely plastered and mad as a hatter. I enjoyed myself enormously as every one seemed to like me and it was all very friendly and great fun. Now it is 5.30 and I have to get up again at eight so as to go to the hospital where we have got lots of new patients now, so I must go to bed.

Saturday, 23 October. At the hospital today there were five or six new Moors in our ward. They arrived during the morning and were absolutely filthy. One could peel the dirt right off and a lot of time was spent scraping their feet and manicuring them etc. I left quite early as the doctor was too busy to give us a lesson.

Sunday, 24 October. I went with Consuelo to Mass at 8.30 and then we had breakfast together and I changed and went to the hospital.[3] There were only three of us in our ward today as it is Sunday and there is no class. I was delighted, as it meant there was a lot for me to do and I love the work. Apart from all the usual dressings there were lots of interesting things amongst the new arrivals. One man is in awful agony and almost paralyzed. It is tetanus from a wound in his back and I think he will die although they have injected him full of anti-tetanus. Another had a hole in his lung with a tube sticking out of a hole in his back which oozed when he coughed. The worst thing of the morning was one poor boy who had a wound right through his calf. It was almost healed but had evidently got an abscess so the doctor, without any warning, got out his knife and cut it right through the whole leg. The boy screamed and had to be held down and cried and blood ran in all directions, and all the time the doctor smoked a cigar and laughed and joked as though he was not doing anything. They were very cold-blooded which is only natural considering what they have to do. The surprising thing is that although I hate to see anyone hurt, the other part of me can look on completely unmoved and very interested. At least that helps me a lot.

3 Though not then a Catholic she always went to Mass with Consuelo.

Monday, 25 October. I was the first to arrive as I got up early and so did quite a lot. Some of the bad wounds were treated today, and leaning over them to hold basins and instruments the smell was grim. It made me feel quite ill. We made some of the beds and they smelt too and were filthy dirty. The doctor was in a bad temper and when he hurt one of the patients by twisting his broken arm, the man let out a scream and the doctor smacked him on the head a great wallop and told him to shut up. The whole thing seemed horrible, sordid, dirty and unpleasant to me.

Tuesday, 26 October. It has rained almost all day again and at the moment there is thunder too. The work in the hospital this morning was splendid as I had a lot to do. All the others went off to do bandages, so I stayed with the doctor and head nurse and did more dressings. The amount of time one has to waste pandering to the patients, making their beds, cutting their toe nails, writing their letters, teaching them English etc.! After the dressings were all done I cut gauze and then helped serve the lunch which was incredibly noisy. About two hundred Moors all shouting and calling one, and a radio blaring out songs.

Wednesday, 27 October. After a boring morning in the hospital and a long wait for lunch, suddenly in the middle of the meal I was called to the telephone. It was Princess Bee at Sanlucar with Ataulfo and lots of his co-officers. The Infanta has invited us over, just Consuelo and I, for two or three days to entertain them. Oh joy! It is not fixed at all yet, but I do hope we go! She also told me my car had arrived in Gibraltar. More joy!

Friday, 29 October. At about 4.30 we set of for Sanlucar. We arrived a few minutes before the German aviators.[4] There are nine of them here, none attractive but all perfectly sweet. Princess Bee seemed genuinely delighted to have me back again and I was awfully pleased to see her as I adore her and have missed her a lot. The Germans can hardly speak anything except German which makes conversation difficult and very funny.

Saturday, 30 October. Though I woke up at 8.30 I did not get up till

4 Serving in the Condor Legion to which Ataulfo was attached.

about 9.30. We did nothing all morning. The Germans went off with Touffles to bathe and I worked. We lunched late and at four we all went off to a fiesta at a *bodega* here. It was the greatest fun. Most of the girls were dressed in flamenco costumes and they danced to Sevillanas and we all ate and talked and drank. By about seven we were all pretty merry and having a splendid time. No one danced at all, so Touffles and I led off the dance with great courage. We had to sign our names on barrels with bits of chalk. The Germans were in splendid form crawling about on top of the barrels. They produced a guitarist and a young man who sang the flamenco, which is the most fascinating noise.

Monday, 1 November. After breakfast we went to Mass as it is All Saints' Day. Then we went round to the Botanico to pick oranges. After lunch they played bridge while I tried to learn it. They played till about five when they had to go and see someone and left Consuelo and me behind. Directly they had gone we put on our coats and rushed out into the rain to buy some cigarettes. There are none in this town except black Spanish, but we managed to buy a few off a boy who had decent ones. Then we played patience and gossiped and laughed until the others came back and we had tea. After tea they played bridge and I sat by Ataulfo and we both sang and yelled at the tops of our voices all the time, which spoilt the game but was most enjoyable. After dinner we played racing demon. There is an awful storm with wind and rain.

Tuesday, 2 November. At about 4.30 we left for Gibraltar where we are now staying the night at the Rock Hotel. As soon as we arrived [*in Gibraltar*] we went to see about my car which is heaven. Black with green leather inside and a dream of beauty.[5] Gibraltar is a strange place. Very small but very *simpatico* and everyone is far more Spanish than English, although they look English enough.

Friday, 5 November. After breakfast [*at Sanlucar*] we wandered round the garden and then went to the Botanico to see about planting some fruit trees. Then Touffles and I played cards until lunch

5 The car, given by her father, was a great joy and she drove incessantly. It became a nuisance when she was pestered to give lifts to hospital staff. There were few private cars in Spain during the Civil War.

time. Two men came to lunch and were terribly boring. I drove over to Jerez in my car and had tea with the Montemars and gave them all their things from Gib. Then I went to my lecture and drove myself back here to dinner. It is about twelve or fifteen miles, so if I do it four times a day all next week I will soon run my car in. After dinner Princess B., Prince Ali and D.T. played bridge while I sat and watched and played my radio. Tomorrow we will all go to Sevilla.

Wednesday, 10 November. I have enjoyed today so much. It is now 3 o'clock but I don't feel in the least sleepy. I went to the hospital as usual this morning and we all worked fast and got the whole ward finished by 10.30 so that we could go and watch the doctor operating. It was the first time I had seen an operation and I was enthralled. There were two. The first was amputating a leg below the knee and the other removing the astragalus. The amputation was given chloroform and was very neat and tidy. It looked so odd to see the foot detached from the rest of the man, sitting on the floor by itself. The second man was scared stiff. He would not have chloroform as he said he would die, so he was given an injection in the spine to deaden his lower half. He could not feel anything much, but howled and screamed and moaned the whole time. I never knew anyone could make such a noise. He went quite mad and shook and fought until finally they forcibly chloroformed him. His operation made a filthy mess with blood flowing in all directions. The most unpleasant thing was the heat and the smell of anaesthetic. I got back for lunch at about two.

Sunday, 14 November. I am beginning to loathe the Moors. They are so tiresome, always quarrelling and yelling at one. It makes me mad to have a lot of filthy, smelly Moors ordering me about. I don't mind what I do for them if they ask me and appear pleased, but the trouble is that they are almost all very low class and just shout and snatch things and swear, or worse, become cheeky and make lewd remarks in Arabic and laugh at one. Every time I had just finished a bandage they wanted a different-sized one and pulled the whole thing off again. The trouble is that they are doing their period fasting and eat nothing till dinner, so are all very irritable. However, I love the work; even if I am getting to dislike the people intensely, I still like their wounds, which is after all the main point.

[11]

Monday, 15 November. Today was my 21st birthday. All the Moors are still in worse tempers due to having to starve for a month during their 'Ramadan'. One of them who was quite wellish has got a fever, and as he refuses even to drink a glass of water before sunset he is getting worse and will die soon if no one does anything about it. In the middle of the morning, Vicky and I wandered out to buy biscuits to eat. We were accosted by a hideous little woman who was scared pink. She said one of the Moors had given her presents of food for her children saying he could not eat it himself because of the Ramadan so she might as well take it. Now he wants to marry her and take her and her children to Africa. She said 'No', and he said he had a right to her after her having accepted his presents. So now he goes and beats on her door every night and says if she does not marry him he will kill her and himself afterwards. The poor woman is terrified. I think it is awfully funny, and she is so ugly.

Friday, 19 November. Being cured of my cold at last I went to the hospital this morning; there were quite a lot of new patients but no interesting ones. Evidently our course has now finished so we ought to have our exam soon. I am terrified, as I don't know anything well enough to explain it in Spanish.

Sunday, 21 November. Here I am back at the Montemars' at Jerez. I was heart-broken to leave Sanlucar and even more so to say goodbye to the Infanta. I think she was genuinely sorry to say goodbye to me too. She sat up till 5.30 this morning writing letters and arranging all her business. This morning was a chaos of tidying, sorting and packing. We finally set off at eleven. I followed just behind the Infanta's car all the way here, and said a last, sad farewell in the road on the outskirts of Jerez. I do wish I could hurry up and go to the front. I'm tired of waiting and doing nothing much. I want action.

Monday, 22 November. Work at the hospital was better than usual as most of the nurses did not come, so there was lots of work. I was terrified at having to cope with pleurisy all by myself, putting a tube in his back etc. I wish we could have our exam and I will be going soon with any luck. The war seems to have come to a temporary stop as there has been no news on the radio now for six days.

Tuesday, 23 November. We lunched with Guy and Nina Williams, the English consul here. It was an awful hurry to get changed from hospital and have my bath in time, but we just managed it. There was a young English novelist, journalist etc. there. He was fat and blonde and stuttered and was quite terrible, in a green suit and a black beret. He tactlessly brought the conversation onto the English point of view regarding Spain which of course induced a heated argument.

Thursday, 25 November. There was an enthralling operation at the hospital this morning when I went in. They were removing a bullet from a man's back. The X-ray gave the impression that it was lying on the ribs, but when they opened him up it turned out to have gone through the ribs and lodged in the left lung. It was fascinating watching it being hoicked out.

Saturday, 27 November. Consuelo and I have decided that if Mercedes Milá[6] says we are not required at the front, we will apply to another woman who runs a different section and get sent to found a small hospital in our own right at the front. A kind of emergency clearing hospital. It would be thrilling as we would be all alone there, the only women and in complete charge and would have to make the thing out of nothing. Hellish hard work but we would neither of us mind that. However, that is only a plan and probably won't happen.

Sunday, 28 November. We spent the afternoon in the country in search of eggs which are almost non-existent here now. We had to drive over the fields and walk through puddles and mud and argue for ages with all the peasants, but we finally returned triumphant with fourteen eggs. This evening we went to the cinema. It was the best cinema I have seen here yet.

6 Mercedes Milá (1895-1990) is harshly treated by Pip. In March 1937 she was appointed by Franco as head of the Nationalist nursing services, the Jefatura General de Servicios Femeninos de Hospitales. She was an efficient organizer who, as Inspector General of the nursing services, found Pip's independent character profoundly irritating; but given Pip's close friendship with the Infanta Beatrice she could not dismiss Pip as a troublemaker. Mercedes Milá went to Russia in 1943-4 in charge of nurses attached to the Blue Division. After the war she became Secretary General of the Spanish Red Cross. Like the Orleans family she spoke English, having been educated at an English convent school.

Monday, 29 November. We had quite a lot to do at the hospital today and I watched one poor man having an operation on his finger to remove a bit of bone. He was howling like mad. It is strange how one can't imagine pain at all. When I got back I found a letter from Princess Bee from Salamanca in which she said that she had spoken to the woman about my going to the front, so I hope we will get an answer to our letter soon. The rest of today I have spent talking, writing letters and working. My exam is on Wednesday so I must do a spot of studying as it would be too ghastly if I failed. How I long to go to the front.

Wednesday, 1 December. Today has been full of spirit. I hardly slept a wink last night from worrying about my exam this morning. Actually it was not too bad. We were examined by the head doctor Romero Paloma, the *commandante* of the Hospital Huerta, and a nun. We were each called up in turn and had to sit in front of the doctors to answer, with the other girls all round. I managed to struggle through more or less all right and think that I have passed. Afterwards I went with Vicky and Piero and Carmen Soto and Maria to Sandilla for a drink to restore our shattered nerves. After lunch Pilar[7] and I and them two set forth in my car in splendid spirits to Seville.

Thursday, 2 December. After getting to bed at 3.30 last night I was distinctly reluctant to get up to go the hospital this morning. It has been a gloomy day. It has poured with rain the whole time and as I am tired everything got on my nerves. I almost hit Pilar on the head more than once and longed to kick the dogs and give the Duchess a good shaking. Pilar is the world's worst if one is not feeling one's usual affable self. Her laugh goes through you like a knife. Her talk is ceaseless and senseless and she never stops asking 'What shall we do today?' when there is nothing to do anyhow. Oh how I want to hurry and go to the front. The only part of the day I really enjoy is in the hospital.

Saturday, 4 December. I stayed at the hospital today till past 2 o'clock watching Paloma curing various people. It is funny how I minded the first time I watched operations without anaesthetic and

7 She was the daughter of the Duquesa de Montemar, and a sister of Consuelo.

now I don't care a hoot. It is extraordinary how much blood people can collect inside them without it showing, and then when the doctor cuts in it all comes out like a fountain. It is awful how much I do on my own, considering how little I know. As the doctor is never there, if one thinks a scab should come off or that there is an abscess under the wound, one just opens it up without asking anyone. I opened two that were apparently healed today and was quite right on both occasions, as there was a great hole inside filled with pus. At last I have mastered the act of painlessly sticking the tube inside the man with pleurisy. The cinema tonight was thrilling. All about a war in Bavaria against Napoleon and everyone was killed. It is silly how in the middle of a war everyone flocks to the nearest gruesome film for a thrill.

Monday, 6 December. Pilar and I and Manolo and a man called Espinosa all went off to Cadiz. When we got there we were given permission to go on board a German warship. The Germans were sweet to us and showed us round a lot. She was a 10,000-ton ship called the *Deutschland*. After we had been shown round all we were allowed to see, we went down to their saloon where we sat and drank beer and Rhine wine till after 10 o'clock. Conversation was very difficult as the Germans only talked German and a teeny bit of Spanish and I understand German and can't speak it much, while the others can't even understand it. At 10.30 we went and dined in a funny little bar, and so at last home at 12.30. I had the greatest fun in making awful vulgar jokes in Spanish all the time pretending that I did not know what I was saying.

Tuesday, 7 December. We went on board the *Deutschland* again. We were all shown round. She is a lovely boat, a crew of 1,054 men, stacks of guns of 28c. and smaller. We went up on to the bridge and saw pretty well everything. Then we went to the officers' dining-room for tea where we all talked and drank wine. It was a very complicated conversation as no one had a mutual language. We were given a lovely insignia and the ribbon with the ship's name on it. After tea, after lots of asking, we were finally shown the engines. They were too enthralling; eight 9-cylinder engines and four auxiliary ones to give oil etc. to the others. She does 26 knots full out. We left the ship at about eight. We wanted to see the only other

[15]

ship in the harbour which was a huge Italian hospital ship, but it was too late and we had no permit so could not go on board. As I left the hospital this morning lots of soldiers marched past with drummer-boys and singing at the tops of their voices all the same old war songs as the English used to sing in the Great War. It suddenly struck me how odd that I should be standing there in a nurse's uniform watching Spanish soldiers marching off to war. It is an odd life really.

Thursday, 9 December. [*To Cadiz to fetch her car from Gibraltar.*] We started off for Gibraltar at 10.30 this morning.

Friday, 10 December. I do wish Mercedes Milá would answer our letter about going to the front. Today there was an air battle in Aragon in which we shot down twenty Reds and only lost one machine. I wonder if it was anyone I know.

Saturday, 11 December. After the usual work at the hospital, a *copa* [*drink*] at Jandilla and a bath, I went with Pilar to lunch at the Ponteras, picking up Vicky on the way. When we arrived there was no one there except Pat, as they had all gone to show three Italian officers round the Bodega. However, after a time they all arrived. The mother, the Duchess of Solferino, the three Italians, Pepe and Marie Louisa, Perico, Manolo and the daughter. We had a huge lunch and everyone was very merry. Afterwards I had to tell every-one's hand which afforded a lot of amusement. Finally at about 5.30 we set off for Sevilla. Manolo and Ena came in my car with Pilar and myself, and the others followed in two others. We were all to meet in the Hotel Madrid, but after waiting for them for a long time we left and Manolo, Pilar and I went to the Andalucia to the bar, leaving Ena with some friends to wait for her fiancé, Perico Pantera. Everywhere we went we just missed them. We went from the Andalucia to the bar of the Cristina and then back to the Andalucia for dinner. Manolo got steadily tighter till by the end of dinner he was quite intolerably tiresome and I was fed up and hating every moment of it all. At about eleven we went to the Cadenas which was pretty full, so we had to sit at the same table as a young officer who soon joined into our party. Then two friends of Manolo's appeared. One was an older man in civilian clothes who talked to Pilar all evening. The other was utterly fascinating, quite the most attractive man I have met out here yet. He is in the Tercio, which is the bravest of all the various units.[8] I am told he is madly brave and always to be found in the very front line – also a first-class football player. He is called Guillermo something-or-other. He is the English idea of an attractive Spaniard, dark, strong and handsome, with nice smiley eyes. I was most taken by him and we got on quite well. Of course I shall never see him again which is a pity, but it all adds to the charm. At about 1 o'clock all the rest of our party turned up. Manolo by then had almost passed out so was no longer being tiresome. Perico was as tight as a tick and most of them were a bit squiffy. We stayed there till after 3 o'clock, dancing, talking, drinking champagne and watching the girls perform their Spanish dances. I could not have enjoyed myself more. Pilar and I came back alone and gave a lift to two miserably cold soldiers who were most grateful.

Monday, 13 December. A completely blank day. There are no interesting wounds. It is rather fun, as I seem to have got a great reputation for being not only beautiful but also extremely clever. I can't think how, except that the beauty is entirely due to having fair hair and my reputation for brains comes from the hospital i.e. from the doctors, which boils down again to fair hair. However, it is fun to be somewhere where people appreciate my charms. But oh gosh! oh gee! how I want to get moving and go to the front.

Tuesday, 14 December. Everyone is in a state of nerves this evening. News has got round that the big offensive on the Aragon front has begun but no one knows if it is true, as the news on the radio is still the usual 'sin novedades en los frentes de los ejercitos'.[9] Also everyone is puzzled about the Italians withdrawing from the League of Nations as there is a rumour that they are being removed from Spain. I don't believe it is true that they are going but it is impossible to know. Anyhow, there is an air of suspense everywhere, and all the men standing about whispering in corners and all the boys who have overstayed their leave are now in a frenzy thinking they are missing

8 The Foreign Legion.
9 The Republican offensive to take Teruel began with Lister's attack on the Muela de Teruel on 15 December. This entry makes clear that this attack was not a complete surprise.

something and will be court-martialled. I do wish I could go to the front and stop idling about here.

Friday, 17 December. When I got back from the hospital I got a letter from Gaenor [*her sister*] in which she says that she and Rosemary are going to Egypt with Mama after Christmas, ditto Ebits and Serge [*her sister Elizabeth and her brother-in-law Serge Orloff Davidoff*] and John [*her brother the present Lord Howard de Walden*] and Nucci. All afternoon I spent cutting sandwiches for the tea party. Blanca Bourbon and her husband came to lunch. About thirty people came to tea and cocktails. It was the greatest fun. I danced and talked and flirted, especially with Gonzalo Segovia who is the most enchanting man. I quite dote on him. That makes two men I have fallen for down here. They all stayed till about 10 o'clock or later. I had read all their hands, which are surprisingly true. It was a splendid party and I loved it. I am furious because I have just posted twenty Christmas cards and now find that all post has been stopped for three days and will not start again for a week or more so that they won't arrive, and also I can't write to Mama before she leaves for Egypt and won't get the news of Elizabeth's child. How tiresome life is really.

Tuesday, 23 December. [*From Merida, en route to Burgos.*] There were complications about having my passport visaed this morning, but the police were very friendly and I managed to get off at eleven. I soon began to run out of petrol and could not find a petrol pump anywhere, so when things were becoming desperate I stopped at a little village and drove all round it on ghastly cobbled roads and mud trying to find some but with no success, so had to proceed on my way without. About five miles from Caceres I ran out but was able to free-wheel downhill till I reached a little aerodrome where I begged some off the soldiers, much to their amusement. One of them wanted a lift, but as it meant waiting half an hour for him I said I could not wait. Then all went well until I reached Bejar at about 2.30 when I found I had run out of oil, as my oil tank has sprung a leak. So I stopped at a garage and filled her up with oil, petrol and water. Everyone was quite enthralled to see a young girl travelling alone and busying herself in the engine of her car. Girls here don't. I arrived at Salamanca at four and tried hard to find Mercedes Milá but with no success, so continued on my way. From Salamanca to Burgos was

[18]

uneventful, and I just drove along at top speed singing to myself all the way. I finally arrived in Burgos at eight, exhausted after driving all day and eating nothing. I trotted into the hotel only to find that Carla [*the Italian wife of Prince Alvaro*] had gone to Aranda, leaving no message for me. I was so in despair that I nearly wept. [*Carla and Alvaro returned later that evening.*] Tomorrow we are all going to Aranda where Ataulfo is going to meet us for Xmas. We have to go in my car despite the leak in the oil tank, as Alvaro's has broken its back axle and Carla's froze and burst and is stuck on the road somewhere. I am so pleased to be here. Also Mercedes Milá is here in Burgos, and the Kindelán daughters say she is waiting to send us to a front line hospital and we will have to wait another two or three weeks, but we are definitely going. So, despite all, the day has ended well. And everyone says I am thinner, which indeed I am.

Friday, 24 December. In the middle of lunch an official came in to tell General Kindelán the news of the day's aviation and said that Alvaro's plane was missing and had been seen going down in a spin with a lot of smoke near the Red lines. Of course no one knew what had really happened yet so we could not let poor Carla know; we all sat and talked to her until at 3 o'clock Ultano and another Kindelán who is in his flight got back. They said they had seen him go down but that he straightened out and landed, so Carla asked where, and they said somewhere a long way off to stop her going to find him, as really no one yet knew what had happened to him. We were all scared stiff and everyone was trying to get news. At last, after about an hour, Alvaro himself rang from Soria. We were all so relieved that we did not know what to do. Carla would not believe it until she had actually spoken to him and then, as a reaction of nerves, she got furious and said she never wanted to see him again and would not come to Aranda with me tonight to spend Christmas Eve with the Infanta and no one could do anything with her. What had actually happened to Alvaro was that his right-hand engine had blown up, and, as on those machines you can't stop the engine in flight, he had got into a spin with smoke billowing all over the machine so that he thought it was on fire. But he let down his slots and got her out of the spin and then, finding she was not burning, very slowly came homewards on two engines. But the third made such vibration that he lost height until he had to land without his undercarriage, in a ploughed field, missing a hill by inches. The machine tipped on its nose but no one was hurt, so there they were stranded three kilometres from the Soria aerodrome. They think it must have been hit by Archie [*anti-aircraft fire*], but Alvaro says no. Anyhow, thank God he is all right. After removing Carla to my room and giving her a brandy and ten minutes' lecture, I finally persuaded her to come to Aranda as a car had been sent to fetch Alvaro and take him there. She was still shaking with fright when we left. We had an eighty kilometres drive in my car in a thick fog where one could not see more than ten yards ahead at the best moments. However, with much care, I finally made it and we arrived at about eight, to find Prince Ali, Princess Bee and Ataulfo here. The Infanta had got a Christmas tree on the table and a present of a belt for Carla and a scarf for me. Then I opened a small suitcase the Infanta had brought for me and found lots of little presents from Mama and some heavenly gloves from Bronwen. Unluckily, when I plugged my radio in, it blew up so I must get new valves from Gibraltar which means a long wait. As my gramophone is coming from Lisbon we had no music. This is a lovely house, and we joined all the family for Christmas dinner, then lit up the candles on the Christmas tree. Then everyone went to bed except Touffles and I who sat up till nearly 2 o'clock playing piquet. I had arranged all about going to the front and hope to leave in a week or two at the most. The Infanta has been telling lovely tales about me in London and says I am now a heroine and spoken of with bated breath. This certainly is the strangest Christmas I have had.

Saturday, 25 December. We all had breakfast in our dressing gowns, then we went to Mass in a sweet little old church next door. Then Alvaro and Carla had to leave for Burgos, as despite it being Christmas Day, Alvaro had to be on guard at the flying ground all this evening and tonight. At 8 o'clock Touffles and Prince Ali left for Burgos de Osma where Touffles is stationed. Prince Ali has gone only for dinner and will be back tonight; Touffles stays there but may come over one afternoon soon. There is no flying at the moment as the whole countryside is enveloped in a thick fog day and night for miles around.

2

El Burgo de Osma and the Battle of Teruel

DECEMBER 1937 – FEBRUARY 1938

On 27 December Pip left Jerez to be near the front. She drove to Burgos de Osma where some of the officers of the Condor Legion were stationed. The Legion had been sent by Hitler in November 1936. It consisted of four squadrons of bombers and a similar strength of fighters together with anti-aircraft batteries and sixteen tanks and crews – some 40,000 men in all. Ataulfo was attached to the Legion. El Burgo de Osma is on the road between Aranda del Duero and Soria.

Pip's arrival in Spain had coincided with the final stages of Franco's conquest of the North. This was a decisive defeat for the Republic. With the resources of the North in his hands (see p. 7) Franco could now turn his attention to Madrid which he had failed to take in the early months of the war. It had been successfully defended by the International Brigades and the Popular Army of the Republic, the creation of General Rojo, the strategic brains of the Republic at war. The capture of Madrid, according to his Italian and German advisers, had become Franco's obsession.

He intended to renew his attack in December. Learning of this, General Rojo mounted an offensive against Teruel in Aragon to draw Franco from Madrid. This the offensive succeeded in doing. The battle, fought in temperatures of −18 degrees and in snow which often halted operations, began with the Republican offensive on 15 December. The heights around Teruel were captured, and the Nationalist garrison under heavy bombardment retired to a group of buildings in the town centre. Without supplies and with the buildings reduced to rubble, the commander, Colonel Rey d'Harcourt, surrendered on 8 January 1938. When Franco mounted his counter-attack on 17

January, the Republicans became the besieged as the Nationalists reconquered the heights, including the Muela de Teruel, which overlooked the town. On 7 February the Nationalist attack north of Teruel, across the Alfambra river, surrounded the town and the Republicans retired in disorder.

The Nationalist casualties were heavy – an estimated 16,000 wounded – and filled the front line equipos. Towards the end of the battle Pip and Consuelo began their first regular work as nurses in the equipo of Captain Roldan. From the beginning relations with Roldan were difficult and steadily deteriorated. Pip's only relief was provided by trips to the Orleans family at Epila and 'shopping' in Zaragoza.

Friday, 31 December. El Burgo itself is a lovely old town. I finally found the old convent which the Legion Condor uses as a barracks.[1] All the soldiers were so surprised to see me that one would have thought they had never seen a woman before. I explained why I was there in my best German to the sentry in a circle of staring soldiers of every size. So I was ushered in and waited in a dirty little office with three German soldiers, a nasty little cell with four wooden bunks and a radio and some broken chairs. If this is how Ataulfo lives I feel sorry for him. Finally he turned up and drove us back to Ventisilla where we arrived very cold and late for lunch. We all sat and talked until after the Spanish news, then returned to our Salon where Prince Ali, Princess Bee and I celebrated the New Year together with the help of my radio and a bottle of Kümmel. Then we got onto a Red station, Radio Libertad, broadcasting in German. They talked the most utter rot I have ever heard, and ended by saying that this triumphant year had ended with the taking of Teruel![2] So evidently both sides are celebrating the taking of the same town. What liars they are

1 Burgo de Osma is an attractive town fifty-eight kilometres from Aranda on the road to Soria. Admiral Canaris had reported that the Nationalists' combat tactics did not 'promise success'. Hitler therefore sent the Condor Legion in November 1936. It consisted of four squadrons of Junker 52 bombers and four Heinkel 51 fighters. The latter were slower than the Soviet fighters of the Republicans. Ataulfo was attached to the Condor Legion. The Republican and Nationalist air forces at Teruel were roughly equal in strength. It was the first battle in which the air force played a decisive role and there were notable dog fights.
2 The Nationalist garrison was in a group of buildings in the centre of Teruel. They were heavily shelled from the surrounding heights, especially the Muela de Teruel. The garrison commander held out until 8 January.

and I have not noticed them having any triumphs anywhere. So exit 1937 and here I am in 1938. I wish I knew what it would bring me, but at least it shows signs of being full of spirit. I have simply loved today and hope that bodes well for 1938.

Saturday, 1 January 1938. It snowed last night so I woke up to a white and frozen world. The English news on the radio is supreme. Today it said we had not entered Teruel when we all know we have, also that we had two hundred machines in the air there yesterday. Actually the weather was so bad that no one flew at all. I have seldom been so lazy in my life. I never do anything except sit in our salon knitting, playing cards, talking and mending my clothes.

Tuesday, 4 January. After tea Prince Ali turned up cold, famished and stone deaf, and added the last straw by informing us that the Jefatura had refused to promote Touffles to the rank he should have. It is a very bad show as he has been in his squadron longer than anyone else there, he has done well over two hundred hours' flying and they leave him with the same rank as the ordinary soldier. It is not only unfair but damn rude to the royal family and even more so to the Germans, as he is the only Spaniard in the German flying unit and they asked for him to be promoted. He pretends not to mind but he really feels it awfully. In the end he was so angry he went away back to El Burgo and refused to stay to dinner. Prince Ali and Princess Bee were both frothing with rage and mortification, Ataulfo saying that, all right, if they did not want him here he would go back to England and enjoy himself. In fact a thoroughly miserable day. (We shot down eleven Reds today.)

Thursday, 6 January. What really makes me angry is listening to the radio for the English news, which is bright Red and lies all through. Today it said that the Reds have taken the last houses in Teruel and are marching on Zaragoza, when I know for certain that we relieved Teruel a week ago and are advancing slowly to the south of it.[3] What with being furious with my country and having to wait so long to go and work, my nerves are getting very uppish and I am usually depressed and fidgety and never manage to sleep. Bloody

3 Completely false. Why did not Ataulfo tell her the truth?

bore. However, after dinner tonight was amusing, as all the lights conked out and we had to fetch candles.

Friday, 7 January. There is still a hell of a row going on about him [*Ataulfo*] being promoted. He is furious because they have refused to take someone into the *grupo* merely because Ataulfo recommended him. The trouble is that one of the men at the Jefatura [*Air Force GHQ*] loathes Ataulfo and is always trying to be nasty. With success.

Saturday, 8 January. After dinner we sat and talked and knitted and played patience until the Spanish news, which was bad. It was not at all clear but I gather that someone in charge at Teruel went over to the Reds and that we have now definitely lost Teruel, because although we entered it on New Year's Eve, we never really got it cleared again.[4] A bad setback, but more morally than practically, I think. Touffles and I were playing piquet and Princess Bee knitting. [*Ataulfo*] told us that two of Ataulfo's Germans were killed today flying a new Heinkel up from Leon. They ran into a hill and two were killed and two wounded. That rather depressed us. So we all went to bed. As it is only 1.30 I am still playing the radio.

Sunday, 9 January. No news of the war except that we have definitely evacuated Teruel owing to the general going over to the Reds. I am awfully happy here, but must go to Salamanca to arrange about the front. I came out here to work and work I will.

Thursday, 13 January. A lazy day as usual, knitting socks. Prince Ali went to Burgos after lunch with Escariot and his three brothers, the eldest of whom only got out of Madrid two weeks ago and still has a sort of scared, dazed look.

Friday, 14 January. After lunch I wrote letters until Princess Bee came in to tell me that Ataulfo had just got back from Sevilla and had rung up. As Carmello was ill in bed, I jumped into my little car and went to fetch him. It was a lovely drive as there was a stupendous sunset and all the world was bright orange. It was dark when I arrived at Burgo de Osma. I told the sentry that I had come to fetch Ataulfo so I

4 The commander of the garrison was not a 'Red' but he was regarded by Franco as a traitor for capitulating. In fact the position of the Nationalist garrison left no alternative.

was then led up to his room along miles of long, cold, stone passages. It is the funniest little room. There were three little bunks, a rickety table, one chair and everything made out of old packing cases with a little stove stuck in one corner and piles of wood all over the floor. We stopped in Burgo to see one of the aviators who was busily trying to arrange the sitting-room which is in a dirty little house a few yards away. It is also made out of nothing and littered with tops of bombs and paint pots. Schiller has arranged one corner of it curtained off with low divans and a dim red light! We finally got back here about eight after stopping in Aranda to send off a telegram to Mercedes Milá, the head of all the nurses. As usual we played cards all evening and finally retired to bed at about 12.30. My radio was maddening, and every time I got into bed it went wrong and I had to get out and fix it again.

Saturday, 15 January. Princess Bee called me at a quarter to six this morning, and after gulping down a glass of milk Ataulfo and I set off for Burgo in the dark. Despite the hour we were in rollicking form and sang and talked all the way. It was just getting light when we arrived at Burgo. We bade each other farewell and I set off back again. I was stopped by a *guardia civil* in Aranda. He was a big, fat, red-faced man, with a curly moustache. First he asked me if I had a *salvo conducto*. When I said no, he became vastly suspicious as a young girl driving alone in the early hours of the morning is unheard of in Spain. So then he asked me if I was German, as I said I had been in El Burgo which is full of Germans. When I said I was English he became more suspicious and asked me why I had to go to Burgo so early. When I told him I had taken an aviator back as his chauffeur was ill, he became distinctly horrified and said was I married. On hearing I was not, he immediately came to the conclusion that I was leading a life of sin and was so horrified he nearly burst. He was so suspicious of me then that I would not have been a bit surprised if I had been marched off to prison as a spy. However, I stated firmly that I was great friends with the *commandante militar*, so finally I was allowed to go, but I am sure the story is all round Aranda already, that I am living a life of sin with an aviator. Princess Bee was awfully amused and told it to the whole family, who for some unknown reason thought it was the best story they had heard for ages, and went on about it all day.

[25]

Sunday, 16 January. This morning I was to go to Valladolid with our hosts to watch a parade etc., but about five miles from here we had a puncture and the jack broke. As no car came by we were stuck for hours, while some of them walked miles to the nearest village to telephone for another car. Then it was too late so we came home after all. Then I went out for a walk with Princess Bee. We met the young *alferez*[5] who said he was leaving, as he had just received the order that all the Junkers were to move at once to Zaragoza. He was almost in tears at going, poor boy. Prince Ali says that we are going to launch an attack near Teruel tomorrow. I hope that it will be a successful one. There is a general atmosphere of unrest around the place so I feel something is going to happen soon. About time too.

Monday, 17 January. Princess Bee went to Burgos with our host. I stayed behind as I had to go over and fetch Ataulfo this afternoon after spending the morning writing letters and working in the factory. It was a dismal, rainy day, but despite that Prince Ali and Ataulfo flew, but not Alvaro. They did advance near Teruel today with great success.[6] Just before I left to fetch Ataulfo a telegram arrived to tell me to go to the hospital at Alhama, so I sent one to Consuelo to tell her to join me here. I want to go and work but, alas, it means leaving Princess Bee again which is hell, but such is life. All the way back from Burgo de Osma we discussed plans of what we would do after the war. A fascinating subject.

Tuesday, 18 January. Poor Ataulfo is here in bed, very ill with a fever and a swollen throat.

Wednesday, 19 January. Prince Ali left with all his men for Casteljón [*the aerodrome on flat land north-west of Zaragoza*] this morning.

Friday, 21 January. Ataulfo is much better today and was more his usual self, especially after shaving off his four days' growth of beard which looked so funny.[7] My cold is cured, but instead of feeling cheerful I am in the depths of depression and so nervous that I don't know what to do with myself. I can't sleep and have not done so for

5 Lieutenant.
6 This refers to the Nationalist offensive against the heights of La Muela.
7 Pip had nursed Ataulfo through a bad attack of pharyngitis.

three nights. Princess Bee told me I was an egoist and an egotist today. I was furious and I consider it most insulting. I don't see why she thinks so. She says I never think of anyone but myself, but it is not true. Or perhaps I am. I don't know, I try to be nice and help other people but it's no good. I've come all the way out here to do something worth while and all I am doing is sitting in great comfort being a thorough bore to everyone. But what's the good of bothering? No one would believe I really did come because I honestly wanted to help. Anyhow, I'm not helping anyone. Oh God, how I hate life.

Monday, 24 January. I am now sleeping at Alhama de Aragon in a hotel where all the nurses live and which is half hospital. I am cold and depressed as there is nothing to do and I want to work hard. This morning, before we left, three fighters came over the house and dived and zoomed at us for some time. They were lovely little machines and I was almost too ill with envy of the pilots. It was Juaquin Velasco on his way from Laon to Calomodo. I took Merucha over to the 'field' to fetch them in my car. Schiller and Oraveurent turned up on their way to Burgos. After packing, we finally left at 2 o'clock. We stopped in Aranda for petrol, etc., and just caught up with Princess Bee in Burgo de Osma where she had stopped to post a letter. She was surprised to see us again and we parted company very sadly. The road from there on was very bad and boring, and as we had had no lunch and had got no cigarettes and could not find any in any town, we were shattered. We finally arrived at 5.30 and located Lolita Kindelán who took us to see the Mother Superior who gave us a teeny little bedroom together. Then we did nothing but talk till dinner.

Tuesday, 25 January. Alhama is a strange little town. Very small, with three huge hotels which are next door to each other and half hospital, half hotel. There is no one in the town at all except nurses, doctors, one or two soldiers and a few sad wives. Our room is tiny, with just room for the two beds, a cupboard and a washstand, no heating, no hot water and very little light, but for a hospital it is jolly luxurious, we expected lots worse. This morning when we got up at 8.30 we nearly froze to death. However, we had a cup of coffee and then went over to the other hospital to see if the Mother Superior had any work for us, but she was still ill and said we need do nothing, so we got into my car and drove to Sigüenza which is about one and a

[27]

half hours away on the Madrid road. It was a lovely drive through mountains most of the time, but I was very depressed and we were both put out by having no cigarettes. We tried to find them everywhere but there were none. Sigüenza itself is a lovely old town, but very dirty and a great deal destroyed. They had an air raid there last night. We went to the Hospital de Sangre where we found Consuelo's old friend. She gave us a cigarette but told us there was nothing for us to do there either, as the *equipos* [*hospital teams*] were complete and they had hardly any wounded. She says that they have nothing to do, that they live in filthy rooms without any heating or any window-panes, and that there is often no food when lots of soldiers come. There were oodles of soldiers and lorries there and it looked quite warlike. We set off back just before 1.30 and stopped to buy cigarettes at Mendinaceli, which was miles up on the top of a mountain with a gorgeous view. When we got back here to our cold little room we fell into such depths of depression and boredom that we nearly wept.

Wednesday, 26 January. We presented ourselves before the Mother Superior once more this morning and after waiting for an hour were finally ushered in; she was sweet and gossiped for a long time. She said there was no work, so she would either put us in the office or in the ward for people who had illnesses but no wounds. We were horrified, but luckily on our way out we met a doctor who said he needed three nurses to his ward, so we two and another who had just arrived were assigned to the ward. It has a 110 beds so is quite a nice lot of work for three of us, but at the moment there are only 56 men which gives us about 18 each. We are each to have our own part of the ward and to do everything for them, curing, washing, feeding, making the beds, assisting at their operations, etc. – today we did nothing much, as it was too late and the doctor had left. So after lunch Consuelo and I decided to go to Zaragoza. We took a girl with us whom we met last night; we did lots of shopping and got back for dinner.

Thursday, 27 January. Things in the hospital are improving and we are gradually organizing ourselves. After watching some blighted girl doing all the dressings we found the lieutenant who is charming and arranged that Consuelo and I should take over half the ward (fifty-eight beds) and the other three the other half. So now we are in full control of our few wounded. We have no interesting ones at all, except one with an abscess on his head, one with a wound in the top of his spine who was operated yesterday and will probably die, and one with seven wounds strewn about him. Our day's work on the whole was tiresome; we were in the ward from 9 to 1.30 and from 4.30 to 8.30 in which time we did nothing of any interest at all except that Consuelo gave the head wound an intravenous injection. As it was in very bad electric light she could not see a thing and took ages prodding around for the vein while he bellowed like an ox. The 'spine' is very tiresome because he messes his bed so we have to change the sheets, which is both difficult and dirty as he can't move at all; also he had no pyjamas and boils all over his bottom which is most unappetizing.

Friday, 28 January. This morning we worked like mad in the ward. We did all the dressings and then washed as many as we had time for and did the beds of the ones who could not move. The spine is worse, and I am afraid he will die tonight, but maybe not. He spends his time moaning and saying he is going to die which is very trying. The big thrill of the day was that Mercedes Milá came to lunch here to detail various nurses to other hospitals. We begged to be sent to the front all through lunch with no effect. Afterwards we all sat round and she told us where the nurses were needed and picked out one or two and asked them if they wanted to go. No one at all was keen to go to the front except Consuelo and I, and she would not send us as she said I was too young to go somewhere dangerous in a responsible position. We went through such a nervous strain waiting to be chosen and arguing about what good nurses we were that I nearly died. At last she said we could leave tomorrow with three others for Cella, which is the nearest hospital to Teruel.[8] Oh, boy, I am pleased. At last we are going to the front. Of course they may tell us there that they don't need so many and send us back, but I hope not. We have to have a soldier to escort us there as all the big roads are closed because of bombardments and if we took a wrong turn we would probably find ourselves in the Red lines. Too thrilling. We were so happy to be

8 Cella was thirteen kilometres from Teruel off the N234 road to Zaragoza via Daroca. She notes the bombing of the roads – not often mentioned in accounts of the Battle of Teruel.

sent at last that we have been hilarious all evening. This evening we just gave a few injections and took temperatures. Consuelo gave two intravenous ones which I have not yet tried. Then we watched an operation to take some shrapnel out of a man's thigh and his ankle and his head. I can't wait to go to the front, my spirit of adventure is aroused.

Sunday, 30 January. I was supposed to take Consuelo and Maria Sala to the Monasterio de Piedra today as we all had leave, but my cold was worse so I did not go. We went to Mass still and spent the whole of the rest of the day lying on our beds reading, writing, knitting and playing the music. We really are off to Cella tomorrow. My feelings are mixed between delight and fear that I know too little, but delight wins. It was lovely to lie in bed late this morning but unluckily we both woke up at 7 o'clock having slept very badly. I was dreaming about the war as usual and was woken by an extra noisy lorry which I thought was an air raid. I was so scared I nearly had a heart-attack. At lunch and dinner the doctors' table sent us a bottle of cognac and one of anis, with the result that everyone was very hilarious. I was quite sorry to say goodbye to them all, especially to the girl who was in our ward with us and is now there alone. She is here by herself and too pathetic; she had four brothers, three have been killed and the last is at the front. Also she is terribly unsure of herself and shy. She must be miserable, poor thing.

THE HOSPITAL AT CELLA

Monday, 31 January. Off we two went in my car with a lieutenant to escort us. As the main road is shut because it is being bombarded, we had to go miles round on bad roads curling up and down the mountains to Eulalia. There the Reds are only about one mile away, but today was peaceful and not a sound to be heard. From there to Cella the road was just a track so full of holes and mud that I could not go more than 10 m.p.h. At last we arrived here. It is a big village, dirty and very destroyed. They say it is bombed nearly every day either by artillery or aviation, but today all was peace and quiet. When we arrived at the hospital no one knew why we had come, and as we had no papers about it we were taken to see the *commandante*. He said that a doctor had asked for two nurses, but that with three others coming they did not know what to do. They are evidently very short of nurses but can't find anywhere to put them up and have no food here. We said we did not mind sleeping on the floor but they would not believe us. We lunched with the *commandante*, our escort and a lieutenant of *intendencia*.[9] It was a crazy, grubby, cheerful meal. Then we wandered about the streets being introduced to all the doctors etc. We have been given a room for the five of us provisionally. It is small and dirty but who cares. The floor is of brick, the wallpaper is all peeling off. The walls and the ceiling are badly cracked, the door won't shut as all the wall it is attached to has sagged in. They produced a double bed and some mattresses which are just sacks full of bumps. We have no pillows, but they managed to produce a miscellaneous collection of sheets and blankets. Apart from that we have five chairs which are distinctly wobbly, one candle as light, and no water. The window has no panes and the worst is the WC. It is so revolting that one can't go there. All the filthy soldiers use it, and from fear of each other's diseases have done everything all over the floor for weeks. The town itself is crammed with soldiers and mules, and ambulances come and go in a continual stream. I am so enchanted with the place that I long to stay, but we are terribly afraid that they will send us back when the others come as they have precedence over us. It is a shame, as they will hate the discomfort and the dirt and cold and we don't mind it. If they send us back to Alhama I shall be blighted for life. Somehow I have got to stay here but it is very difficult. However, we start work tomorrow and work from nine till nine, then twenty-four hours off, then nine at night till nine in the morning. A good arrangement which gives us time to roam between whiles. They say that one sees lots of air battles and bombing here and that one day there were ninety in the air at once. The lieutenant of *intendencia* came to see how we were at about eight and found us sitting round a candle stuck on a chair. He says we are only five or six kilometres from the nearest front and that our only line of communication with the outside world is the way we came, so if the Reds succeed in cutting the railway and the road we are stranded. The *equipo* we are trying to get into is probably leaving here for Villaquemeda in a few days which is even nearer to the front.[10] I do hope they take us. We dined with the *commandante* after slipping and sliding our way along dark, muddy alleys. The *alferez*

9 *Intendencia* is the Army Service Corps.
10 Villaquemeda was ten kilometres north of Cella on the N234.

[31]

and another attractive one were there too. Afterwards we came back here and the *alferez* knelt on the floor by the light of a candle writing us out our permission to fetch our food rations tomorrow. I really began to feel I was in a war. It has been the funniest day and I hope and pray we stay here.

Tuesday, 1 February. We did not sleep badly last night despite the floor and the cold. We got up at seven, frozen stiff. A little later I went out and after picking my way over dozens of sleeping soldiers on the floor I got to the balcony, where the *alferez* turned up and we went to the station in the car to fetch our food for the day. However, there was none yet, so at nine we went to the hospital. We had only just got to the *quirófano* [*operating theatre*] when we were told that the other three had arrived. Then ensued anguishing moments of waiting for the doctor to make up his mind whom to take, and finally he chose the other three as they had precedence. We were almost in tears, and just as we were leaving we met a *teniente* who said he thought his *capitan* needed two more. So we waited not daring to hope, until he came. And without any hesitation he took us. We were so thrilled we nearly died of joy. So then we started to find a room, and with great luck met a kindly peasant boy who said that he knew a fat woman with six cows who had a room with two beds that had just been evacuated. So we leapt on it and it is splendid, large and clean, with a double bed and a single one and a washstand. No other furniture and no window-panes but definitely luxurious for this place. The family is charming. Nice pleasant peasants who are willing to help us in every-thing. So far we have no light but a candle, but that also we will arrange. Our food turned up in time for lunch and we sat on the floor of our old room and cut up the raw meat and cooked it over a candle. Tough, but good, when one is hungry. Our *capitan* is a most energetic and efficient man and takes lots of trouble to make us comfortable, but he scares us stiff. All day has been spent getting our room, moving our luggage, finding our food and generally settling in. Our *capitan* thinks we are both real nurses, so I am terrified of having to work in front of him in case I show how little I know. There are two other nurses in the *equipo*, both very common. The old lady who owns this house cooked us some fried potatoes for dinner and then we went to the hospital to do night duty. As there was absolutely nothing to do we were told we could go to bed at two, having spent the night knitting and gossiping.

We were both dead tired and got back shivering with cold as we have to walk quite a bit from the hospital here.

Wednesday, 2 February. We got up at seven in the icy cold and after dressing I went to see my car. It took me more than half an hour to start her up, but finally at 9.30 Consuelo and I and Capitan Roldan set off for Calatayud. We went from St Eulalia along a very bad lane to Villafranca where we joined the big road. We gave the Capitan Portela a lift to Camino-real as we passed through it. I wish he was our *capitan*. He is good-looking and pleasant. Roldan, in command of the *equipo*, is very common and treats us as if we were his soldiers and orphans. He is very abrupt and rude, and watching him eat nearly killed us with suppressed laughter. We got back at about seven, I was dead tired and flew into a temper about everything, what with cold, hunger and exhaustion my good temper finally gave way. Consuelo teased me which made it worse, so finally after eating some beans and potatoes which our old girl had kindly cooked for us, I went to bed at nine feeling like hell.

Thursday, 3 February. We were on duty at the hospital today and sat in the dirty *quirófano* all day from nine to nine except for a hasty lunch. During the morning one man came in with a bad head cut from a motor accident. In the afternoon three head wounds. One had smashed his skull and all his brains were coming out. When they sliced him open to take out the smashed bits of bone he bled like a pig and one could see his brains pulsating. Apart from cleaning and preparing the instruments and cutting gauzes we had nothing to do, so spent most of the day knitting and writing letters. The few wounded there were due to the Reds making an attack on the Muela at Teruel. I was absolutely horrified at the dirtiness of the doctor. His ideas of antisepsis were very shaky and it gives me the creeps to see the casual way they pick up sterilized compresses with their fingers, etc. I am not surprised that so many of the wounds get infected.

Friday, 4 February. We neither of us slept much; I coughed all night as I have a bad sore throat. We spent the morning buying various bits of stuff and miscellaneous plates and glasses and begging empty ammunition boxes off soldiers to make a cupboard, and getting our

[33]

electricity fixed up. After lunch we joined the other nurses and went for some exercise. We climbed up onto the top of the hill behind the town. From there one can see all the strategic points of interest except Teruel itself which is in a declivity. There were occasional shots from one side or another, otherwise nothing doing. Then we visited the cemetery which is as neat as one would expect. Rows of little numbers without even crosses or names, and big trenches dug ready for the next. Yesterday a poor man was looking for his brother who died here three months ago. As they are unnamed, he had to disinter a hundred and twenty three-month-old corpses. In the end he never found his brother. Horrid, sordid parts of the war. We spent the evening talking to the other nurses in their quarters, ironing our uniforms and generally arranging our room. After dinner I brought my radio down to give the peasants a shock. We have been told by one of the soldiers in the house that he is leaving at two this morning with the 84th Division for the hill near Villaquemeda where there is to be a surprise attack tomorrow.[11] The 83rd Division moved yesterday and I think the 88th is here too, so they are evidently all going into action. As it is only eight or ten kilometres from here and we are the nearest hospital, we should have lots of work tomorrow. I am glad it is the day that our *equipo* is on duty.

Saturday, 5 February. I am very tired after a long day's work. We went to the hospital at nine and did not leave till 9.30 this evening except for half an hour for a hasty lunch of beans. It was continual hard work without sitting down for one moment. My work only consisted of washing endless quantities of instruments and rubber gloves. But standing up all day in a very hot room full of the smell of chloroform does one in. My feet ache like mad, my head is bursting and I am semi-chloroformed. We had nine operations which is a full day's work. One elbow shrapnel wound, three amputations, two arms and one leg; two stomach wounds, one head and one man who had shrapnel wounds in both legs, groin, stomach, arm and head. They were vile operations. The stomach ones were foul. One had to be cut right down the middle and his stomach came out like a balloon and most of his intestines; the other had a perforated intestine so

11 The Nationalist attack came to the north of Teruel where the Republican defences were weak (7 February). In two days the Republican line was broken. It saw one of the last cavalry charges of the war.

had all his guts out, looking revolting. One amputation was just the hand, another above the elbow was an old man of seventy who had been hit in an air raid in a nearby village, the other was cut off at the top of the thigh. He swallowed his tongue and had to be given artificial respiration. Then he was given a blood transfusion but I don't think it will save his life. The most incredible one was done by another *equipo*. The man had shrapnel wounds in his back and had got gangrene as he had lain out for two days before he was found. The gangrene had spread all over his back and the doctor had to take off all the flesh so that one could see one side of his spine, all the ribs down to the waist and his shoulder blade. It was beautifully done by a young doctor of twenty-five, but the man died later in the day. Our doctor [*Roldan*] is foul. He was in a bad temper all day as usual, and is perfectly brutal with his patients. Also I don't think he is very good. It is perfectly grim having to work as an operation sister to a man whom one does not trust, who is brutal and shouts at one all the time. It is nerve-racking and leaves me all of a flop. The young doctor of twenty-five wants us to join his *equipo* but alas we can't change now though I would far rather, as I don't know how I shall stick working for Roldan. The advance which caused all our work was a success and we advanced ten miles. I was told that one could hear the shelling all day but we, shut in the *quirófano*, heard nothing. There were two air alarms to which we paid no attention, but nothing happened. If they had bombed we could not have done anything so it is of no interest to us. We have now installed electric light in our room which is a great improvement. To celebrate I washed my feet for the first time for fifteen days. What a pig I am, but under the circumstances it can't be helped.

Sunday, 6 February. We got up slowly, about nine. We neither of us slept last night as usual but it does not seem to affect us at all. My cold is worse, and when I got up I had a little fever but it wore off. After cooking our coffee we went to Mass and spent the morning strolling about the town in the sun. After lunch of lentils we arranged our room, changing the furniture round, nailing the packing cases together for our cupboard and draping with splendid blue curtains. It now looks very superior. Then Tomasa and Carmen (two of our fellow nurses) came to fetch us and we went out for a walk along the road getting run down by all the lorries and ambulances. It was a lovely clear, sunny day and we counted sixty-two of our machines flying over to bomb, etc. All very high like little dots in formation in the sky. Unluckily we could not see the bombing as it is too far away, but we could hear the occasional distant bangs of cannons. They say we have advanced further today and that the aviation have done deadly work. At four we went to the blood transfusion people who travel round in a beautiful little caravan and conserve the blood for transfusions. After being shown over the caravan we had our blood tested. Consuelo had 'B' which is only used for her own type, which is rare. Tomasa and I had 'O' which is the universal one and can be given to everyone. So the day after tomorrow we are to go and give some. I now possess the medal and will be given the bar after the transfusion. I am delighted that I am 'O', as now whenever an urgent transfusion is needed I can give my blood safely.

Monday, 7 February. The news of the war last night was stupendous. We have advanced to Alfambra, twenty kilometres in two days, taking fifteen villages, 2,500 prisoners and 3,000 dead, not to mention lots of war material. They say two *equipos* are to be sent to Alfambra which we took today. I wish ours could be one of them. We are probably going to move soon anyhow as this is no longer really the front. We were on duty in the hospital all day. This afternoon we had three operations, The first was a Red prisoner with a bad head wound, the second was one of the most fascinating things I have ever watched; an operation on an eye. They had to take out some shrapnel and then sew up the actual eyeball. The needles were so small one could scarcely see them. The third was awful. A head wound from shrapnel. It had slit up his cheek and right across the top of his head. When they cut him open there was a hole in his frontal lobe about three inches in diameter; of course when they took out the chips of bone his brains all oozed out to such an extent that one could see right down inside his head to the back of his left eye. One of the nastiest things I have seen yet. The man can't possibly live, which for his benefit under the circumstances is all for the better. Capitans Segrave and Wals spent most of the evening in the *quirófano* with us and were quite mad. I can't stand either of them and what is worse is that they are both careless doctors. Wals always goes away to sleep and lets the patients wait, and Segrave has not the remotest idea of antisepsis.

Tuesday, 8 February. We arrived at Alhama nicely in time for lunch. Josephina had my parcels for me, also letters from Mama and all the family. Charmian has sent me stacks of new records which I am playing at the moment, also chocolates. She is awfully sweet. Mama was definite in both her letters that I should come home on 20 March for three weeks and I don't know how to explain I can't. I can't ask for leave so soon after joining the *equipo*. I must wait for a few months unless we have absolutely nothing to do which is unlikely as we always move up with the troops.

Wednesday, 9 February. I hated today at the hospital more than I can say. Three people came in to be operated this morning. The first was a devastatingly attractive man who looked like a blonde devil or Hamlet, with a little beard and beautiful eyes. He had to have two fingers amputated and was very brave. The second had a stomach wound. He had lost so much blood that he was as white as a sheet and too weak to operate, so was taken away to have two blood transfusions. After him came a tough with a shell in his kneecap. Just as he began the operation the doctor nearly fainted. I suffered agonies watching as the local anaesthetic didn't take properly and the doctor was so ill he kept fumbling and dropping things and had to do it sitting down with big rests at intervals. It was nerve-racking to watch. It appears that our *capitan* has false teeth and that he has broken them; until they are mended he can't have anything solid and as the food here is so limited he can hardly eat and is terribly weak. After lunch Capitan Wals carried on in his place with three operations. First, a stomach wound which had hit the spleen. It was so badly damaged that we had to take it right out. He did a beautiful operation and is obviously a far better surgeon than Roldan, but it was nasty to see the spleen sitting on the table like a piece of liver in a butcher's shop. After that there was a ghastly one. A poor man who had all one side of his face shot to bits. His whole jaw was just a mass of flesh and teeth and splinters of bone, and his mouth was hanging loose by one strand. As he had no mouth left he could not speak and anything he wanted to say he had to write down on my pad. He could hardly breathe because his throat was all full of bits of face. It was awful, and when he was finally patched up he looked so frightful that one could not look at him. After that came a man with five wounds in his head, a fractured upper arm and a fractured femur. Holding his arm to be bandaged gave me the creeps. As the bone was smashed his arm was quite limp like a sausage and sagged everywhere. Then Roldan came back and operated on the poor boy with the stomach wound. At that one I actually did cry despite trying my best not to, but I hope no one noticed. He was so white and pathetic with an expression of such pain and sorrow and he never made a sound. He almost died under the anaesthetic. It would have been better [*if he had*].

Sunday, 13 February. We are both quite hysterical with mirth, partly due to tiredness but mostly to the stupidity of the day. We were supposed to be going up the Cero Gordo to watch the battle for Teruel, but as it snowed and the weather was impossible for flying, they put off the battle so we did not go to see it. We got home after Mass at nine, and had breakfast.

Monday, 14 February. We slept moderately badly last night as it was bitterly cold and, although the bed is big, the blankets and sheets aren't, so can't be tucked in and slip off one side or the other. We got up at nine to find the world under snow and beastly cold and windy. We hardly had the courage to get up but finally cooked our coffee, dressed and went to visit the others at their house. It was so cold out we nearly died in the street.[12] We sat in their sitting-room in a thick fog of cigarette smoke huddled round the stove, most of the *equipo* were there including Ramon, who twanged the guitar all the time. Toni García told us yesterday that our *capitan*'s brother-in-law was shot a little while ago for being a Red and that his mother-in-law has just been fined 40,000 pts. for the same reason. The *capitan* does not know yet but I bet he will be mad when he hears! We spent all afternoon ironing and knitting and shivering with cold. I never thought I could survive living in a room with no heating and snow coming in at the windows as there are no panes to keep it out.

Tuesday, 15 February. We froze all morning and kept ourselves warm by being rude to each other. Consuelo, with a smarting sore throat, proceeding to wash her hair while I tidied and cleaned the whole

12 − 18 degrees. Operations frequently had to be postponed when intense cold immobilized lorries and aeroplanes. A four-day blizzard cut both armies off from their supply depots.

room, sweeping the floor, dusting everything, nailing bits of material onto tables etc. After lunch Tomasa and Felicia turned up to go to the *intendencia* to buy some food, so we went to start the car with jugs of boiling water.

Wednesday, 16 February. (Day) It was even colder today and we both shivered round the stove all the time. In the morning we cleaned, dusted and tidied. After a lunch of fried eggs, potatoes and some foul tinned meat we retired to our room again and spent the afternoon knitting and talking, too cold to do anything else. After tonight we have two days and two nights free unless there is a lot of work, so we amused ourselves by imagining we could get leave to go and spend the night with the Infanta. The thought of a hot bath, a comfortable bed, a good meal that we did not have to cook ourselves, and a WC instead of a pot seemed distinctly pleasant. This evening we spent making hot chocolate and fried bread, then dinner of the hardest, saltiest chick-peas I have ever tasted, and off to the hospital. It is difficult to be gay when one is frozen all day in a store-room with no window-panes or heating. However, it must be very healthy.

(Night) We were told the offensive on Teruel was to begin tomorrow so all our plans to visit the Infanta went flying, and now we are all going up a mountain to watch the battle. At about three a patient came in who had to be amputated above the knee. Ramon operated with Pepe Louis as assistant and me as anaesthetist. I assured them I knew all about it and had done it before, which was a lie. I don't think I have ever been more frightened. As Ramon is not a very good surgeon the man was under ether for an hour and a half and would keep coming to life and trying to swallow his tongue. However, I accomplished it all right despite acute nerves, and by 6 o'clock we had everything cleaned up and ready again. Then Consuelo went off to church and almost immediately a stomach wound was brought in. He was obviously fatal but they sent for the *capitan* and at 8.30, after having been confessed by the priest on his stretcher on the floor, he was operated. He had a hole in his side with all his intestines hanging out. He had one completely parted and two perforations but surprisingly did not die under anaesthetic.

Thursday, 17 February. Ramon turned up at 10.30 and helped us start the car. Once more we had to push her out into the road and run her down the hill, as she was frozen stiff. Pushing, swinging the starting handle and running backwards and forwards after all night of thirteen hours' work and no food nearly laid me out. However, we finally got off and found our way over tracks in the hills to our destination. When we stopped the car in a dip we could hear the roar of the cannons quite near. So we left the car and climbed up the hill to where lots of German anti-aircraft guns were placed. The Germans were amicable and lent us glasses and explained what was what. The noise was incredible, a continual roar like thunder with intermittent different-toned bangs. The sky was full of aeroplanes shooting up and down the Red trenches and the whole landscape all around was covered with pillars of smoke. Bit by bit we wandered from one hill to another amongst all the anti-aircraft and look-out posts until we finally arrived quite close to the action, though out of danger as all the firing was aimed elsewhere. At about 11.30 the bombers began to arrive and came in a continual stream for hour after hour till the Red lines were black with the smoke of the bombs. The roar of machines continually coming and going and cannons without cease was deafening. From one hill we could see almost all our batteries firing and the infantry moving up to the front. Occasionally a Red shell would wallop down about a hundred metres away aimed at the battery. One could hear it whizz through the air with a high-pitched scream and then crash! and a huge cloud of smoke down below us. We stayed there till 1.30 watching, too enthralled to leave. One could see Teruel about ten kilometres away hidden in a cloud of smoke. It was so strange to sit in the sun watching it all going on and recognizing the aeroplanes and thinking 'There goes Ataulfo, then Prince Ali, over there Alvaro, etc.' It seemed like a strange dream. When we left, the air was still full of planes and the roar of cannons as intense as ever, but the Red shells were falling nearer so we decided that discretion was the better part of valour and packed off home again to peaceful Cella about six kilometres away. When we got back we suddenly collapsed, and after eating our lunch of lentils we retired to bed and slept from four till eight.

Friday, 18 February. We slept like rocks till eight which worked off most of our tiredness. At nine we sent the boy round to find out if we were to go on duty or not. The answer came back by the orderly that not until either this afternoon or tonight, so we decided to go and see the battle again. He said he would come too, so left us to dress. We dressed and heated water and after the usual struggle to start the car, we set off at eleven. We left the car as before and picked our way through barbed wire, trenches, unexploded shells and all the litter of war including a dead mule or two, to the aviation look-out place which was a little more to the front than where we were yesterday. There was infinitely less shelling than yesterday and the Red shells were falling a bit further away. However, the noise was continuous from one side or the other. The extraordinary thing was that no one minded us being there. The Germans, after photographing us from every angle, asked us to sit down so as not to block their view, which we did. Aeroplanes came over in swarms, though less than yesterday. All the time the Germans were 'phoning back to headquarters receiving and giving information and orders. Once I heard them 'phone Neudorfer who is head of the unit Ataulfo is in, arranging that they should come at two. At 2.30 when we were back I heard them pass over and then go back again. It would amuse Ataulfo to know that I was in his front line look-out hearing them give him orders. I should have loved to 'phone him from there. We stayed till 1.30 when a Spanish general turned up and politely told us to scram. So we came home to lunch. All the time aeroplanes were passing overhead so we guessed there was lots of activity going on.

Saturday, 19 February. A hard day's work at the hospital. We never stopped all day. Ten operations: 6 stomach wounds, 3 heads, one arm amputated and one man who was wounded in the lungs who died on the stretcher before they could operate him. We had just got back from a hasty lunch of fried potatoes and foul tinned meat and found him on the stretcher obviously dying. Consuelo sent for the priest to give him the Last Sacrament and we could do nothing at all, just sat around miserably watching him die. He was unconscious and as pale as a sheet. We looked through his pockets to see if there was any address of his family to write to, but only found one pathetic crumpled letter from his fiancée saying that, after all the difficulties there had been with her family, when he came back from the war they would let them marry and how happy they would be. It was pathetic reading it with him dying at our feet. As there was no address we can't even write to tell her what has happened to him. The worst was that there was a hurry to start operating another, the *capitan*, who is a brute, got angry and told them to take him away to the mortuary for the dead and the man was still living. Suppose he came to life to find himself just thrown anyhow amongst the dead corpses or buried alive. It must happen to lots of them. I have seen them being taken away to the cemetery just piled anyhow half-naked in a lorry. It is foul and not necessary. All morning aeroplanes were roaring overhead but I had no time to watch them. Twenty-one Red machines came over but we did not know it till after as they did not bomb us. I don't know where they went to. A head of Sanidad turned up to take a registration of all the *equipos* and told us that now there are only to be ten movable *equipos* and we are one of them, which means we will always be sent to wherever the war is hardest, which is exactly what we want.

Sunday, 20 February. We slept soundly until nine. Then we went to Mass where we met Tomasa and Felicia. We all went to the hospital to see what was going on. There we met the rest of the *equipo* who said we had entered Teruel. We decided to go after lunch in the car to see if we could enter it too or if it was not true. Finally we set off, Tomasa, Felicia, Consuelo and I in one car and Roldan, Ramon, Pepe Louis and their old host in another car in front. When we got to within four kilometres of Teruel we were stopped and told we could go no further. Then we decided to go ahead on foot. The guards tried to stop us saying women were not allowed past, but Roldan firmly asserted that we were not women but nurses, and strode on. The ground was covered with shell holes and barbed wire and trenches. The air was full of machines which did not appear to be doing anything but were actually bombing the Valencia road out the other side of Teruel. Our troops are in Teruel but have not taken it. We looked at it through glasses but, apart from a lot of burning houses, could see no signs of action. It appears to be very destroyed and none of the big buildings have roofs so have probably been gutted.

Monday, 21 February. A hard day's work at the hospital. Until twelve nothing happened. They brought one man in with a head wound but he was inoperable, he had a big lump of brains the size of a fist or more sticking out of the top of his head which made both Consuelo and me feel rather ill. So they just had to leave him to die.

From 12 till 9.30 we worked without stopping. Eleven operations: 5 stomachs, 1 back, 4 heads and 1 arm amputation. They were all very bad and difficult operations. There was such a rush that the operations just followed on one another without a pause. While one was on the table the next was on the stretcher being prepared, while we hectically sterilized the instruments for the next one and washed up the one before. Except for ten minutes for lunch I never stopped or sat down for one second all day. I like to have to work as it gives one no time to think and get depressed. There is no doubt that it is demoralising to live in an eternal whirl of blood, pain and death. One of the heads had to have an eye removed which was out of the usual form. Otherwise they were more or less routine operations. We calculate that of all the men we saw today, about nine out of ten will be dead before tomorrow morning. It is depressing when it goes on every day. I don't know how there is anyone left. Apparently we have not yet succeeded in taking Teruel although our troops have been in it for two days. They are having to take it house by house. However, tomorrow we are going again to see what is going on as the radio says we have taken it but the wounded say not, and they should know.

Tuesday, 22 February. We got up at ten to the sound of the bells ringing the capture of Teruel. Guns are firing, people shouting, soldiers letting off rockets and aeroplanes zooming over. Actually the radio said Teruel was only completely ours at 1 o'clock, and at 3.30 Consuelo and I and Maria and Sala and most of our *equipo* were there [*in Teruel*]. As we had decided to go after lunch we spent the morning with the blood transfusion *equipo* firing at stones with rifles and pistols. After lunch we went off to Teruel. The town is utterly destroyed. I didn't see a single whole house, they are all covered in bullet holes and shot to bits by cannons with great gaping holes from air bombardments. The filth was incredible, dust everywhere. The streets littered with paper and rubbish and sandbag barricades in all the side streets and squares. The shops were just a shambles and the soldiers were busy looting all they could, which was very little. We wandered in and out of all the shops and collected a bracelet and some much-needed field-glasses. In one bar in the middle of a complete shambles was an untouched grand piano which I played tunes on for fun. Everyone was crazy with joy and all the soldiers were dancing about in the streets with queer straw hats on which they had looted. The air as usual was full of planes and we saw one small one going down leaving a trail of smoke. Unluckily our *capitan* was impatient as usual, so we had to leave sooner than we wanted to as there was lots we had not seen. All the time there were cannons firing not far off all around, and one hand grenade went off accidentally just near us by the roadside and whistled past my head so close that it blew my hair. When we got back we invited Maria Sala to tea and we sat talking about the war and our strange life here until eight. A brass band played patriotic tunes outside in the pitch dark so we shot out onto the balcony to hear. They played very well. Then at eleven all the family, the soldiers and various neighbours came up to our room to hear the news. Evidently we have gone on advancing south of Teruel taking 3,000 prisoners, 2,000 dead and 11 machines shot down. Our mishaps are obviously not mentioned. The soldiers stayed on listening to the radio so late that it is now 1.30 and I am awfully sleepy. A gorgeous day full of spirit and interest.

Wednesday, 23 February. It was snowing hard when we got up at seven this morning and as we stepped out into the street to go to the hospital I slipped up and went head first into the mud. I was filthy but as I had no uniform to change into I just had to go dirty. By the end of the day the mixture of blood and mud on my apron was positively fascinating. Nothing happened all morning till one leg amputation at lunch time. Then nothing more till four, so we cleaned instruments and folded gauze. From four on it was a continual rush. First an arm amputation with gangrene, then two more heads. Both amputations and one head were Reds. Consuelo and I had to clean the instruments and were terrified of getting gangrene as both our hands are sore and raw from so much cold and manual labour. However, by washing in alcohol afterwards we should be all right. The doctors were exceptionally cold-blooded and did two wounds without anaesthetic which resulted in a series of bloodcurdling howls from the unlucky patients. I did the anaesthetic for one with an elbow wound with great success. When we got home at 9.30 we ate some tinned salmon and then I washed up and tidied while Consuelo had a much-needed bath in our little basin. I am filthier than I have ever been before.

Thursday, 24 February. We went to Teruel on our own and explored it thoroughly. It certainly is a frightful wreck and the Seminario is so surrounded with wrecked houses that one can't reach it.[13] We went across to the new part to see some friends of Tomasa's family who had a shoe factory and are some of the few remaining inhabitants.[14] They live in the cellars below the factory which is utterly destroyed by shells. At first we left Tomasa and Felicia to see them while we explored the Plaza de Toros next door which was the Reds' last stronghold. Then we joined the others who were being given a present of bedroom slippers. The women were thin and pale and crying almost all the time. Suddenly the hell of an uproar started. It sounded as if a cannon was going off a few yards away. Actually it was anti-aircraft fired at twenty-one Red machines who tried to come and bomb but were driven off. Stones were flying all over the place and the row was colossal, so everyone beat it hastily for the refuge with Consuelo and I reluctantly following. When we got halfway down we decided the our caution did not equal our curiosity so we went up again. It all appeared to be over so we wandered about outside asking what it was, when suddenly the Reds started to shell us. One could hear the cannon bang off and then a pause, then suddenly a loud whistle and with a hell of a smack the shell would hit the ground, a cloud of smoke, stones and bits of shell flying all around. The first we watched from an open space. It landed about twenty yards in front of us but luckily behind a little hillock so that the bits of shrapnel did not come our way. For the rest we joined some soldiers behind a wall where we just heard it and got covered in dust and falling stones; we only had time to peep round the corner to see where it had landed before ducking back for the rest. It was too exciting and amusing. After about ten minutes it stopped and the others came, pale and trembling from their cellar. They were more bruised by falling down the stairs than we were by stones falling on us. Then we bid the people goodbye and wandered off towards the car. About 5.30 we came back home again, vastly amused at our afternoon which was full of spirit. Tomasa and Felicia were scared pink at the shelling, I admit I was terrified myself, but I like being frightened and certainly would not show it like they do.

(Night) The *capitan* has forbidden us to go to Teruel any more as

13 The garrison had held out in the Seminario till the surrender on 8 January.
14 The civil population had been evacuated in January.

evidently this afternoon, as well as shelling the town while we were there, the Reds also shelled the road between Cella and Teruel killing quite a few people, so we had a narrow escape without knowing it. Unless any unexpected orders come, Roldan, Tomasa and Felicia are going for ten days' leave on Monday leaving Ramon, Consuelo and me here. As we can't work without the *capitan* there will be nothing to do, and as we can't leave here in case orders come to move we will just be stuck here for ten days. Depressing thought.

Friday, 25 February. We were woken at ten by a loud crash and all the doors and shutters being blown open. I suppose someone accidentally let off a hand grenade in the vicinity, anyhow the uproar successfully got us out of bed. All morning we did nothing but clean, tidy and knit. After lunch we heated water for the car which started like a dream, and roared off to *intendencia* to buy some stores. We got oil, dried figs, coffee, cheese, tinned salmon, sardines, jam and tinned meat. Everyone was very amiable and said they were sorry they had given us nothing good last time but that Tomasa had been so rude that they did not want to give her anything. So to make up they produced a box of butter which was a luxury we had never dreamed of here, then one of them said he would take us to the slaughter-house where they would give us brains and tongues whenever we wanted them. We were delighted and shot off with our kindly friend. At the slaughter-house they had neither brains nor tongues so instead made us a present of an enormous slab of perfectly delicious fresh meat, some of which we ate for dinner. After having the car filled up with petrol which I got free being a nurse at the front, we came home and had a large tea to try our butter which we have not eaten since over a month ago. At about seven our friend the *alferez* of *intendencia* turned up to see us and we talked for a long time about Teruel. We were very lucky, as evidently the first time we went there it was full of corpses in all the trenches round it and behind the barricades, and we never saw a single one of them except a lot of blood in the streets. After a time the *alferez* became very cheery and insisted on dancing to the gramophone. On a stone floor full of mountains and holes with nailed boots it was too funny for words and we kept nearly falling over. Then we talked about bullfights and he leapt about the room demonstrating with his cloak. He left at about 8.30 and we went down to cook our meat for our dinner. The kitchen was full of soldiers who were eating pancakes which they had made, they offered us one each and they were delicious. They were all a bit squiffy and made us hysterical with mirth. One little one was prancing round the room singing and playing the violin with the bellows and a piece of wood, then they all sang songs in parts and roared and laughed. We did not go to bed, or rather to sleep, till two as the *alferez* came at eleven to hear the Spanish news and stayed until 12.30. Then we went to bed and played the radio and gossiped and laughed.

Saturday, 26 February. As we were leaving the house I was given a letter from Princess Bee in which she said she had just been to Teruel and was sorry she had not come to see us but Prince Ali would not let her. She was in Teruel Wednesday and we were on duty that day and in Teruel Tuesday and Thursday. She enclosed two letters for me. One from my cousin said that when Mama left England she left John in charge of me and he says that he disapproves of my being here and is going to get me back. Bloody interfering nonsense. I should like to see him try anyhow. The result of all this is that I was in a bad temper all through a very good lunch. However, afterwards I cheered up and we went off with two of the men in their car to see Albarracín which is a funny little town twenty kilometres away. It was nice drive through the mountains. Albarracín itself is perched round a corner up on the mountain and the road goes under it through a tunnel. One can only go about on foot after climbing miles of steps. All the houses are rickety, dirty little buildings perched on the edge of a cliff. The streets are very narrow and dirty and dark with the overhanging houses almost meeting above. We were shown round the cathedral and the Dominican monastery by the priest who could speak of nothing but the war, as Albarracín has been taken twice by the Reds. The last time was in July when the entire population shut themselves in the cathedral and managed to hold off the Reds for seven days without food or water until they were relieved.

3
The Aragon Offensive
March – July 1938

THE ROLDAN EQUIPO AT CELLA AND CALCEITE

After Teruel, with his armies concentrated in Aragon, Franco exploited his success by mounting an offensive towards the Mediterranean and the River Ebro. It began on 7 March. The Republicans were demoralized after Teruel; units gave way exposing those which resisted. Rojo reported on 13 April a 'total crisis of morale'. On 10 March the Nationalists recaptured Belchite. On 15 April the Navarrese Brigades reached the sea at Vivaroz, cutting the Republican zone in two. By the end of April Gandesa, Lerida, Fraga and Tremp had fallen and the Nationalists had reached the Ebro and the Pyrenees.

The isolated Republican resistance brought casualties. Pip's equipo was working flat out. She had only twelve hours' sleep in six days. There was no hot water (she had no bath for two months), little food and operations were performed with oil lamps. She arrived in Morella a week after its capture on 4 April. Throughout, the only relief was occasional trips to Epila and Zaragoza.

Franco, with his armies on the Ebro, took a decision that was much criticized by General Kindelán and others, who favoured an advance on Barcelona. Instead of advancing into Catalonia, in April he turned towards the Republican capital, Valencia. His troops met with stiff resistance through difficult terrain. The Nationalists reached the Valencian huerta on 23 July after suffering 20,000 casualties in five days. Pip was convalescing in England from 7 July to 23 August.

Her stay in Aragon was the most miserable of Pip's time in Spain. Overwork stretched all the equipo's nerves to breaking point and squabbles were the result. How far were Pip and Consuelo's difficulties with the equipo chief, Captain Roldan, of their own making?

[48]

Roldan, like many Falangists, was hostile to the monarchy and aristocrats in general. Consuelo and Pip were both aristocrats and ardent monarchists; their connection with the Orleans family must have grated on Roldan. Her frequent visits from Ataulfo and others was an irritant as was her 'mad' behaviour with Consuelo. She was accused of flirting with the sympathetic doctor, Magallon. Almost continuously ill and run down, she reacted violently against her detractors.

Thursday, 3 March. We are going to move at last. We don't know exactly where or when yet but it will be tomorrow or the day after to somewhere near Belchite which the Reds took from us last year and we are now going to take back.[1]

Friday, 4 March. Consuelo and I are having an arduous fight to save ourselves from a fate worse than death they say. After waiting all day for the order to leave which never came and packing etc., at about five we sat down in our room to rest. Suddenly in at the door came four strange soldiers. As Consuelo was so hoarse she could not speak, I asked them what they wanted. They said they were looking for two nurses but we were not the ones. So I asked what they were like and they said one fair and one dark. We immediately thought it must be Felicia and Tomasa. They said that was it, but undaunted by that they firmly came in and sat down and asked our landlady to fetch them some bottles of cider. We were mildly surprised, but as I had said Felicia and Tomasa were coming over later it did not strike us as particularly odd, especially after all the odd things that happen with soldiers here. The landlady was shocked and refused to go away or fetch anything, but alas after a swift passing of money she trotted off. Then I realized that things were not as they should be, but always hold that one can get out of everything peaceably in time which is better than rushing into a row and everyone knowing about it afterwards. So they stayed drinking cider and talking and becoming more tiresome. The leader sat on the bed beside Consuelo and tried to paw her about, while the other three were harmless, except one who poked and prodded me a bit. However we kept them in order more

1 Belchite had been taken by the Republicans during the ambitious but ultimately unsuccessful Aragon offensive (August – October 1937). Belchite surrendered on 6 September after a fierce battle. It is notable that Pip knew of the proposed attack on Belchite.

or less until Tomasa and Felicia appeared. It was then perfectly obvious that our suspicions were correct, as they had never seen each
other before. After they had gone the soldiers became worse, so we
said we had to go down to dinner. It took us about half an hour of
alternate gentle persuasion and forceful measures when driven into a
corner and seized upon, to get them out. However, at last they went.
The leader asked me again and again if he could come come back
after dinner, to which I said certainly not. Five minutes after dinner
suddenly the door opened and in came the two tiresome ones again.
We were definitely disconcerted, not to say frankly frightened. We
neither spoke to them nor answered their questions for about ten
minutes but they just sat themselves down. If our friends the soldiers
had been downstairs I would have called them, but tonight they were
all new and might well have taken sides against us if a bit tiddly, so I
did not dare as I can cope with two but not more. They stayed and
stayed despite us saying we were tired and would they go. So then we
all four played cards while they kept asking if they could sleep here
tonight. There ensued a heated argument on the subject. They would
not take no for an answer and said there was plenty of room in the
bed, so we said that was not the point and would they please go. This
went on and on despite my going and opening the door and saying
good night. At last at 12.15 they left very reluctantly but quietly.
They said they were coming back at nine in the morning. We said
they were not to, but they will come for a certainty. The result is
that we are both sleeping with the window firmly shuttered and our
bayonets beside us.

Saturday, 5 March. We slept late. I had just got out of bed at 9.45 and
Consuelo was still snoozing when suddenly there was a knock at the
door. I opened it a little putting myself firmly in the gap, and there
were the two tiresome men. However, as I did not let them put a foot
into our room and was rather rude, they soon went away to my great
relief. All day we spent waiting about for orders to move which never
came. Suddenly at about five there was a knock on the door and in
walked Marie Angeles and Alvaro. Alvaro brought us some assorted
food and me lots of letters and a telegram from Mama asking for my
address. All my letters were from family. Mama is frantic about the
way I have disappeared as she evidently does not get my letters.
Unluckily Alvaro had to go very soon but it was a lovely surprise to

see them again. This town in crammed with a new lot of soldiers who are foul drunks. It scares me pink every time I go out, especially in the night. However, my loaded pistol [*given her by Ataulfo*] cheers me up.

Wednesday, 9 March. We are raging and wrathful. The attack on Belchite started yesterday and here we are in Cella doing nothing.[2] BAH!!! And the *capitan* asking for leave with the radio giving out glowing reports of fighting and advancing eleven kilometres and shooting down two machines. BAH!!! I want to go there quickly but here we sit idle.

Thursday, 10 March. After a boring day as usual we decided to go to bed early. At nine we had just got into bed when the old landlady came trotting in to tell us a boy had come round to say that we were to leave at once. She was so vague about it that we thought it was not true. However, we got up again and rushed round to ask the others if it was. They said that the order had come to leave immediately for Cariñena where we would be given further orders.[3] We went to start the car, and load it up with all the delicate things in packing cases, gramophone, radio, records, glasses etc. We tried to unlock the door only to discover that some soldiers, in trying to open it with a key that did not fit, had broken the lock. The result was that I broke the key. There was only one thing to do, so armed with a stick and distressed to a degree I smote a window with a mighty biff, shattered it, strewed the car with glass and cut my hand. Then, of course, great oaf that I am, I remembered that the broken key was also for ignition and consequently I could not start her up. I made a futile search with Tomasa in the cases to see if there was another key and finally had to ask the soldiers to make a contact with a wire instead. After hours of fiddling with the engine and a bit of wire at last it was fixed up, and we shot off round to the other house at 11.30 to collect the others. They were waiting to hear the news, so we hoicked out the radio and sat down to wait. The news did not come till 12.15, an hour late. It was perfectly stupendous. We have advanced enormously and taken

2 Belchite was retaken by the Nationalists on 15 March. It had been preceded by heavy bombardments. This was an early battle in Franco's Aragon offensive (March – July 1938). The Republican armies put up little serious resistance.
3 Cariñena is seventy-six kilometres east of Zaragoza, through wild, mountainous country.

Belchite again as well as millions of villages, prisoners, arms, etc. At last we set off for Cariñena after fond farewells from everyone. We were so happy we laughed and talked the most utter nonsense. We decided after the war we would all go to London: Consuelo to work in a travel bureau, Felicia in a dress shop ending up as a second Schiaparelli, and Tomasa as a chorus girl ending up by marrying a rich marquis and eating caviare. We arrived at Cariñena at 3.30.

Friday, 11 March. We started off to Belchite for miles along a bumpy, dirty road. We passed soldiers, cannons, cavalry, trenches, lorries, barbed wire entanglements, etc. till at last we arrived here. The town is a mess. Very destroyed, not a decent house anywhere, all in pieces and filthy. The hospital is a large house that was a casino.[4] We trotted round looking for a house to live in but they all had holes in the floor, walls or roof and were uninhabitable. Finally we found one opposite the hospital which was ankle deep in dirt but quite passable and big enough. We requisitioned it and lots of plates, pots, pans and so on that we came across. Then we unloaded the lorries which went off to Zaragoza to fetch our beds. We cleaned the room to be the operating room, scrubbing the floor and the furniture and unpacking the things out of the cases. We four lunched at 4.30, having eaten nothing all day, on our tinned food and biscuits, perched on packing cases in the ward. All the time the batteries of cannons outside the town were booming off as the Reds are only two kilometres away, but we were much too busy to pay any attention. All afternoon Consuelo and I were on our knees with buckets of water scrubbing the floor which was thick with mud and filth. We took about three hours to do it, as it was a huge room. By the end I was just about dead. Then we went off to the only water supply to get water. It is a fountain in the middle of the town with a quantity of soldiers all round fighting to get water. We are pretty well the only women here. This morning we were photographed for the press with the only two surviving civilians, an old lady of about seventy and one other of about forty. Apart from them there are nothing but swarms of soldiers of every kind. One talked a little English and told me that there are eighty-five prisoners here of the International Brigade, mostly Americans and some English. They will all be shot as the foreigners always are. After they went we did a certain amount of tidying and

4 Not a gambling casino but the local worthies' social club.

washing plates, then cooked coffee in the machine for boiling the instruments and dined on coffee and tinned fish. The *capitan* produced cognac and everyone got very gay. We laughed and joked and all became very lewd. It was very funny and we are all in a stupendous temper. I have never enjoyed a day more but I have never been dirtier. After dinner we sat talking till 12.15, waiting for the beds to arrive, by the light of a petrol lamp as there is no electricity here now. At last the lorries arrived with forty beds and some very tired orderlies. Then we worked like lunatics putting beds together and making them up until 2 o'clock in the morning. A short interval for cognac and a cigarette and on with the work till 2.30. So far we have not had time to see to our house, so are all sleeping together in the ward in our clothes. A crazy life, and they say in a few days we are to go further forward!

Saturday, 12 March. After breakfast the great tragedy of my day happened. I discovered someone had been in our room and stolen a case of records, 1,000 cigarettes, my pistol and worst of all my radio. Exhausted as I was I thoroughly disgraced myself by crying, which made me lose my temper. Next time we came back to our house poor Felicia discovered they had been again and broken the lock of her suitcase and stolen all her clothes, her coat, a bracelet, 250 pesetas and the photo of her fiancé who has died. At the last she very nearly cried too, poor thing. They also took Tomasa's coat, two uniforms and various clothes and Consuelo's fur jacket and broke open my suitcase but luckily took nothing. We were all furious, and every time we had to go over to the hospital something disappeared. We told the *guardia civil* and complained to the *capitan* of Estado Major. I got my records back and they have found the cigarettes but I have not got them yet. But, alas, not my poor dear radio I loved so much. Roldan caught two soldiers in the act of stealing and they were removed. As there was no other food we peeled and cooked potatoes for lunch and again for dinner. After lunch Consuelo and Felicia stayed in the hospital to cope with an amputation while Tomasa and I went off to the river to wash all the bloody operation sheets and clothes. We knelt on the bank amongst a crowd of soldiers and scrubbed all afternoon till my hands and knees were dead. Then more cooking and hospital and washing up till dinner. Then after all day of deep depression and exhaustion without stopping for one moment, suddenly came the news that we are to leave tomorrow for Escatrón which we took to be about forty kilometres away.[5] So tomorrow off we go again. What a life. I like moving. The culminating depression was to hear that Germany and Austria have declared war. God knows what will happen now, but as I don't approve of unnecessarily depressing oneself I refuse to think about it at all. Tomasa has been quite maddening all day, grumbling about the few unimportant things of hers they have stolen. I can't stand that woman. On the other hand I am getting more and more fond of Felicia. Consuelo and I have decided never to feel tired, never to feel hungry, and never to grumble, but my God it has been difficult to stick to today. Poor Roger Radio!! I am afraid I will never see him again. These last few days we have worked so much under such strange conditions that we have no time to wash or change and making up has gone completely. Oh, God. I hope there won't be another war. What can I do if there is? What hell life is. Now it is 1 o'clock and we have to get up early to work, so I must try to sleep.

Sunday, 13 March. Once more in a different place. Tonight we are in Escatrón, right at the front. We got up at seven, dressing in the usual rush that does not allow for anything elegant like washing. We had to collect and pack up everything. The others did the hospital round after taking coffee to the four wounded. The other whom we operated yesterday with the bad stomach wound died last night and his corpse was still lying in the passage on the stretcher. All morning I stood guard on our house while packing up the bedding and kitchen things. I caught at least six hopeful thieves who had sneaked in. Consuelo went off to the battery where my gramophone records have been found to see if they had the radio. We went to the mayor to agitate again where I found a most attractive German. After that came an officer with the radio saying he had just found it, so all is well in the end thanks to Consuelo.

About three we set off along a dreadful stony, dusty road. Half way, we came across the blood transfusion ambulance again and stopped to say hello. A little further, after passing hundreds of trenches, dead horses, barbed wire, batteries, soldiers and so on, I suddenly saw Schiller in the side-car of a motor-bike coming out of a side road. I stopped to say hello and discovered that he is now liason officer between the aviation and 5th Division and is living in Escatrón, so I hope we meet again. Along the last part of the road we passed five or six corpses strewn about which was rather an unpleasant spectacle.

5 Escatrón was on the Ebro.

Finally at five we arrived here. It is not at all destroyed, and all the inhabitants look well and happy and have no complaints about the Reds except lack of food. However, they all seem delighted to see us and to be on our side now. We sat about doing nothing for two hours while the horses arrived and we unloaded, then made up beds etc., dined off tinned tunny in the ward and all went off to bed in our various houses. I have never been so dirty or lead such a rushed and hectic life, but it is all the greatest fun except when I am very over-tired.

Monday, 14 March. A perfectly splendid day. After a morning of putting up beds and counting sheets etc. suddenly Ataulfo appeared to visit us. I was so surprised to see him that I nearly fell down the stairs. He laughed to find us so dirty, as my uniform was black, and my hands too, as well as swollen and rough, my face dusty and unpainted and my hair all dirty and tangled. But what does it matter how I look? He was looking very clean and smart. Maybe it is the effect of living so long with dirty soldiers, but I thought him devastatingly attractive and good-looking.

The Reds seem to be running like hares as we are the nearest hospital and have not had a single casualty yet. The enemy are about two hundred yards away, and all day we have heard shooting and machine-guns, but no one seems to get hurt. I believe actually with the continual rattle going on they have killed one and wounded eight slightly, and that with pistol shots actually falling in this village. What a strange war this is! Our billet is clean and pleasant, and our landlady very nice. She says amongst the Reds there were an enormous amount of French and Russians and a few Germans, but no English.

Tuesday, 15 March. At 8.30 I wandered out onto the balcony to admire the sun, when suddenly shells began to whistle overhead. I listened enthralled until they began to get their range and fall close, when I beat a hasty retreat indoors with the orderlies. Then for about half an hour the shells fell all round us. I was scared pink, but of course did not say so. Tomasa turned up, having been fetched by Felicia, in a state of collapse from terror. Then Consuelo came running in. A shell fell just near her as she was coming and the man in front of her collapsed in a pool of blood. A few minutes later he was brought in with a smashed leg and a hole in his throat. He was the first to be operated and died on the table. Five came all in a rush from the near vicinity, pouring blood in a ghastly mess. It was a hectic business tying them up, mopping blood and getting them into bed. The bombardment went on all day, and about fifteen wounded came in, almost all very bad. The whole populace retired very wisely to the rcfuges while we worked all day without stopping. At about five they got our range again and the shells began to fall in the next door houses. It was petrifying having to stay here unable to do anything. Why we were not hit I don't know, as there was hardly a house near us without a shell through it. When it got really bad so that the windows were breaking and bits and pieces falling all around the house, everyone went downstairs, and moaning and calling for us all the time. Poor things, it must be awful for them. I must say I don't know why we weren't hit as, one after the other, shells exploded within a few yards of us. The bombardment stopped at about eight, but who knows if they will start again tonight, certainly tomorrow. We are all sleeping in the hospital. As everyone else leaves the patients when there is any real danger I am sticking to them. At the moment we have just evacuated six and are waiting to see two more, meanwhile cleaning up by the light of a little oil lamp which is all we have. I am going to bed now but expect we shall be up again soon, except that as the *capitan* says he is too ill to operate we can't take in any really serious cases tonight. Once more I sleep in my uniform in the ward. This is one hell of a place. Today they hit Ramon's room just after he left, and burnt *intendencia* so that we have no food for the wounded or ourselves, and as the road is under fire all day no one can come or go, except at night with no lights and risking a smash in a shell hole. What a life!

Wednesday, 16 March Last night everyone slept down in the refuges except a few orderlies, Consuelo who was on duty and I who slept in the operating room, not in the ward, so as to keep Consuelo company if the Reds start bombarding again. However, I got to bed at eleven on a mattress in all my clothes with two blankets and slept without stirring until six, when a casualty was brought in with a thigh wound of no great importance. Then I lay down again and Consuelo who was tired out used my feet as a pillow and went so sound asleep that she never stirred when I moved her and gave her the pillow. All night she had to go from one to another and two died. Another died this morning, and one who came in this morning died in the afternoon; a poor boy of seventeen with all his intestines out, too bad to operate. He bled so much it went through the mattress and made a pool on the floor. We are all over-tired and depressed. The Reds bombarded us again in the morning but only four or five fell really close. It is awful being here bombarded all day in a ward of wounded begging to be moved, and so petrified that they pretty well die of fright. The *capitan* is ill and can't operate. The others are cowards and fly down to the refuge leaving a dressing half done. We have no food or anything to give the wounded. Our last condensed milk has gone, ditto our coffee. The women who come to clean the floors and the linen are all in the refuges. The whole situation is quite impossible. The other three slept all afternoon. Consuelo on some packing cases, and the others in the refuges. We might be quite all right if only we could sleep and eat, but there is no time to sleep and hardly anything to eat, and a terrific nervous strain all the time into the bargain. Well, everything stops sooner or later one way or another, though I hope this won't stop by us all being killed, which is quite probable if they go on bombarding every day. Another patient with a wound through his neck died this evening. After a dinner of rice we evacuated all except two stomachs, one of whom is more tiresome than twenty put together. I think he will die tonight and I am ashamed to say I shan't care a damn if he does. He never stops shouting for things every minute and then swears at one and uses filthy language and disturbs all the others. It is not that he is worse than the others, just his character. Tonight I am on night duty as Consuelo and I take it in turns and only sleep every second night.

Thursday, 17 March. All morning I spent in the wards tidying up and looking after our two patients. The delirious one got worse until he suddenly had a fit and sat up in bed clutching madly onto me, and moaned and yelled until he stopped breathing. I thought he had died, but when I laid him down he suddenly came to life again and, completely delirious, wanted to get up and go out to lunch. We stayed with him all morning while for two hours he talked complete nonsense till finally, just before lunch, he went to sleep and died.

After lunch I spent the afternoon repairing and cleaning my poor car. There was a certain amount of bombarding all day but only a few fell close to the hospital. At about 6 o'clock suddenly came the order that the *equipo* was to move to Hijar. We were both very depressed to think that we were going further back from the front, as we had expected to be sent to Caspe which was taken last night. About two hours later a lieutenant-colonel arrived with the order that instead of going to Hijar we were to go to Caspe. We were thrilled and danced round the hospital with joy. The main road is impassable as there is a flooded river and no bridge, so we have to go along a small lane and get to another road. At about 10.30 at last the lorries were loaded and everything ready despite the drawback of not being able to use lights or make a noise in case of being shot at. We set off with the others in front and me following, with the ambulance and the lorries bringing up the rear. As the road was shut from being under fire we could use no lights, and had only the light of the moon to help us on our way. The result was that on the most open part of the road both the *capitan*'s car and mine hit a big stone beside a shell hole in the road. Their car broke down completely, but mine, although it had smashed the oil tank, jammed the brakes and squashed the exhaust pipe, could still go on, so I abandoned the other car and inmates and beat it for the refuge of an olive grove, leaving them out in the open to be shot at. Luckily the Reds were feeling lazy and did nothing, so they were able to get their car in tow behind a lorry and come and join us. The *capitan* came in my car the rest of the way. We were jammed in a long line of lorries and cannons moving slowly down a twisty, muddy lane. What with the breakdown, swinging car, the lorries and the state of the road we took seven hours to do twenty-five kilometres, or less! Sometimes we stopped on the way to wait for the lorries or let a battery go past, or a long line of cavalry. Finally, exhausted, we arrived at Caspe at 4.30 in the morning, shivering with cold and famished with hunger. It looked extraordinarily unattractive. We stopped on the outskirts as the streets were full of bomb holes, and one or two houses were burning merrily.

Friday, 18 March. Directly the lorries arrived at six we went to see the new hospital. It is a college, large and pleasant with a patio and cloisters all around. Naturally it was quite filthy but full of things we wanted to requisition like bedclothes, cooking utensils, a sewing machine and gorgeous books. We set straight to work cleaning every-thing up, sweeping out the filth, collecting help from the town, putting up beds, unpacking beds. With a short interval for coffee we went on until 10.30 when everything was done. Just as we were about to take a rest, casualties began to pour in and the wards filled up and I rushed round giving injections, making coffee, changing and heating beds etc.

till I was nearly potty. After lunch, three-quarters dead from exhaustion, Consuelo and I decided we must get down all the bedclothes from upstairs and count and tidy away. We worked all afternoon sorting and carrying them downstairs, getting more miserable every moment. Everyone was dead tired and bad-tempered so no one would help us. Finally it was all over, and the few more casualties that came in the evening were all finished, so I sat down at last for a rest on the verge of tears from sheer exhaustion when suddenly I was informed that my car has been stolen. It was a fitting end to one of the worst days I have passed in my life. So now I have no car and my dear little Fiona has a new owner. What swine people are, stealing everything from under one's nose. I frankly broke down and cried, more from tiredness than anything else, and where no one could see me. I finally got to bed semi-conscious at about eleven after more casualties had arrived. If life goes on like this much longer we will all die. It is more than any one can stand.

Saturday, 19 March. I woke at eight feeling tired but a new woman. More casualties had just come in, after leaving us a peaceful night, thank God, so went to find the ward in the most appalling mess with pools of blood everywhere, all the beds dirty and unmade. I went to our small ward to fetch more sheets and found five dead corpses strewn anyhow on the floor, which made a pleasant aperitif to breakfast. We worked all morning straightening things out, giving injections etc. A few new patients came in and one or two were operated, but too much happens here for me to remember it all. By midday we had everything tidy so went to sit on the patio in the sun making numbers of the beds and lists of things, when Ataulfo appeared. He was very worried about us having been in Escatrón during the bombardments. He was quite right to be worried as he came through there today and says that there is scarcely anything left of it, and he would not have recognized it as the same town. He said that Princess Bee disapproves of my leading this life and thinks it is time I went away. I said she was quite wrong, and we argued a lot about it. He threatened to send the Infanta to fetch me, but I begged him not to. I do hope he won't as I can't say no to her, and yet I have no intention of leaving. Maybe if he had asked me to leave yesterday evening I would have done so with joy, but last night I slept and now things are very different. He brought us biscuits, chocolate, shortbread and wine, but alas no cigarettes and he has run out too. He has promised to see what he can do about my stolen car, as of course it has not turned up. At about six three or four wounded arrived. Two were operated, which meant everything was just nicely finished off for dinner. All through dinner we were saying how gorgeous to go to bed in peace when suddenly a head casualty arrived, followed quickly by a stomach, two legs, a hand and an arm. As they all arrived at once and we have only a limited quantity of oil lamps it was complete chaos. The floor was covered in stretchers, blood everywhere, everyone shouting, the poor patients moaning and screaming, and so instead of going to bed it started all over again. One thing is that though there is a certain amount of bombarding here and lots of shells fall in the town, so far none have fallen very near us. One or two did yesterday and a few this afternoon, but nothing to worry about. Three patients had to be operated, one stomach, one hand amputation and one arm. At 3 o'clock I went to bed as everything had settled down again. Consuelo stayed to cope till it was all finished. She had a bad time with a head who died screaming and fighting and cursing. Most heads seem to go mad, they are the ones I loathe as they have a glassy look in their eyes and make awful noises and are quite crazy. I don't really see how we can go on like this, working all day and all night with never a rest.

Monday, 21 March. Six months today since I left home and it seems like six years! Home seems so far away, and such a completely different world that I cannot imagine ever going back. How strange it will be. Luckily no new patients arrived last night and we slept peacefully till seven when one arrived with a hole in his neck and out of his back. He was operated later, but after spending a few hours roaring like a tubed horse and trying to throw himself out of bed, he died. No others arrived all day until one just after dinner. He also was operated. A bullet had entered the top of his head and was lodged in his neck. Incredible as it seems, despite the bullet having gone straight through his head, behind his eyes, through the back of his palate and past his spine, it appears not to have touched anything vital so he may live. Some have died and five have been evacuated and now we have only eight here, of which five are almost certain to die in a day or two. One is a head wound who is half mad and quite terrifying. He appears to be over-sexed and masturbates to such an extent that we have to tie him down. He imagines himself to be sleeping with a certain Conchita, and makes the oddest remarks to her, also sometimes with a Maria just to vary things a bit.

Wednesday, 23 March. We were both shattered today. While I was washing, Consuelo had to aid a stomach-washing which she said almost made her vomit. My unpleasant experience was very funny. The over-sexed head wound suddenly threw off his bedclothes, let out a wild shout and produced his penis, he then left it to its own devices and proceeded to spray fountains in all directions. I rushed for the pot and chased after the fountain, but it was so damned elusive that I finally had to grab the damn thing and hang on. I thought he would never stop. How any nurse can look at a man, let alone touch him, I don't know after all the unattractive things one has to do with them.

Thursday, 24 March. I had just got to bed last night at about 10 o'clock when an ambulance arrived. Four patients had arrived but one was already dead when brought into the hospital. Of the three others, one was just a knee wound of no vast importance who did not have to be operated and was evacuated tonight. The second had a lot of shrapnel wounds in his torso, one leg and one arm; the worst was a hole in his chest which had penetrated his right lung, and through which he breathed and frothed blood. He was operated but died early this morning. The third was a lieutenant with a bad wound in his forehead which had made him lose his sight. All of them had been sitting together in the kitchen of a house a few kilometres from here when it was shelled. The lieutenant who is unpleasant and tiresome is all right so far, but almost sure to go crazy. The day passed as usual with nothing of any interest and no new wounded till about five suddenly Mercedes Milá appeared unexpectedly. We had to show her round the hospital. She found fault with lots of things: one ward was too hot, our beds were untidy in our bedroom, and the thing that annoyed us was that she said we were too made up. After all the weeks of filth we have been through, the very first time we have time to make ourselves respectable she has to come and tell us we are too painted. Quite untrue anyhow. She said we were only to have fifty beds here, so we only have to put up twenty in the dining room upstairs. Half of them we did directly she left but as we have no lighting we could not do the rest. Evidently a big advance is starting from here tomorrow and our *equipo* is likely to stay here for about two weeks. Too bad to be left at *retaraguardia* again.

[61]

Friday, 25 March. After talking in my sleep most of the night in Spanish about blood, and moaning, I duly overslept again and was not up till nearly nine. What with arranging the new ward of twenty beds and changing sheets and all the other things, we were busy all morning. One new patient arrived with a bad wound in his side on a level with his ribs. I don't know what happened inside, but I gather from the treatment we gave him that it missed his lung but hit his guts. Anyhow he moans all the time, tries to fling himself out of bed and vomits blood. I hurt my ankle somehow and could hardly walk all afternoon. No one was at all sympathetic and just laughed every time they saw me hobbling about. Really very irritating considering how much it hurt. Finally we went to bed leaving an orderly and the young nun on duty. Ten minutes later I had to go down for water and decided to see if everything was still peaceful in the wards. Both the people on duty had disappeared, everyone was vomiting and it was a colossal mess. By the time I had cleaned them up, the ones on duty came back. I was in a rage and blew off at them in a big way, and told them never to dare to go away both at once, whatever the reason. It made me laugh afterwards to think of me blowing the heads off a man and a woman both at least eight or nine years older than myself. My God, how everything smells in this place. The patients nearly knock one down with their aroma whenever one approaches them.

Saturday and Sunday, 26 and 27 March. Once more I am dead tired and God knows if I shall get to bed tonight. I sincerely hope so as I look like a dead cat and my ankle hurts so that I can hardly walk any longer. Saturday was an ordinary day though a bit busier than usual. We were trotting from ward to ward all the time. At about four we had everything nice and settled and were contemplating a well-earned rest when suddenly along came an ambulance bringing us four very bad patients. Before we could get going with them five more came, and so it went on all night. The most awful rush and hurry which has kept up ever since, operating one after the other, ambulances rolling up continually with more and more, stretchers of moaning people all over the floor, and me diving amongst them behind the new Lieutenant Mirat, clasping a bundle of compresses in one hand and splints and cotton-wool in the other, with my pockets stuffed with bandages, sticking plaster, scissors and so on. Consuelo was frantically giving injections of antitetanus etc. and everyone tripping over everyone else. Pepe took charge and put a spot of order into the business, and we went on all night. At about 5.30 they stopped operating, as they were all too tired to see, and we went to bed. Consuelo and I stayed up, as there was still a lot of work in the wards straightening everything up again. I really don't know what happened as it is now four days later, and we have never stopped day or night, so I have had no time to write this diary and am in such a whirl that I honestly don't remember what happened when. Today was the same again. Despite not having been to bed the night before we stayed up till the early hours still working. Finally I retired to bed exhausted at about three, leaving Consuelo on duty. Four times she came up to bed, but every time an ambulance arrived and she had to go down again. She finally got to bed at 6.30. It was all such a rush that I shall never be able to remember what happened. I only know that we all worked day and night without stopping for a single moment.

Monday, 28 March. Amidst all this rush and hurry things are gradually getting settled very nicely. Pepe, who is perfectly charming, is in charge of the wards, and is a heavenly doctor to work under as he helps and teaches one and does not shout often or get impatient. Needless to say I overslept last night and did not get down till nine, to find all the wards in a fearful mess. The *capitan* turned up soon afterwards and was furious with me, quite rightly, as I had no business to wake up at nine when I meant it to be 6.30 even if I have not slept for thirty-six hours before. However, with great energy I got everything cleaned and tidied and by the time poor Consuelo got up at twelve it was all tidy. The wounded rolled in all morning in twos and threes. There was one poor patient, the first to come, who was an *alferez* of aviation. He was shot down yesterday in flames by anti-aircraft, and was terribly burned. All his face black, one leg and both of his arms. The forearm and hand on his left side were burnt to a cinder and was just a nasty shrunken black stick. I had to help do his dressing, which lasted two hours, as Ramon and I were the only ones who were up and about except Consuelo, who was vastly busy feeding patients. I took a great interest in my aviator, who could talk English and was very brave. He looked like a snowman wrapped from head to toe in bandages. However, some relatives turned up and took him away to Zaragoza in the afternoon, so my big interest was removed. I hope he lives, as he was so sweet despite looking like something out of the chamber of horrors. At about four

[63]

once more the stretchers and ambulances began to roll up, and off we went again to work. This time it was not so bad and all got fixed quite happily and peacefully. However, once more I was working all day long without time to sit down or anything. As there are so many wounded and all so bad, we have to do night duty as well as day. We take it in turns, Consuelo and I, with the result that tonight I am on duty. We have girls from the village to help in the wards, but they are quite hopeless as they always do everything they should not, so that one has to be constantly watching them. Tonight the *capitan* was too exhausted to operate so Ramon and Pepe did it. Pepe is a very good doctor and a joy to work with. I am so glad he has taken charge of the wards, as he lets us do all the bandaging and a lot of the dressings, and organizes everything beautifully. After the operations were over at about 1 o'clock we all sat down to talk. I had made some coffee which I brought down for everyone, also my last bottle of wine. Gradually everyone went off to bed till there was only Pepe, Tomasa and I.

Wednesday, 30 March. I had meant to get up at 6.30 but overslept until nine, which is not surprising if one thinks that I only sleep every second night and even then don't go to bed till after midnight. However, I arose with my eyes glued up with sleep, to find Consuelo had done all the beds and had everything tidy, and was going round with the *capitan* and most of the *equipo* to see all the men. Most of the morning was spent doing injections and salines, and the afternoon all the usual work of changing sheets, etc. Then I had to take all the temperatures which, with forty-nine patients, is a distinctly lengthy job. Then we evacuated six and after a few more injections it was dinner time. So as usual the day passed with no time to rest or wash. However, no wounded arrived all day and so far have not arrived tonight either. I am so sleepy that I can hardly see to write, but it will wear off. Tomasa and Felicia have quarrelled again and now Felicia says she can't stand it any longer and that she is going to leave the operating room, as she won't work with Tomasa. I must say that I don't blame her, as Tomasa is unbearable and never does a stroke of work. A general whose name I don't know came to visit the hospital this afternoon – this influx of generals is very trying.

Thursday, 31 March. After a valiant struggle not to go to sleep, at last the daylight arrived and I could start making beds and taking

[64]

temperatures. Consuelo turned up at seven, and by the time the *capitan* came to see the patients we had it all clean and finished off. Then one or two injections and all our work was over, so we started sorting clothes from under the beds and labelling them all, etc. We were busy all morning, although only two new patients arrived. After lunch we were sitting out in the sun on the patio, revelling in having nothing to do, when suddenly three casualties arrived, swiftly followed by five more, and so it all started again; the rush and muddle and blood and screams. Luckily this time I had everything ready for dressing the wounds, and it all went off splendidly. We paused for dinner at about ten, and then on again operating till two in the morning. In all we have had about twenty wounded, which is a lot if they are all very badly hurt. One, a captain with a stomach wound, will die, and a head has died already and another stomach, so the hospital empties again. How we succeed in living this life without dying of exhaustion I don't understand. During the last six days I have been to bed exactly twice, for about six hours each time. I must admit that I am terribly tired as we never stop working all the time, but it is most enjoyable and I like it much more than when there is very little to do. I finally went to bed exhausted at 2 o'clock, leaving Consuelo on night duty.

Saturday, 2 April. I am too utterly exhausted to write anything at all. A day like the others, work like blacks without stopping, no sleep, so tired that we are only semi-conscious. For more than a week now we have gone on working forty-two hours on and six hours off. Enough to kill one. This evening some friends of Consuelo's who are ADCs to General Monasterio turned up and asked us to dine.[6] As lots of wounded had been evacuated and the remaining thirty were peaceful, we accepted and went off to dine with General Monasterio. It was great fun, and he is a charming man, though very quiet and rather serious. He is easily the best-known general in Spain, and I was delighted to be able to meet him. He told me my car had been found and was in Zaragoza in the possession of a certain lieutenant-colonel, who came to explain to me how he found it abandoned on the road (oh yeh!). The evening was great fun. We dined with about fifteen majors, generals, lieutenant-colonels, etc. One young major played the piano very well and the priest sang, and we all drank cognac until 1.30

6 General Monasterio had led the rising in Zaragoza. He commanded the Nationalist cavalry in the famous charge on the Alfambra.

when we came home. I stayed up on duty till four, almost too tired to keep my eyes open, then called Consuelo and fell thankfully into bed.

Monday, 4 April. After a moderately idle day, just after dinner came the order for us to move to Gandesa.[7] We shot to work and collected up everything that was not in actual use. Then after dinner till 2 o'clock came the ghastly business of moving our twenty-seven seriously wounded patients out of their beds and putting them in every kind of makeshift bed that we could find, as we had to take away fifty-five beds. Also sorting blankets so as to leave only the dirtiest and most torn behind. All this by the light of a candle or a little petrol lamp. With great genius we managed to arrive at Caspe with thirty-two beds and depart with fifty-five, leaving twenty-seven behind us. Not a bad bit of requisitioning at all, especially considering we also have an abundance of linen for our additional twenty-three beds. By 8 o'clock we were almost crying with exhaustion. After the last ten days of work and no sleep it almost killed me. However, at last the lorries were loaded and away, and the *capitan*, thank God, told us to go to bed and not do night duty. It was a good thing he did, or I should probably have passed gently on to another world.

Tuesday, 5 April. [*On the road to Gandesa*] we laid out two mattresses and relaxed in peace, with a bottle of wine, a loaf of bread and some cigarettes. It was the greatest fun, and we all sang and laughed as we bumped our way along rivers where the bridges had been blown up, or rumbled over dusty roads through bright green bits of country and cypress trees. At last we arrived here and had to start in making beds as usual. However, the *capitan* was merciful and at 10.30 sent us to bed, to our great relief. The hospital is quite good. A school, as usual. Half is ours and half belongs to an Italian *equipo*. The operating room is large and light, and there are three big wards and a room for the chemists, but alas nowhere to live, so we all live out except Ramon and Pepe, who sleep in the chemist's room. Our house is two small bedrooms with a double bed in each. In there live the four of us and we eat in another house opposite the hospital, but naturally we don't eat there tonight as there is no food and no fire. However, with any luck, we will have something tomorrow.

7 Gandesa, recently captured from the 15th International Brigade, was sixteen kilometres from the River Ebro.

Wednesday, 6 April. One thing for this place is that there is a lot of perfectly excellent wine. This afternoon we went to drink some wine in huge barrels about twenty feet high or more. We had to climb up a ladder and then walk about on top from one to the other trying them. All the soldiers were quite tight and it was awfully funny. I don't know whether I like Catalonia or not, but I do know that the people irritate me, and that they speak such a different language that we can't understand a word they say. The Italians are very amiable and fearfully smart, but over-amorous.

Thursday, 7 April. Christ Almighty, what I have felt like today! Consuelo, Felicia and I were all in the worst possible fit of despair and depression, feeling we were fools and idiots and no use, which is of course true, and we became quite desperate. I got up at five as I was supposed to leave for Zaragoza at six with Ramon to fetch my car, but when I got to the hospital I was told we were not leaving till eight in the lorry that takes the post. At eight we dashed off to find it, but it was only going to Alcaniz. So it continued all morning. We could find no way to go and so here I am, still in Gandesa. However, I have written to the garage to tell them I am coming soon to fetch the car and not to let anyone else take it. By lunch time, after losing my temper with everyone including the *capitan*, and shouting at them all morning, I was in the depths of despair, sick of life and all I am doing, and wondering what has happened at home. I decided I was either going to go crazy or get tight. So I sat down with Consuelo, Felicia and Pepe, a bottle of Jerez and one of cognac and drank hard. Just as I was getting thoroughly bottled a casualty arrived and we trotted over to the hospital to plug a few injections into him. Then I lay down on a bed and suddenly went white as a sheet and felt terribly sick. Consuelo gave me one look and wisely accompanied me home, where I was promptly very sick. What I am turning into I don't like to think, getting so tight that I am sick at 6 o'clock in the evening. I went through half an hour of pure hell, being sick at intervals, with the world spinning round me.

Friday, 8 April. We did not get up till eight and arrived at the hospital to find the most ghastly mess. The Italians had had so many patients during the night they had ended up by putting them on all our forty-nine empty beds. The result was that the beds had to be remade, a lot were stained, and all covered with the Italians' blankets. As usual, neither the woman or the man to wash and help had come, and everyone got furious and had rows. However, at last we got things going, and by twelve, everything was spick and span and going swimmingly. The rest of the day passed in peace. The Italians were moderately occupied, but we had nothing at all. We work quite apart from them; they only look after their own men, and we the Spanish. They have a continual stream of wounded, but all very slightly damaged. However, at about seven suddenly they had a colossal influx and the hall was full of some thirty or more groaning corpses on stretchers, looking exactly like films of the Great War. Such was the overflow that we had to set to work to help. The *capitan* started to operate a stomach and another with a thigh, while I madly undid about thirty-five of our beds for the Italians to take over the wards. I collected everyone in sight, and had the whole thing fixed in the most beautifully organized manner in no time at all. Then I had to rush in to the operating room in a hurry to give an injection of saline to the stomach, and of course it all went wrong. The needle jammed, the spare was too small and so on, but at last I got it going and patiently pumped it in while they were operating the other. During the second operation three Spaniards who are with the Italians turned up, so we said we would take them over. Pepe, Consuelo and I sallied out to cope. One had nothing except a foot of no interest. The other was burnt by a tank and we pomaded him, and Consuelo bandaged him while we went to the third. He had a shot through his behind, resulting in the fact that he had split a bit and done all his doings in all directions. That little joy was left to me to clean and bandage. I was damn nearly asphyxiated and my hands still smell despite a thorough scrubbing. I always seem to get the choice bits of work. At 10.30 we went to have supper and a heated argument about Spiritualism. Then another stomach operation and a dislocated shoulder, who nearly yowled his head off and had to be chloroformed. And so to bed at 1.30. I was supposed to be going to Zaragoza tomorrow but can't find any means of getting there at all. We are leaving for Morella either tomorrow or the next day anyhow, so I guess it will have to wait, like most good things.[8]

Saturday, 9 April. It appears that Ataulfo now commands a flight of three, and that a few days ago the other two ran into each other

8 Morella is (or was) one of the most picturesque towns in Spain.

landing, and they were killed. Poor Ataulfo, having all his friends killed. I slept most of the way to Zaragoza, where we arrived at about 11 o'clock. It was so late that we decided to stay there instead of at Epila.[9] I was very ashamed of turning up to dinner at the Grand Hotel in my filthy uniform, with burst shoes and torn stockings, my face unpainted and my hair on end. We joined Arnold Lunn for dinner. He is out here writing articles about 'Red Horrors' and collecting more material for speeches. It seemed very strange to be sitting in a large hotel talking to Arnold and eating good food with the right amount of knives and forks. I saw Ataulfo over the other side of the room with some other aviators and a lot of empty bottles. He came over to talk to us, and was quite bottled and in splendid form. Then he tootled off with his friends to beat up the town. The Kindeláns were all there and pretty well everyone I know in Spain, including Mary Angel who is awaiting the return of Santa. Princess Bee is in Lerida doing her charity things, Ataulfo is living in Zaragoza, and Prince Ali, Alvaro and Carla in Epila, which is about three-quarters of an hour away. After dinner and coffee and cognac we went on to Epila, where we arrived at 1.30. It is a perfectly huge and beautiful house. I am exhausted, but quite hysterical with joy to be back to normal life just for a short time.

Sunday, 10 April. I lounged happily in bed until 11 o'clock, despite waking up at eight. It was heaven to know that there was no reason at all to get up. Finally I got up and went across to Carla's room to have my first bath for more than two months. I drank Carla's hot chocolate with *churos*, which brought gladness to my heart, and flung myself joyfully into the bath. While I was splashing and Carla smoking in bed, Ataulfo turned up, and after saying good morning through the door, also went to have a bath. When I was ready, we collected some chocolates and cigarettes and cards and went off to sit in the little enclosed garden in the sun and play cards. Bella Kindelán turned up and joined us, later Prince Ali arrived. I was delighted to see him again after such a long time, and he wanted to know all that I had been doing ever since I went up to the front. We were all in the

9 The Orleans family lived in a requisitioned house. It was near the aerodrome where the bombers were stationed. The house was 'Moorish' and belonged to a local aristocrat; it was alleged to be haunted. Conveniently near Zaragoza, it was frequently visited by Pip. She describes Epila as a village 'built on the side of a hill and most of the houses are underground or caves burrowed out of the hillsides'.

best of tempers, and at lunch spent our time roaring with laughter and throwing things about. I sat between Prince Ali and Alvaro and thoroughly enjoyed myself. Afterwards they all played Lexington, while Ataulfo and I lay on our tummies on the floor playing patience like in the good old days. At about four we decided it was time to ooze off to Zaragoza to look for the car. We spent nearly three hours driving round and round the town, trying to find the wretched garage. It was so small and unknown that no one had ever heard of it, and it had no sign up. We both got more and more bad-tempered and despairing about it until at last, about 7 o'clock, we ran it to ground. It was a relief to find it at last. It still has no window panes and no key, and starts with a couple of wires one has to join up. Also it lacks its number plates and some tools, all its papers and my passport; but who cares, now that at last I have found it again. We intended to go to the cinema at seven, but it was too late, so we went back to the Grand Hotel instead for a drink or two. We joined Ultano and Manolo Kindelán who were there, and later were joined by Senora Kindelán and Bella. I shocked them all horribly, as they would talk about hospitals and corpses so I made a few jokes about dead corpses which were not approved of by Senora Kindelán. We stayed drinking cognac with everyone till about nine. I did not know I knew so many people in Spain. The place was crowded with my friends. By 9 o'clock both Ataulfo and I were quite tiddly and in definitely good form, and set of in search of a good restaurant. It was bitterly cold and we nearly froze to death and sincerely wished we had taken his car. All the restaurants were crammed, but finally after waiting about for a bit, we got a table and settled into a good feed. I felt even more ashamed of my strange clothing, a thick brown tweed skirt and navy jersey which I have used to sleep in all winter, a pair of very dirty and torn stockings and high-heeled white shoes. A strange get up, but the only things I possess at the moment. We talked a lot about what we would do after the war, and how strange it was to be here living this peculiar life just like a cinema. After dinner we decided to look for a cabaret, so trotted round all sorts of back streets looking for Ataulfo's favourite haunts; but, alas, they were all shut, with fierce policemen standing outside. Finally, we gave up hope and retired frozen stiff to the nearest cinema, where we saw a very good German film. It was the greatest fun to go to the cinema again after such a long time. It was not over till 12.30. Then we decided to look for a bar, but they too were all either shut or shutting, so we retired to the hotel for a cognac. There were still some groups of people about. One German fetched a piano accordion and started to play on it, so we went and sat with them, and Ataulfo joined in on the piano. I knew most of them already as they were all aviators, and I think I know almost all the aviators in Spain, at least the ones in bombers; the party finally broke up about 2 o'clock and I trotted up to bed. As my only luggage consisted of a lipstick and a broken comb, going to bed was neither a lengthy nor a complicated business.

Monday, 11 April. These few days of leave are a short piece of heaven to me. To go to bed with the certainty of not being called in the middle of the night, to sleep as late as I like, to be with people who are pleasant and kind, to eat well, sleep in a comfy bed and, most of all, to be clean. It seems untrue, just a short and oh, so pleasant dream, but also it ends tomorrow as I really must go back to my *equipo*. I often wonder how poor Consuelo is bearing up on her own. I know I could not stick that *equipo* for a week alone. However, I have only been away for two days so far. As my car refused to go yesterday driving back from the garage and stopped every few yards, I decided that something definitely had to be done about it. So when I finally got up at about 10 o'clock I went with Manolo to find a chauffeur to look at it. The Kindeláns very kindly lent me one of the aviation ones, and I spent all morning with him overhauling the engine, There was something wrong with almost every part of poor Fiona's guts, but the chauffeur finally located the main fault. I lunched with the Kindeláns, the General, his wife, Bella, Garcias Vegas and his wife and Major Lopez Ayala, who is very nice. After lunch I had to go off to the hairdresser for the first time for over six months. After that dreadful ordeal was over and I had almost choked myself to death under the dryer, I returned to the hotel to see if I could find anyone who would come shopping with me. I met Ultano Kindelán in the hall who had just got back from flying. He said he would come with me if I gave him time to have a bath. I said I would not wait that long, so he decided only to change into his proper uniform. So we set off up to his room. On the way we met Kiki Mora and Alphonse Domecq, who were both tight as usual and had just bought a large white rabbit and a white duck. The two wretched animals were lodged on the roof of the dome of the hall, where they were galloping round, chased by the buttons who was in charge of them. We laughed ourselves silly clambering about the roof in pursuit, with all the inmates of the hotel leaning out of the windows, quacking loudly. Ultano had caught the duck and had brought it up to his room, with a string tied round its neck and wings so that he could take it for walks. The rabbit subsequently became the possession of Bella, who keeps it in her room. All aviators seem to be completely crazy. Finally we set off shopping. I bought six bottles of very good cognac and lots of food. When I got back to the hotel I met Ataulfo there in a very bad temper. I don't know what he was angry about, but he would hardly speak to me. However, after wandering about from group to group of friends drinking cognac or sherry I was distinctly in form, and when I joined Ataulfo again found he was also a changed man and in the pleasantest mood. Ataulfo and I, comfortably seated on a sofa, proceeded to make rude remarks and discuss everyone's charms. Of course one man turned out to speak perfect English, just after I had said he was completely lacking in sex appeal. I have never hated anything more in my life than the idea of going back to the *equipo*. I don't want ever to see a hospital again in my life.

Wednesday, 13 April. Today I disgraced myself so thoroughly that I shan't forgive myself for a long time. I was called at six so as to have time to reach Zaragoza at 7.30 to leave with the Italians for Morella. Like a great, slob-faced, hopeless ass I failed to wake up, and slept peacefully till 8 o'clock. I shot from my bed and roared off, flat out, argued my way past the guard who did not want to let me pass, and arrived at the hotel at nine to find, of course, that they had all gone without me. In a way I was relieved, but they had left no message or anything to say if they had left a chauffeur or anyone to go with me. I was in despair, as all my friends were either flying or had gone to Sevilla for Holy Week. When men say women are hopeless and can't do anything they are quite right. After all these months of having to get up at all hours of the night, I can't even get up at six when it is important. I was livid with fury against myself and almost in tears. I did not want to go four hours over a road I did not know, covered with lorries, in a car that does not go very well, and with no spare wheel or tools to mend a puncture, but there seemed to be no alternative. I had just decided to go when Lopez Ayala turned up.

He said we would wait till General Kindelán came down and see if he could lend me a chauffeur. He appeared at about eleven and immediately gave me one of his chauffeurs to accompany me. So off I set, thoroughly miserable and ashamed of myself. I arrived at Morella at last at about 3 o'clock, to be greeted effusively like a long-lost daughter by the whole *equipo* to my great surprise. There is nothing much to do, so I spent the day settling in and locating everything. One head and three probable stomachs. This is a sweet little village on a hill, with a wall all round it and a castle almost entirely ruined on top of the hill.[10] The village as usual is all wriggly little streets, but very pretty and festive, with flags on all the balconies. I arrived at exactly the same moment as an ambulance. How I hated the jerk back to this life, stretchers being carried in dripping blood all over the front doorstep, the smell of anaesthetic, the moans and shouts. I have gone all squeamish in my few days away, and felt almost as though it was the first time I had been in a hospital. I remained depressed all day and very tired, mostly I think due to the drive here; four hours over narrow, bumpy roads with no brakes and lousy springs.

Thursday, 14 April. All today I remained in the depths of depression and feeling vaguely ill. I simply could not jerk myself out of my mood. Everyone laughed at me and said that was what happened to people who went back to *retaraguardia*. I spent the morning occupying myself with anything I could find to do, but there was not much work, so I retired to the roof to sit in the sun amongst all the washing. After lunch Tomasa, Pepe, Seminario and I went to explore the castle and sit in the sun. It was lovely being up there on top of the world. There was quite a lot of shelling going on all around, which we watched, but it was all very far away. There is a certain amount of war around the place here. The day before I came back there was lots of fun. The Reds counter-attacked and reached to within about six kilometres of Morella, then came the Red aviation and bombed our troops who were gathered in the fields outside the village. Consuelo watched most of it from the roof, but went indoors when the aeroplanes came, which was lucky for her as a bit of anti-aircraft fell

10 Morella, when I visited it in 1950, still had a night watchman singing out the weather at every hour, and an artisan who made beautiful saddle-cloths. It is now a tourist attraction. In 1950 there was only one inn with no sanitation.

[73]

just where she had been. I was sorry to have missed all the fun. However, this morning at 3.30 Consuelo had just come to bed when some Red planes turned up and proceeded to bomb us. Actually they only dropped three small bombs in the village which did no harm, and the other thirty were aimed at an ammunition dump just outside which luckily they failed to hit. It was really awfully funny. As Consuelo was still dressed she ran up to the wards and found the nurses who help us all in tears, and all the *sanitorios* in their pyjamas rushing downstairs. Felicia got very nervous and dressed in a hurry, and ran in and out of the room doing nothing. I personally was far too sleepy to do more than yell at them to shut up and go back to bed. It was the first time I have been in an air raid, and I must say the bombs make a hell of a crack. We spent a long and pleasant afternoon in the sun which made me hate the hospital even more, especially now that one of the patients is dying of gangrene. It smells so foul that it almost makes one ill to go into the room. By dinner time I was dead with exhaustion, but it is a sort of unwritten rule that one can't go to bed without dinner, so somehow I struggled through it and got to bed at eleven absolutely dead.

Friday, 15 April. I got up to deal with three wounded and found that my head was spinning round and round and my knees would not hold me up. As I had been aching from head to foot all day I began to suspect myself of being ill, so took my temperature. I was quite right as I had a bit of a fever, so with a sigh of relief I went to bed. I don't know what is wrong with me, but I feel like pure hell and have a temperature of 38.8, which is quite high enough for my liking.

Saturday, 16 April. I seem to be firmly fixed in bed. I am exactly the same as yesterday. Of all the places to be ill in bed, I really could not have picked a worse one. The four of us share a room which is so small that there is just room for the four beds, and we don't possess so much as a chair between us, let alone a table. The room leads off the hall and is next door to the operating room, so that I can lie in bed to the gentle accompaniment of a continual uproar, and patients groaning and grunting on the operating table. My bed is a hospital bed of the lower order, which to be in all the time is not of the most comfortable. This morning was dreadful. I had a cracking headache and felt like hell, and all the time everyone came bounding in, leaving the door open, shouting at each other, singing, banging everything down on the floor. Doctors are strange creatures. They know I have had a fever now for two days, but no one has even bothered to give me anything to make me better till later this evening Consuelo bullied Pepe into prescribing me various things. Ramon says we may be going to move tomorrow to somewhere near Tortosa.

Easter Sunday, 17 April. After lunch Roldan, Plaza, Pepe Louis and Tomasa went off in the car to collect the post. The rest all came and sat in my room and drank my cognac till they were moderately squiffy. Seminario got completely bottled and roamed about shouting at the top of his voice. All afternoon they stayed here playing the gramophone and behaving like lunatics till finally, after they had polished off a pot of my *foie gras*, what was left of my ham, two bottles of my cognac and biscuits, I decided that even for the sake of their celebrating Easter I could stand it no longer. I was so hungry and could not eat anything. I started the afternoon with a temperature and ended up with 38 degrees and my head spinning round in circles. So I just pretended to go to sleep, and they all got guilty consciences and went away to play cards. After a bit of peace, in which I rested and Consuelo slept like a rock, there came one wounded, so she had to get up and cope. After that the others arrived back from church with the post and news that we will probably go to Vinaroz tomorrow or the next day, and after that the *equipo* will be given eight days' leave. I don't believe it.

Monday, 18 April (written on Tuesday). A day I shall never forget in all my life for sheer unpleasantness. The morning was peaceful as usual, but when Pepe came to visit me I decided that it really was time someone found out what was wrong with me. Consuelo evidently had the same idea, so we bullied Pepe till he eventually agreed to take charge and do something. Of course, all the others will be filled with medical jealousy and say everything he does is wrong, but I am tired of lying in bed with a temperature with no one bothering to find out why. After the usual poking and prodding he took a blood test to analyse, and gave me a bottle of medicine and a box of injections and various other things. The result was it wrecked me, and I don't think I ever felt iller in my life. If I live to be a hundred I shall never let anyone look after me again.

[75]

Friday, 22 April. Today at last I really am much better. What is more, I have finally been given some food so that I feel in snorting good form, having woken up weak and exhausted. It appears that what I have had was the beginnings of paratyphoid, but with my inoculations in London and the aid of all the doses, injections, etc. which I have been given these last few days, it has been successfully sent packing. Thank God for that. I have my usual amount of constant visits from all the men of the *equipo*. Ramon talked for an hour about the royal family (he is a rabid anti-monarchist) and Rafael and Escalada talked about food for three hours. I end the day with castor oil! Ugh!!!

Saturday, 23 April. I have got incredibly much thinner considering that it is only a week. I must have lost at least eight or ten pounds, which is a great improvement. My lunch was delicious, cooked for me by Consuelo: broth, chicken rissoles and fried brains. A clever girl, old Consuelo. She went off in the car with Felicia to a nearby village and returned with twenty-four dozen eggs to keep the troops going for a bit.

Sunday, 24 April. I have decided definitely that directly Roldan comes back I am going to ask him to let Consuelo and me go to Zaragoza. There is nothing to do here and I anyhow can't work for a few days, as I am awfully weak at the moment. The main point is that I must get my car mended, as it has a completely broken back spring and definitely something wrong with the gears or clutch. I say that I can't go without Consuelo because first of all I can't drive all that way myself, and also supposing Princess Bee is not there, I can't stay a whole week in Zaragoza all by myself. It just isn't done in this country. So I hope he will let us go. He can always send us an official telegram if we have to come back suddenly. Consuelo informed me that Felicia had told her that I say awful things about her whenever she is not there and don't like having her doing things for me at all. Felicia said that she did not see why Consuelo went on being such friends with me considering the things I had said to her behind Consuelo's back. What an old mischief-maker that girl is! But luckily Consuelo has got more sense than to believe any of her nonsense, so it does not make any difference.

Monday, 25 April. This morning Consuelo and I decided definitely that if the *capitan* did not come back today we would leave for Zaragoza tomorrow morning at 8 o'clock. As Roldan was due to come back, we spent all day in a frenzy of anticipation waiting to see if he would come and spoil our plans or not. I had acute neuralgia again till about 4 o'clock. When it finally stopped I decided to see if my gramophone was really broken or not. I found that it worked admirably, so took it to the operating room and danced like a maniac all evening without stopping, by myself. It was great fun until suddenly at about 8 o'clock the door opened and in walked Roldan with Ramon and Pepe Louis. I was horror-struck at all my lovely plans disappearing. However, I plucked up my courage, and directly I got an opportunity I asked Roldan if he would give us leave, explaining that the car simply had to be mended once and for all. He started by saying no, but then after a bit said, very bad-temperedly, yes, if we were back on Thursday. We said it was not possible to get it done in one day, so he grudgingly gave us till Friday, with dire threats if we were back later. Roldan is quite intolerable, and I thoroughly dislike him.

Tuesday, 26 April. We got up at seven, meaning to leave at eight. We actually got off at nine after much pushing of the car and packing in all our luggage. The car was pulling even worse than usual, and bumped horribly all the way over appalling roads with a broken spring. However, after five hours of bumping and neuralgia, we finally arrived dirty and tired in Zaragoza at 2 o'clock. We made our way in the pouring rain to the Grand Hotel and arrived there, wet and dishevelled, to find there was not a soul there that we knew. We were still trying [to contact Ataulfo] when we saw him come in. So with a shout of joy we shot after him and bewailed our lonely fate. He immediately relieved us of all our troubles by saying he would take us to Epila in his car and hand mine over to his chauffeur. So we sat down and drank a cognac while waiting for the chauffeur. When he arrived he said he thought there was very little hope of getting anything done in Zaragoza as everything was requisitioned, but he would look around. So we left him to it and set off for Epila. On the way Ataulfo told me about his Easter. The poor wretch was sent off with all the Germans on Saturday to Grenada, from where they were to bomb Cartagena. The weather was foul, they all got stuck in

Sevilla in the pouring rain, and of course in Holy Week there was not a hope of finding decent rooms. Altogether the whole thing was a mess, and although they did make a very successful bombardment on Sunday, the journey cost them, as far as I can make out, six men killed and three or four machines lost. Ataulfo was indignant about the stupidity and waste of it all. We arrived at Epila at about six to find Princess Bee and Alvaro in the drawing room. I was delighted to see Princess Bee again after three months, and she seemed pleased to see us. She has been having a terrible time in Lerida for the last few weeks.[11] The Relief Fund has set itself up in a huge asylum there in the middle of the town, they have the Reds fifty yards away shooting explosive bullets up all the streets, no doctors or help of any sort and about four hundred old freaks to look after. The filth was evidently terrible, as these wretched old people had been completely deserted for ten days and naturally had messed their beds and stayed there, till finally Princess Bee and her helpers removed the mess. The place was full of corpses. There were dead people sitting at tables or lying on the stairs, as the Reds shot a lot of people before leaving. The town has been completely left to us as a punishment to the first Catalan capital, with the result that there is no one to take away the corpses and bury them, no food, no doctors and no organization of any sort except Princess Bee and the Relief Fund. She just had to act as doctor and do whatever she thought best with the few things she happened to have with her, and no light, no water and everything filthy. However, now I think she has cleaned it all up a lot. I do wish we could have been there to help her. It would have been just our form, although awfully grim. Prince Ali turned up after a bit and we all played cards till dinner time, then dined, gossiped and to bed, very tired indeed, but awfully pleased to be here.

Wednesday, 27 April. It rained nearly all day, so Alvaro and Prince Ali came back to lunch. We spent the whole morning, after getting up very late, sitting in Princess Bee's room having breakfast, baths and gossiping. Princess Bee told me that Mama had written that as there seemed to be no hope of my coming home, she thought that she might come out here and pay us a visit. It would be fun if she did. I

11 The Princess organized Frentes y Hospitales. Its purpose was to enter Republican towns immediately after their conquest by the Nationalists in order to look after the old, the women and children. Lerida was the capital of the Catalan province of that name.

must write and ask her to, as I don't see how I can go home, it takes too long. If the war goes on into next winter I will go home in the autumn to get more warm clothes, but otherwise I shall just stay out here. We spent all day playing cards. Ataulfo turned up at about 4 o'clock and left again at seven, as he had to dine with his Germans to celebrate the birthday of his *capitan*. He finally retired to bed at about eleven. I was most awfully tired. I get tired so easily nowadays, I must be weaker than I think.

Thursday, 28 April. The weather continued lousy, so no one flew, but they all had to go to the aerodrome, and only Alvaro turned up for lunch. Spent the morning in Princess Bee's room where we bathed, breakfasted, dressed and gossiped, cured my neuralgia once more with Princess Bee's Algocratin and let her cure the abscess on my arm. I feel it is very low to sink to these wartime things like abscesses. Ataulfo was supposed to be coming over to take us to Zaragoza to a cinema but he did not turn up. At 8 o'clock he rang up to say he had just woken as he had been up till six in the morning, and consequently had slept all day. Poor Princess Bee has been awfully worried about him all evening, as he definitely said he would be coming. It was a gorgeous let down when he rang up. So we continued playing cards till dinner. After dinner the order came that Prince Ali's group need not be on the aerodrome tomorrow until 9 o'clock. The result was that Prince Ali was hilarious at the thought of being able to stay in bed till 7.30 and pranced round the room doing gymnastics. They then discovered a piano hidden away in an alcove behind a curtain which delighted Princess Bee, as Ataulfo will be able to play it. We ought to be going back to Morella tomorrow, but as the car won't be ready in time, thank God, we have an excuse to put it off for another day. I could not want to go back less. Ataulfo told me his chauffeur is mending the car, as no one else will do it. That it has its main foundation rods bent, which of course puts all the braking out of order and the springs, also the entire engine has collapsed off its supports and fallen forward onto the chassis. No wonder it would not go properly. We finally went to bed at about 11.30, poor old Consuelo with a cracking pain in her side, so that she could hardly move.

Friday, 29 April. After the usual lazy morning and curing my abscess which is the disgrace of my life, Ataulfo rang up to say he would come to lunch and that eleven Germans were going to visit Prince Ali's aerodrome and would be coming here to tea afterwards. Ataulfo duly turned up and after lunch he and I went off to Zaragoza with Carmelo to buy bits of food to make the tea. When we got to Zaragoza we bought sardines, anchovies, *chorizo*, olives, tooth picks, wine, tunny and butter. Then we went to the market and after walking all round it, returned to the first stall we had seen and bought two large baskets of strawberries. The journey home was most enjoyable. We ate strawberries without ceasing and discussed where we would go to ski when the war was over and what clothes we would wear. We finally decided on St Moritz and against plus-fours. When we got back we found that Carla was already there and that Princess Bee and Consuelo were hard at work in the kitchen, cutting bread and making sandwiches. Consuelo and I set to work to de-stalk the strawberries which kept us busy until the Germans arrived. The tea party went off quite well though not vastly exciting. When they had all gone, Ataulfo played the piano for a bit and then set off with Consuelo and me to Zaragoza for a binge.

Princess Bee has firmly stated that she won't have any nonsense and that we are all to stay here till Monday. As we can't let Roldan know and he expects us back today he will be furious, but as he is always bad-tempered anyhow, it does not make any difference.

We dined at a funny little restaurant where they gave us very bad food. Then we went in search of a nightclub which we finally found after losing our way about three times. It was awfully funny. An old theatre with semi-naked women who came out on stage and who could neither dance or sing. A fair smattering of peroxided tarts and swarms of dirty, tight and noisy soldiers. It was quite amazing and just like an old war film, dirty soldiers all singing and shouting lewd remarks at everyone. After half an hour we got bored with it and decided to look for some other place, but we could not find one and all the decent bars were shut, so we retired furious, for a drink at the Grand Hotel. We had just sat down there when one of the Germans of this afternoon came across and asked us to join them. There was no alternative but to do so, so we trotted over. There were about twelve of them drinking some perfectly foul sweet liqueur; later it changed to beer which was better. We stayed till 1 o'clock rather bored, but it was very funny. Three of them played the piano accordion which they did in unison all the time, making a colossal row. At intervals, one or other would get up, bow stiffly at another German the other side of the room and drink his health, bow once more, click his heels and sit down again very solemnly. Consuelo was very bored as she can't deal with Germans. I sat beside the major who got very tight and started slanging the English royal family, saying that except for the Duke of Windsor, they were all lousy and enemies of Germany. I got very angry but could not succeed in changing the conversation.

Saturday, 30 April. Life went along peacefully as usual. A woman called Pilaron and her husband, Juan Antonio Ansaldo, who is one of the most famous aviators in Spain and has the Laureada, which is the equivalent of our VC, came to visit Princess Bee.[12] Pilaron, who is an aviatrix and nurse, told us that she had been asked to go and work in the Ciudad Universitaria next month.[13] Evidently, now they have started to send nurses there. Up to now no woman has been allowed to go there, as it is continually under fire and everyone lives in cellars and never goes above ground, except to come and go at night under fire of machine-guns. Consuelo and I feel that it is just our form, and asked Pilaron to let us know if one volunteers for it or what, as we would like to go. It would be very exciting and not permanent as one is only allowed to stay one month, working one week and the next not. I suppose that is because it must be an awful strain on the nerves. I should love to be able to volunteer for it.

A little after lunch, Pilaron and Ansaldo left, leaving behind them a box of Chesterfield cigarettes to our great joy. We settled down to play cards, when suddenly Carmelo came in to inform us that some Germans had turned up with a ping-pong table and that Ataulfo would be coming later. Then my car turned up, looking very clean and smart and perky. I was just admiring it and thanking the chauffeur, when up rolled Ataulfo with two Germans – Von Sichert, who was in Sevilla with Ataulfo and took me up for a flight, and a mad

12 Ansaldo, a strong monarchist, had been the pilot who was assigned to bring General Sanjurjo from Portugal to head the Nationalist rising in July 1936. Overloaded with Sanjurjo's dress uniform, the plane crashed into a tree and caught fire. Sanjurjo was burned to death, leaving the rising without a leader and the monarchist cause weakened. Ansaldo published his memoirs ¿Para que? in Buenos Aires in 1951. For Ansaldo's role in the rising see Raymond Carr, op.cit., 84-5.
13 After Franco's failure to take Madrid in 1936 the battle line was stabilized in the University City, which had seen some of the bitterest fighting.

but amusing-looking one called Schultz. We all helped to put up the table in the big room and had ping-pong tournaments, played the gramophone and drank whisky.

Sunday, 1 May. We had to get up a little earlier than usual so as to get to Mass at eleven. It was the day of rest for the aviation, but Prince Ali had to go to the aerodrome and afterwards to Daroca for the day to see Kindelán. So Princess Bee, Alvaro, Carla and we two went to Mass together at a huge church here in Epila, which one reaches by climbing up a long path made of stone steps. The whole village is built up the side of the hill and most of the houses are underground or caves burrowed out of the hillside. I was most depressed all morning, as we were supposed to be leaving tomorrow.

Alvaro had forgotten the injections for Consuelo, so to our great joy we now have to stay a day more and can't go on until the day after tomorrow. We all played dice till dinner, at which the Italian always won. As everything was explained in Italian, Consuelo and I understood very little of what was going on and became quite hysterical counting and trying to talk in a language of which we did not know one single word. Ataulfo and the Italian left almost directly after dinner, and again Princess Bee and we two played cards. Prince Ali, Alvaro and Carla all went to bed, leaving us to it. I am glad that we need not go tomorrow. I loathe the thought of going back to that awful *equipo*.

Monday, 2 May. Our really last day here. I am miserable and bad-tempered and would like to hit Consuelo over the head and cry all night, but these little things are sent to try us, and they do. However, despite the continual thought that it was the last day which spoilt a lot of my fun, today was very amusing. We went along to our breakfast and baths with Princess Bee as usual. Consuelo had to dress in a hurry to go to the aerodrome to be injected by the doctor there. I stayed talking with Princess Bee; I adore gossiping with her. After lunch, we started once more playing cards, not expecting anyone to turn up. Consuelo and I were supposed to go to Zaragoza about four, to do some shopping and meet Ataulfo for a cinema, but at about 3 o'clock he appeared unexpectedly with his usual two Germans. It became the most awful muddle, because they did not know the game, and with the small amount of German I knew, I could not explain it properly. We got in such a muddle, and Ataulfo who was playing the piano would not come and help us out. Then Ultano [*Kindelán*] turned up, very pleased with life as his English fiancée Doreen is probably coming out here next week. It must be very awkward being engaged to someone who can't speak any mutual language. Dinner was very funny. We were thirteen, so Ataulfo sat at a separate table beside Princess Bee. Everyone was very gay, but they all left soon afterwards.

There was great excitement today, as Alvaro and Prince Ali were flying near Teruel and got caught in bad weather. Alvaro and his lot got back all right, but Prince Ali and his people had to land at Vello and only got back here at about tea-time. Princess Bee took it all in her usual calm way and Carla was very upset and nervous, but as everyone was all right it was OK. God – how I wish I didn't have to go back tomorrow.

Tuesday, 3 May. We had a very amusing breakfast with Princess Bee, and later were joined by Prince Ali who was in his usual good form. Of course, what with talking and Princess Bee curing my abscess, and all of us forgetting everything, we only just got to the car at 11.30, after saying goodbye to Carla who gave me some stockings and hand-kerchiefs. And then the car wouldn't start, and for half an hour Carmelo and Jesus struggled with it. We were still sitting dismally there, when Ataulfo and the two Germans turned up very amused to find us still there. However, finally the chauffeurs pushed the damn car out and shoved it down the hill till it started. So after another round of farewells, at last we set off. We arrived at Zaragoza just as the shops were shutting, and just had time to buy some soap, cognac, cheese and sardines before we were locked out. Then we paid a visit to the patron saint, Pilar, who is very well known. She is a teeny wee little saint, only about six inches high, but with a lovely halo and lots and lots of candles. After that we went to the Grand Hotel to see if there was any message for us, but there was only the long-lost note from Esalada. So we set of in search of a place to eat. All the res-taurants were full and my temper got worse and worse. So finally, we had to go back to the Grand Hotel and eat there, despite the fact that Princess Bee had assured us that the food was poisonous. We saw a few people that we knew, but that did not deter us from a well-needed cigarette. After we had finished Consuelo saw some royalty or other behind her and went to say 'How-do-you-do?' like a polite girl. And there at the table was the Duchess of Victoria, who is head of the Red Cross and who gave Consuelo a great ticking-off for smoking in uniform, and said she could make a great row about it in Burgos. We were furious not to have seen her before. We sat in the hall for a few minutes, when in came Sylvia Larios, out of uniform. We chatted to her a bit, then set off for Morella.

We finally got off [*from Zaragoza*] at three and by seven were in Morella, after a tiresome journey. We rolled up at the hospital, to be greeted by Carlo, who informed us that everyone except Ramon, Plaza and Seminario had gone off on leave and would not be back for two days yet. We decided to turn the car round and go straight back to Epila, but alas, out came Ramon and said that we must stay. We were furious, but there was no remedy, so we stayed. Actually, there was no need to keep us; it is just that Ramon is so desperate after sitting here for four days more or less alone, watching the rain and the cypress trees that he does not know what to do with himself. When we arrived Seminario was out, Plaza was writing letters glumly, and Ramon looking as if he would like to jump off the roof at any moment. So we produced cognac, sardines, coffee, cigarettes and the gramophone, and swallowing our disappointment at having to stay here, soon put them into better form, till Ramon was dancing with us and making jokes and Plaza chuckling to himself in the corner. Seminario turned up in splendid form, having visited a friend here and got tiddly. We all sat and talked in the *quirófano*. We were joined by a very nice vet who brought along a man who had to have an intravenous injection, which Ramon gave really well. Soon after dinner, we gave up the unequal struggle of being cheerful and retired to bed. I hate being back here with nothing to do. This is the gloomiest place in the world, and what fun Epila was. There are occasions when I hate being appreciated.

Wednesday, 4 May. Morella is the lousiest, most boring place in the world, and not a thing to do all day. Up at about twelve, lots of bombers came over very low, accompanied by swarms of fighters. We watched them bombing way off on the horizon, and little puffs of black smoke from the anti-aircraft. But it was all so far off that it was not of vast interest, and there was such a bitterly cold wind that I soon went in again.

[84]

We had just finished lunch when Mercedes Milá and Milagros Santa Cruz turned up to see how things were going. Ramon told Mercedes Milá about the business of Escatrón and she said to tell the *capitan* to propose us for the Merito Militar with *distintive rojo*. We were hilarious with excitement as it is the best medal a woman can get. We were fairly dancing about with joy, but now on further thought it seems very doubtful that Roldan will do it, as there is too much favouritism around, and he can't possibly propose the other two as they spent their time sitting in the refuges. Hell's bells! Anyhow, even if he did propose us, we probably would not get it, as we really have not done anything vastly brave yet. Soon after Mercedes Milá had gone there began a colossal hailstorm and then a hell of a row, which I thought was thunder, but everyone else said it was the Reds bombing us. I tried to see what was going on, but the hail was too thick and one could not see anything. The storm did not last long and soon afterwards a wounded man was brought in; a German with a wound in his neck. However, it was nothing much and he only had to be cleaned and sewn up. The rest of the day absolutely nothing happened, and we got more bored and depressed. Despite the excitement of the medal and a probable bombardment, I feel acutely depressed. This evening is was very foggy and we listened for a long time to a miserable aeroplane going round and round, completely lost and very low, unable to see anything and right in amongst the mountains. I expect it hit one of them in the end, but I hope not.

God how I wish something would happen and get us into action again.

Thursday, 5 May. That only nice thing today was that I got a letter from Mama, in which she seems to be frightfully pleased with me, says she will probably come out here after 21 May. She also says that she saw my photo and headlines about me in all the papers, but does not say what they said. Then she says, 'When you come home I will give you a beautiful new car and fill up your bank account.' Evidently she is pleased with me about something. Maybe the papers did good propaganda for me. Anyhow, I am delighted that she really is coming out here.

Friday, 6 May. Today was a fatal day for poor Consuelo. Roldan and the others arrived back at about five in splendid tempers and laden with parcels. I had to go and put my car away. When I got back Consuelo informed me that she had been scratching her ear with one of my little pencils and the rubber had got stuck right inside. She had tried like an idiot to get it out with a hairpin and had just pushed it further in. She asked me to see if I could find it, but I could not even see it. I suggested that she should ask one of the doctors to do it so we went to ask them. Roldan had gone to bed, so Ramon tried. He saw it for a moment but could not catch it with the pincers, and after hurting her considerably, he told Pepe to have a try. Pepe made one wild dig at it, which completely wrecked Consuelo, who fled from the room. I found her in one of the empty wards with the whole of her head and neck hurting like hell and her ear bleeding a little. I tried to console her in my usual unsuccessful way, and then told her she must go to Zaragoza at once and get a specialist to take the rubber out. She said that she would not go, and we argued for a long time. Finally, I left her and went and woke Roldan up and told him what had happened. He said he would look at it, which is not at all what I wanted. However, he sent me to see if there was a frontal mirror. As there was not, that gave me an excuse to go back. Plucking up all the courage I possessed, I said I wanted to take Consuelo straight to Zaragoza to see a specialist. He was in a very good temper and just said he would look at her first. I was terrified he too would start trying to take it out without suitable instruments, but he only looked at it very carefully and hardly hurt her at all. Finally he said that Ramon was to wash it out with hot water and if that did not succeed, then we could go to Zaragoza. He was awfully nice to us about it, to my great surprise and relief. After waiting a long time while the water was boiled and cooled again, poor Consuelo, who was still in agonies, duly had her ear syringed by Ramon, who did it more brutally than I would have believed possible. God – these doctors are swine, and he spent all the morning making a fearful fuss because he was putting hot compresses on the back of his neck, where he had his own abscess. Consuelo became quite hysterical in her efforts to bear up under his syringing; what she has had to suffer today! Anyhow, despite her arguing all the time till about 11 o'clock at night, we are going to Zaragoza tomorrow, where they will fix it up.

Roldan was very nice about letting us go to Zaragoza and says if we can't come back comfortably tomorrow, to come the day after. It looks as if there will be lots of work again, so we must get back as soon as we can. Also, a new nurse is joining us tomorrow. The wife of a major in *aviación* who is liaison to our division or something. I resent her, as she has forced herself unwanted on us and will probably be tiresome and bossy and pleased with herself.

Saturday, 7 May. We meant to get off at 6.30 but what with sleepiness, the garage door jamming and the car refusing to start, we only left at seven. The car was not on its best form and groaned along, making strange grinding noises. I am sick of driving along the road from Morella to Hijar. It is so full of holes and bumps and curves and lorries that one can't go more that 20 m.p.h. for three solid hours or more. In Alcaniz we stopped for petrol and had to give a lift to a lieutenant-colonel and his batman. He was quite a sweet old boy, and when we finally arrived at Zaragoza he directed us to the Red Cross hospital. Consuelo, having suffered acutely from her ear all the way and after the mess of yesterday, was very nervous and begged me not to let the doctor touch her. We asked for the doctor on duty and explained the matter to him. He was quite a nice, cheerful man and had a squint at the ear, but of course could see nothing. So then he deigned to recommend an ear specialist, whom he rang up for us to say we were coming round. He was the vaguest person. He asked where we came from, so we said Morella, and he looked very surprised and asked if we had taken it yet, when it has been ours for nearly two months now. Finally, we got away from the hospital and drove to the house where the specialist lives. After climbing miles of stairs in a large, impressive building, we finally reached his abode and were ushered into a room rather reminiscent of a dentist's operating room. He immediately sat Consuelo down, popped his little trumpet into her ear and there was the rubber at the end of it, just visible. He made six or seven attempts to get it out but with no success, and poor Consuelo writhing in silent agony at each attempt. Finally, he said the only thing to do was to give her chloroform, as the rubber was jammed through the ear-drum and no one would stand the pain of having it touched without moving. At first Consuelo said that she would not, but I finally persuaded her that it was the best thing to do. So we set off once more to the hospital. When we arrived we found our specialist waiting for us, and we all trooped into a very elegant operating room. After a time, when the doctors had all stopped gossiping, Consuelo was laid out on the table and the boy who was anaesthetizing set to work At first she held my hand and breathed it in great form, but once she became semi-conscious she began to shout and groan and quite stopped breathing, and started fighting so much that we all had to fling ourselves on her and hold her down. Despite the fact that we were the specialist, a young *practicante*, the anaesthetist, a nun and I, she succeeded in tearing the mask off her face and sitting up in a daze, making strange remarks about carrying her on a stretcher. However, after about ten minutes with her strapped down and everyone shouting at her to breathe, while she turned purple in the face, she finally went sound asleep. The specialist, after two attempts, finally dislodged the rubber which had evidently gone straight through her ear-drum. I was very frightened, as when she was asleep he said that he did not think he would be able to get it out and if not, would have to do an intervention behind her ear to get at it. My relief when the little blighter finally came out was colossal. Her ear bled a lot and has been bleeding ever since, but hardly hurts her at all now. What agonies she must have been through with her ear-drum burst.

After a short time she woke up, completely vague, as if she were drunk. She could not talk straight, and kept on asking me what I had given her to drink, as she was quite tight. After a time I left her with the nun, while I went to see if I could get hold of Ataulfo but he was out, so hoping that we would find Princess Bee still in residence we got into the car, Consuelo still distinctly dizzy, and off we set on the three-quarters of an hour's drive to Epila. I thought maybe Consuelo would be sick or something, but she survived the drive well and we arrived in good order at Epila.

Sunday, 8 May. We got up at 10 o'clock and dressed. I was ready first so I went along to write my letters before having breakfast. However, I met the Infanta and had to leave them till afterwards and go and have my usual chocolate and *churos* with her. After Mass we said goodbye to everyone and, complete with a box of lunch given us by the Infanta, off we set. Coming into Zaragoza I very nearly ran over a small boy. It was raining torrents and the road was very slippery, I did the most colossal skid and almost turned round and went back the way I had come. Consuelo almost passed out from fright but I did not mind as I knew it was going to happen. We had a wet and boring drive but at least the car was going well. Just outside Alcaniz a car full of soldiers drew alongside and made silly remarks at us. After a time it passed us, splashing us with mud, so I returned the compliment when I met a large patch of muddy water. We continued chasing each other and racing along the decent bits of road until we hit the bad road and had to drive sensibly again. We arrived here at Morella at five expecting to find the hospital full of wounded and moans and blood. To our surprise only four more had arrived, two of which had already died. All the ones we left are well and healthy on the way to recovery. The new nurse, Pilar, is definitely unpleasant of first impression. Ugly, peroxided and very tidy, unfriendly and abrupt with a bass voice, and rather pleased with herself. She spends her whole time in the wards but does nothing at all as far as I can see, except put on airs of the 'please don't serve me first' type when no one was going to anyhow, and says that she regrets coming here as there is no work for so many people. Of course there is not work at the moment, but there has been and there will be again. She stays here all day and goes away after dinner in her husband's car. I don't believe she has ever been in a front line hospital before for all her talk, because she is horrified by all the little things that we don't have and considers the whole thing untidy and badly run, like everyone who has worked in a regular hospital before. We were tired and after putting up two salines after dinner retired comfortably to bed.

Monday, 9 May. [*She gave a lift to hospital staff to Alcorisa.*] We collected petrol and set off along a nasty, narrow windy road full of holes. It might have been a nice drive as the country was lovely, but the road was frightful and it rained all the time. I thought it was quite near, but it took us two and a quarter hours to get there. When we arrived Pepe Louis went off with the *capitan* to find out about repairs [*to Roldan's car*] and Consuelo and I were immediately surrounded by a swarm of small boys who hung on all over the car making stupid remarks about us. They said we must be men disguised, as we drove and smoked. After buying some biscuits and perfectly foul chocolate, we set off back. There is something radically wrong with my car. She just won't go properly and groans and squeaks and can't get up the hills, apart from her shock-absorbers being in a dreadful state. By the time we got back at 8.30 after four and a half hours driving over wicked roads, I was both bored and tired.

Tuesday, 10 May. It was my turn to get up and deal with life, so I very reluctantly left my bed at eight little knowing how long it would be before I saw it again. I took the temperatures, made the beds, gave the breakfast and bullied the women who come to clean and are the most idiotic lot of old witches I have ever seen. I meant to start a diet today but luckily there was no food to diet with. Until about 4 o'clock there was nothing to do at all and we just sat about, bored as usual. Then an ambulance rolled up with one Red prisoner with a head wound who was dirtier and smellier than anything I have ever seen. He had lots of letters on him full of 'Viva Russia' and 'Down with the traitorous Italians' etc. After he was operated Consuelo and I retired to the kitchen with sardines, cognac and the gramophone, where we stayed all evening talking with Pilar who was ironing. She is not so bad really. She is thirty-four with four children, the eldest fourteen years old. She has the right spirit as she hates her husband being a liaison officer and wants him to start flying again soon. She was quite pleasant and amusing.

Wednesday, 11 May. From 11 o'clock last night when the first batch of wounded arrived, until twelve this morning Roldan operated without stopping. 14 operations in 13 hours and all very bad. Altogether 18 wounded arrived during the night, only three of which were not operated, one who did not need it and two who died before anything could be done. We all had to work like blacks. I don't know how Roldan stood thirteen solid hours operating. By about three in the morning he had a temperature, Pepe who was helping him went green and had to go out for a breather and everyone was wearing down. However, they had to go on, so that was that. Consuelo and I spent our time heating water in the kitchen for the beds, giving injections and all our normal work on these occasions. Between whiles we sat in the kitchen for about ten minutes to smoke a cigarette. From about 6.30 there was not a moment to spare, despite the fact that no more wounded arrived. The mornings after a night's work are always grim because the hospital is disorganized, full of bloody sheets and bandages, everyone dead tired and a million things to do. However, by 12.30 it was all over and everything tidied up, the linen folded away, the beds numbered, the charts up and all running smoothly. Roldan had lunch looking frightfully tired, ill and dishevelled and went straight to bed. Tomasa came to bed too later. I slept like a log from two till nine when Consuelo called me. Then I got up and she went to bed. This business of going to bed and getting up again all the time is very tiresome, but I learnt my lesson in Caspe and now sleep whenever I get a chance as no one knows when the next chance will come. It makes life very 'topsy-turvy' but luckily I don't mind when or where I sleep. At the moment I am waiting for 3 o'clock with impatience as I am bored. Pepe, Plaza and Seminario, who had got up for dinner, stayed here in the operating room talking about how truly nasty Roldan is till about 11.30, since when I have sat up here on my own by the light of a candle drawing charts as usual. About every half hour I go round all the wards but there is nothing to do. We have girls from the village in each ward with either a man, also from the village, or an orderly. However, the two orderlies are both sleeping despite being on duty, one in the hall on the floor and the other in one of the wards. I know I ought to wake them up but there is really no need as there is nothing to do. All the wounded are very well and not moaning too much despite giving hardly any injections of morphia. One very unpleasant thing happened last night. One of the men who was operated, when cut open turned out to be an impossible case. He was dying so they sewed him up again, and finding him dead sent him off to the room where they deposit the corpses. An hour later someone heard him yelling and found he had not been dead at all. The poor wretch had woken up to find himself lying on the floor amongst the corpses. Of course, he was very cold and died an hour later, but it was all very unpleasant. Almost all the wounded who came were from three Red aviation bombardments on our lines. At about 9 o'clock this morning we watched some aeroplanes bombing a line of trenches about seven miles away. We have not stopped arguing yet as to whether they were ours or Red. I keep hearing ambulances at the bottom of the hill and wondering whether they are coming here or not. They ought not to be, as we and the other hospital are working alternate twenty-four hours and until tomorrow morning we should be left in peace. But if they get too many to operate they will probably push them on to us. Well it is fun to be working again at last.

Thursday, 12 May. I awoke at about 9 o'clock in good form and after washing my feet which was very necessary, I dressed and went to help Consuelo with the wards. No wounded arrived except one lieutenant directly after dinner who died almost as soon as he arrived.

At 3.30 I was just going to go to bed when we heard an ambulance. They brought three wounded, two prisoners badly wounded and a *requeté*.[14] The *requeté* was sent upstairs as he did not need operating. One by one everyone turned up and after much discussion one was pronounced inoperable. The other Red was operated by Pepe aided by Pepe Louis. The *capitan* went back to bed and we all sat in the operating room while Pepe operated. I was filled with curiosity to see how Pepe worked. It was a head wound and though rather slow he did it very well. By about 6 o'clock it was all over and nothing left to do except clean the operating room. We all sat down drinking coffee till everyone had gone back to bed except us four and the two operators. Suddenly Consuelo got into one of her crazy moods and started quarrelling with Feli. She chased her round and round the operating table shouting and laughing. They were like a pair of lunatics. Feli got terrified and hid in our room till Consuelo got in, climbing over the glass partition into the hall. Feli hastily fled back into the operating room and jittering with fear, tried to lock the door, but in haste none of the keys would fit. Finally, after about half an hour of fighting they began to make too much noise, and although we were hysterical with mirth Pepe sent me to tell them to stop it. I went into our room where the noise came from and found Feli alone and shivering with fright. I delivered my message when suddenly Consuelo leant over the glass partition, seized a handful of my hair and nearly pulled me off my feet.[15] However, in the end she calmed down and about 7 o'clock Pepe and Pepe Louis went off to bed. Tomasa and I wanted to go off in the car round the countryside to look for eggs, but Feli said there was no need so at 7.15 I at last went to bed, not actually feeling at all sleepy.

Friday, 13 May. As I only got to bed at 7.15 this morning I did not get up till 10 o'clock when I arose feeling full of beans but did nothing all morning. Tomasa said in the middle of lunch that she had been told that we intended to leave the *equipo*. We said it was rot but no one believed us and later in the afternoon the *capitan* came and asked us if it was true, saying rather nastily that he had no reason to send us away, but if we wanted to go we were quite at liberty to do so.

14 The Requetés were Carlist volunteers, mostly from Navarre. They were among the best troops of the Nationalist army.
15 This was the behaviour that irritated Roldan.

However, we managed to persuade him that it was all a lie and we didn't want to go. We were furious at Tomasa's deliberate malice.

Thursday, 19 May. I have not written this for ages but nothing much has happened. We are still in Morella. It has been one of the worst weeks I have passed yet in the *equipo*. Everyone seems to be against Consuelo and me. Poor Consuelo has been in bed since Sunday evening and only got up this morning. I was awfully worried as the others thought she was just pretending to be mad. I knew she was suffering from acute fever but could not persuade them to believe it, and they were teasing her and being as tiresome as possible until I nearly slaughtered them all. All this week Pilar has become more and more tiresome, pushing herself forward and pretending that she has done all the work. With Consuelo in bed I have to stay up till about 2 o'clock on night duty and get up again at 7 o'clock while Pilar comes on at 9.30 and goes after dinner. Despite that she pretends she has done everything and everyone plays up to her. Tuesday and Wednesday at about 8 o'clock [*more*] wounded turned up, most of them from our own aviation which made a mistake and bombed a position we had just taken instead of a Red one. Of course as the wounded always arrive after dinner Pilar went home and I coped by myself, which I loved. Poor Consuelo hated to have to stay in bed when there was work to do but just had to put up with it. Pilar has done so many stupid things this week that it is quite unbelievable, but everyone is tactfully blind; because she is the wife of the major who is liaison officer to our division she can kill as many patients as she likes and no one will do more than praise her, while we get rows for things we have not done. I got so angry one night that I positively sat down and cried. I had been working very hard, apart from sleeping a lot too little having to be on night duty as well as day duty. Everything I did Pilar went and told the *capitan* that she had done it, until finally one evening Roldan was going out to dinner and in front of me handed over the responsibility to Pilar while he was away. It is silly to get hurt by things, but after all Consuelo and I have worked here in the wards for three months or more and organized the whole thing, while Pilar has been here ten days and done no work and not even offered to help me with the night duty knowing I had to do it every night. In a short time she has been shoved over our heads as chief. If she was a good nurse it would be quite understandable, but she is hopeless.

One day she let a newly-operated stomach fall out of bed while coming round from the anaesthetic, another day she gave a glass of coffee to someone who was only allowed a teaspoonful of water; another she forgot to take the temperatures, another she was told to give a drug and gave it to someone else; another time she got a recently amputated arm out of bed so as to make his bed more easily, which is unforgivable. And she gets away with it all. This morning Consuelo got up and went to the hairdresser. The order has come that we are to leave here for Iglesuela del Cid, so this morning early we evacuated almost all the wounded back to Alcaniz.

In the middle of it Pepe brought me a telephone message from Prince Ali telling me to ring him at 4 o'clock. I spent the day in a frenzy wondering what had happened. Consuelo and I went to the other hospital which has a telephone to see if we could get a call through. We sat there dismally from 3 o'clock till 8 o'clock with no success till I finally gave it up in despair and we went back to our hospital. Then suddenly I was brought a telegram saying that Mama was arriving in San Sebastian on Sunday and could I go and meet her. I was delighted to find her really coming but did not know what to do. As we are moving on Saturday I finally decided that I could not leave until we were settled into the next place as I want Consuelo to come with me. So I decided to ring up tomorrow morning and let them know. Directly after dinner Consuelo went to bed like a good girl and I joined the troops in the operating room after doing my rounds. Seminario turned up at about 11 o'clock with three friends of his whose brother had just died in the other hospital, so we had to turn off the radio and be consoling, which is one thing in the work that I hate above everything else. It is so awfully grim to have to talk to heart-broken relations. Finally they retired to bed in an empty ward here. The little Moor with the bad stomach wound was dying in agonies, so Pepe told me to give him a double dose of morphia which is another thing I hate doing as it is just cold-blooded murder. At 2 o'clock I decided to go to bed, even though the Moor was still alive, because I was terribly tired. As we went out into the hall we met a lieutenant of the Legion who had had the Moor as his batman for months. He was almost hysterical and begged us to do something to save the Moor's life, which made me feel even worse about the morphia. It is silly to mind that, as it merely means he will die quickly and painlessly instead of slowly and in agony. Pepe and Tomasa and I stayed for about half an hour calming him down and assuring him that there was absolutely nothing to be done. The man was crying and shouting and making a terrible fuss, till finally he went back to the Moor and we went to bed. I should have stayed too till the Moor died, but it is not humanly possible to go day and night without sleeping and I was terribly tired, so I neglected my duty and went miserably to bed with a guilty conscience.

Friday, 20 May. The usual work of collecting the hospital and tying everything up in bundles to be put in the lorries. I tried before lunch again to ring Princess Bee so as to tell her I could not meet Mama, but could not get through. So after lunch I went with Consuelo to the *commandancia* to get permission to send an official telegram. Every-one was sleeping, but finally a guard was dug out of his siesta on a pile of straw and told us we had got to go upstairs. The *comman-dante* was very amiable and gave us permission at once, to our great relief. When we got back the rest of the wounded were evacuated with the usual muddle of missing clothes and not enough stretchers. One was left behind looking frightened and miserable in the deserted ward, all by himself in the corner. However, he died about three hours later so his misery did not last long. The mess of leaving was colossal, the women from the village washing madly all the dirty sheets, the wards empty except for a miscellaneous collection of rejected clothes and belongings of the late patients which were too bloody and torn to be worth taking away. The smell became more offensive and finally, when everything was finished, we opened all the windows and retired to the kitchen which was also in a state of chaos. All the men of the *equipo* went out to a farewell dinner with the crazy Lieutenant Hermoso. We five dined in solitary glory with the priest. I had been setting my hair for lack of anything better to do while waiting for the iron to get hot to iron my uniform, so came in for a lot of teasing as I had to wear a turban with one big curl sticking out of the front of it. After dinner the priest went to bed and Pilar left as usual, so we four determined not to be done down. I sent a boy out to buy two bottles of cognac and one of anis and we settled down in the operating room with the drink, my radio and the infallible iron. After a drink or two we became much happier and I got quite 'tiddly' as I am so thoroughly over-tired, and could not stop dancing. At 11 o'clock when our party was in full swing, the lorries arrived so we sent someone over to fetch the *capitan* and the others, and another to fetch the prisoners who were to load up for us. Soon the hall was filled with about thirty prisoners and guards and the work started. The *capitan* arrived in a furious temper and all the others as tight as ticks, complete with Hermoso who sat firmly down on the floor, all the furniture in the operating room having gone, and set out to drink some more. The *capitan* stayed in the hall shouting, while I rushed from overseeing the loading of the lorries to serving out more drinks. Finally, despite the muddle and rain, it was all finished and everyone went off to bed. I chased after the *capitan* and buoyed up by cognac asked for a week's leave once we were settled in Iglesuela del Cid to go and see Mama. He gave it to me grudgingly, but to my request to take Consuelo said no. However, I was feeling brave and said that I saw no reason why, if Consuelo and I had run the wards for three months, two proper nurses like Pilar and Lon's wife could not do it for a week. The argument was undefeatable so he had to give in and say she could go with me.

Saturday – Sunday, 21 and 22 May. Saturday morning we left Morella for Iglesuela del Cid. The lorry and ambulance were expected to come for the last things at 11 o'clock, instead of which they turned up at 8 o'clock. We were all just beginning to get up when the *capitan* called us in a fury. It was awful chaos. We had to collect the washing of the day before despite the fact that it was still damp or even wringing wet, there were lots of things which we had forgotten or purposely left quite apart from our own luggage. I was only half dressed and hastily shoved a pair of stockings into my pocket and threw everything else in any trunk I could see. Roldan was storming with rage and shouting at everyone and I had no time for breakfast and was very sleepy after my first decent night's rest. However, at last everything was ready and packed on to the lorries. Roldan saw our puppy sitting forlornly in our room, and flew into such a rage that he swore and cursed at the luckless Consuelo and almost gave himself an apoplectic fit. So I threw the poor little dog out for the last time and ran to the kitchen to see if I could get at least a cup of coffee to bear me up. Roldan came storming in and said why was I wasting time and that I was to go at once and get my car out. I asked mildly if I could finish my coffee, whereupon he flew into a rage and I had to content myself with one gulp and fly. By 10 o'clock we were off. All the men and the precious Silvestra [*the cook*] and her daughter in the ambulance and lorry, Roldan in the front of the lorry with we five squashed into my little car bringing up the rear. As usual the damn thing would not start and we had to be pushed by a lorry for a mile to get her going. Then we had to go and fill up with petrol. It was about an hour's drive to Iglesuela over a windy, bumpy lane right up in the hills and over makeshift bridges, and up such steep and strong inclines that I wonder how lorries ever manage it. A few kilometres before Iglesuela there was a destroyed Russian tank in the middle of the road. The lorries going round had made such deep ruts that I knew it would wreck my poor little car, but with a precipice the other side there was nothing to do but follow the ruts. So I bust my exhaust pipe and finally arrived at our hospital making a noise like six motor-boats. The first sight was distinctly depressing. A dirtier, more ramshackle house I have never seen. There was a howling wind blowing and it was very cold, so I parked the car and fled to the shelter of the house. I spent most of the day exploring the village or sitting in the car. I cheered everyone up by producing *foie gras* and sardines for tea. At last Roldan came back with the news that we were to stay in this house. He started allotting rooms for wards and operating room and then sleeping quarters. To the other three he gave a large, airy room with a balcony next to the living-room. To us two, a filthy little dungeon off the operating room which is so dark that one has to light a candle during the daytime to look for anything. Typical unpleasantness on his part. Our room had two doorways with no doors in them which the carpenter fixed for us and a kind of wire meat safe which was removed next day for firewood. Our only furniture all the time we were there was two beds and a table we managed to steal. On Sunday we worked like blacks putting up the beds and getting everything clean. So as to simplify life we left Pilar and Feli to their own devices upstairs while we arranged the ward downstairs. I am glad to say we had ours all spick and span and the linen stored while they were still only half way through. By the end of the day we were tired and bad-tempered due to trying so hard not to quarrel with the others. Anyhow I was cheered by the thought of leaving the next morning for Epila to see Mama and wrote out a long list of things I was to get for everyone in Zaragoza. Then we went to pack and suddenly Consuelo said she was not coming to Epila. I did not know if she was serious or joking, but after quarrelling till about 1 o'clock in the morning I was furious and nearly strangled the girl. Of course she was joking.

Monday, 23 May – Thursday, 3 June. We started out early on our journey to Epila, leaving at about 7 o'clock with Plaza, who was going on leave and wanted to be taken to Zaragoza to catch his train. I drove all the way as we were in a hurry, and if anyone is going to break the car it is simplest that it should be me. We had to be towed by the ambulance to start her, but once going she roared along in good form making a colossal row with her burst exhaust which was tied up with a piece of wire. We made record time and reached Zaragoza at 12.45 and Epila in time for lunch. It was grand to see Mama again. She and my brother John were sitting with Princess Bee and Prince Ali in the little garden when we pranced in absolutely filthy. As they had not expected us till the next day they were all very surprised. I was rather ashamed of my dirty uniform stained from head to toe, no make-up and my hair long and untidy, but Mama did not seem to mind a bit. She was looking so clean and cool and elegant in a smart dress and a white straw hat with a big diamond brooch in it. It seems all out of place to see anyone so clean and smart here, and it seems even odder that the people should be Mama and John. They stayed till Saturday which seemed a very short time. We always spent the day at Epila and usually I went back to Zaragoza where I shared a room with Mama for the night in the Grand Hotel. Sometimes I stayed here but most nights I went back to the hotel with Mama. We were very idle and happy and did not do anything. Mama brought me letters from all the family, lots of gossip and my press cuttings which were a hoot. Headlines and talk of Escatrón, and about my courage, etc. In the mornings Mama and I would have breakfast in bed. She told me all the family gossip and London scandal. I told her all about what I had been doing and what it was like and the sort of work and general mess, until to my great surprise Mama begged me to stop telling her so many horrors or she would feel ill. It is evidently quite true that one gets so used to it all that one forgets what a normal idea of a horror is. Our days in Epila were peaceful and pleasantly idle. Sometimes we stayed to dinner and sometimes we dined in Zaragoza where I met Peter Kemp, the good-looking Englishman I once saw in Salamanca ages ago.[16] He is now an *alferez* in the Legion. He took me out to dinner one night. Peter and I dined at a strange little restaurant behind the cathedral of the Pilar and above a garage. I was the only female there, and it was full of Moors and a variety of

16 Peter Kemp had joined the Foreign Legion. See Introduction p.1.

soldiers. We finally got back to the hotel at about 12 o'clock and sat drinking until 1 o'clock. Peter [*in Zaragoza*] told me a very sad tale illustrating the sadism of his colonel. Evidently one day an Englishman passed over to them from the Reds. Peter was sent to talk to him and found out that he was a sailor. His story was that he had gone on shore in Valencia and got tight. The next thing he remembered was being taken up to the front in a lorry. He could not escape, so at his first opportunity he had passed over in the hopes of getting sent home. Peter repeated this to the *capitan* who said it sounded alright but he would have to ask the lieutenant-colonel about setting the man free. The *terriente coronel* said it was OK by him but that Peter would have to ask the colonel. Before he was half way through the story the colonel just said, 'Shoot him.' Peter sort of gaped and the colonel got angry and said, 'What is more, shoot him yourself or I will have you shot.' He even sent an officer after Peter to see that he did so, with orders to shoot him if not. So Peter led his Englishman off into the countryside. The man realized what was happening and asked if he was going to be shot, so Peter said yes. The man just answered 'Gee, that's tough.' Then Peter said if he wanted to die properly he was to walk quietly away in front of him. So the man shook hands with Peter, said, 'Thanks anyhow', turned round and walked away and was duly shot. A nasty thing to have to do. Having power, especially over human lives, seems to go to people's heads and make them horrible almost always.

When Mama left on Saturday I did not go to see her off at San Sebastian as she left at 7 o'clock in the morning and it is such a long way away, so I just said goodbye to her in Epila the night before, and to John who had been in great form saying that he was going to stand for Parliament in the next elections and become Dictator of England and shoot all the Reds, and that if he were not married he would stay here too and join the war. We meant to leave again for Iglesuela and the beastly *equipo* on Monday, but due to various reasons it did not work so we decided to go on Tuesday instead. But the next morning Consuelo woke me at about 6 o'clock with the most awful headache having been sick all night. The next day she was better but not well so we only left on Wednesday. We were miserable at leaving because the Infanta was almost in a state of collapse from looking after Carla who has got paratyphoid. However, the parting was made slightly better by the arrival of the first instalments from Mama of the enormous lists she had taken away of what everyone wanted. For Princess Bee there was a lovely little silver lighter, tea and biscuits. For me, a fountain pen, a gramophone and needles and *foie gras*. For Ataulfo, a fountain pen, apart from which there were one dozen books, two boxes of chocolates, twelve bottles of whisky for Epila and twelve for me. Not bad on the whole. So at last we set out for Iglesuela, loaded with food and drink. We took seven hours to get there and drove through the most awful rain storm with such a wind it nearly blew one off the road. When we finally arrived we were greeted by a singular lack of enthusiasm by most of the *equipo*. It was a pity, as we had decided to have one last try at getting on well with them but they never gave us a chance. We were ignored, Pilar in her usual affable way refusing even to say hello. We gathered from the orderlies that there had been a certain amount of work and that Pilar had been useless and they were all furious as they had to do all her work which has never happened to them since we joined the *equipo*. The wards were in an awful mess with beds not done, no alcohol with the injection paraphernalia which was all dirty with the needles jammed. However, we said nothing, determined to quarrel with nobody. The next day we set about tidying up without interfering with the five or six wounded whom Pilar considered her property. Suddenly Roldan burst in on us and shouted out that from now on Pilar should have full control of the upstairs ward where all the wounded were so far, despite its having the worst beds. I was to have charge of the downstairs ward and Consuelo of the linen. He is a swine because he knows there is nothing to look after with the linen, and gave that job to Consuelo just as a way of being beastly and stopping us working together as we have always done. And apart from that he can't fail to know that Consuelo is much the best nurse amongst us and that Pilar knows nothing at all. However, what does it matter to him if some of the patients aren't well looked after as long as he can work off his spite on Consuelo for being the daughter of a duchess and an ardent monarchist. I know that we shall have to leave very soon if Pilar stays because the favouritism makes working impossible. We decided to stay as long as we had work, but now that Consuelo has been pushed out of it and no doubt I will follow soon, we can leave at last. God, how I hate them all.

Friday, 4 June. Consuelo now seems completely resigned to her fate of sticking to this dreadful *equipo* and keeping me company. I am awfully glad but I wonder if I was right to persuade her [*to stay*] out of sheer selfishness. Today passed peacefully but dismally. For once in my life I lost my patience and decided to leave this *equipo* once and for all, but now I am not so sure. I have five patients in my ward who have come in the two days since we arrived back. An appendix, three chests who were sent on from the new *equipo* in Mosqueruela which is nearer the front, and one little girl of twelve who was playing with a hand grenade and got blown up. I think I minded seeing her being treated and operated more than anything else I have seen so far. I can't bear to see children hurt. She was blood from head to toe, her whole body one mass of burns and superficial wounds, both her knees had to be operated, one arm amputated above the wrist as her hand had been blown clean off, the thumb of the other hand (or what was left of it) amputated and two holes in her forehead and all one side of her face sewn up. Apart from which she is temporarily blind in one eye and permanently in the other. She is getting on quite well now but moans and shouts all day, as naturally she is in awful pain. I had a terrible quarrel with Roldan yesterday evening to get him to allow her aunt to stay with her all night. The appendix is thirsty and yelling for water all day, which I can't give him, and shows signs of pneumonia. The three chests are peaceful and chatty. A lieutenant was brought in at about 7 o'clock this morning and operated later for a bad face wound. The bullet had taken off half his ear, gone through the cheek and out beside the mouth. He certainly will be no beauty from now on. This afternoon two of the chests evacuated leaving the third firmly convinced that he had been left behind because he was going to die. Actually he won't die but I can't convince him of it. After that I retired to my room and bemoaned my fate to Consuelo. We got very dismal and depressed. Then poor Tomasa came in almost in tears saying she could not stand it any longer and Feli and Pilar are both foul to her, which they are, and that she is going to leave and go home. I have been shivering and feeling a little odd all afternoon and began to feel worse, so after dinner I went to bed and took my temperature to find that I have a fever of 38 degrees, which won't do at all. I can't get ill again. I must be going downhill badly. The big excitement of the day was that just as it was getting dark we were told that the electric light was working again. Everyone was thrilled and rushed about getting bulbs out. So far we have no light in our little dungeon but they say that the electrician will run the current in from the operating room next door tomorrow. Anyhow it is a sign that we will soon be moving again, because we always do either just before the light comes or directly afterwards.

Saturday, 5 June. After a depressing morning in which nothing happened except the resetting of the leg of a man who arrived at 11 o'clock last night, and the evacuation of him and the lieutenant, we went to lunch. The afternoon was even more boring. One wounded turned up but went to Pilar's ward after being operated. He had a hole in his back which may have hit the lung, a hole about six inches deep in his bottom, and his testicles all shot to bits. At about 6 o'clock I took my temperature, and finding it 38.8 degrees decided upon bed, although I hardly feel ill at all. I had just taken off my uniform when Tomasa came rushing in to tell us that we had been given the order to move. So I dressed again hurriedly and went to find out when and where. It is to a place called Vistabella, two kilometres from the front and so completely cut off from everywhere that we have to go from Mosqueruela on mules as the road is destroyed. Of course that means that we can't take more than a limited amount of equipment and we will be entirely cut off from everywhere, probably under fire, sleeping on the floor, with lots of work, too few beds and no evacuation. We were so thrilled at the thought that we were fairly dancing with joy. I went off to bed in the best of tempers, when suddenly came the depressing news that only two of us five nurses were to go. It is impossible that it should be us two, although we are the only ones who really want to. Perhaps one of us might, but it is more likely to be Tomasa and Feli. Anyhow I refuse to be depressed and will just live in hopes until Roldan delivers his verdict. How I would love to go, especially in a train of seventy-five mules!

Monday, 7 June. I have never met such a day for changes. When I awoke I had a temperature of 37.9 degrees but was cheered by the fact that as the order has not come to move yet, the *equipo* would probably stay till tomorrow. Pepe Louis was waiting for an ambulance of evacuation to get a lift to Zaragoza. He was in deep despair as, after hiding successfully from his battalion for two years, he has finally been called up and has to leave for the front as a soldier. He is the world's greatest coward. I hastily started a letter to Princess

Bee. Then came the order to dismantle twenty-five beds that were to go as the lorry was on its way to fetch them. Still no one knew if they were going or who was going. At last at about 10 o'clock came the order for the entire *equipo* to move. Roldan came to see me and said that Consuelo and I were to stay behind until he sent for us. He also told Consuelo later that if I had not been ill I would have gone and she could have stayed behind alone to look after the linen until it was sent for. The man is a sadistic swine. The things he does are not vastly important, but the continual flow of small unpleasantnesses is more than I can stick any longer. The *equipo* finally left at 12.30 taking everything to do with the kitchen with them, refusing even to leave me a cup to drink out of. Nice thoughtful treatment with me in bed with a fever which no one cares to bother about more than to say I have some infection. They cheerfully say, 'Oh, you can go over to the other hospital to eat.' I suppose they expected me to walk through the village in my night-gown every time I wanted a glass of water or something. Anyhow, Roldan repented a bit and left us a cup that belonged to us, said that when I was well and Consuelo had the linen ready we could let him know and he would send for us. He even said goodbye to me nicely, hoping I would get better soon. However, Pepe produced a friend who is the director of the other hospital and immediately said it was a disgrace to leave us abandoned completely with me ill, and said we could live at his hospital which we duly accepted to do. Just after they had all gone, feeling sad at the thought of having to walk nine kilometres up and down a ravine, Plaza turned up and came to see us with Pepe Louis who told us that a new order let him out of going back to his battalion for a few weeks yet. So I abandoned my letters, which I had just revised for the fourth time, and they went off in the lorry with the orderlies. Then came our last farewell to dear, sweet old Silvestra who was returning with her daughter to Morella. She burst into tears and so did we nearly. Finally there we were all alone with one orderly. We relapsed into a fit of desperation and agreed that this last piece of barefaced treatment was the end. One can't stick this sort of thing for ever, one must crack up under it one day.

At about 5 o'clock, despite a temperature which had risen to 38.5 degrees, I dressed and walked over to the other hospital to take up residence. We sat in the doctor's room talking for a time. It is the choir of a church and overlooks the nave which is a ward. Everyone was very nice to us and finally when our room was ready I retired to bed again. After I had been inspected by the doctors, we had a long conversation with our protector who hates Roldan nearly as much as we do. He told us how he had rescued two girls he knew from the *equipo* who, after being there four days, had seen him pass and rushed out crying and begging to be taken away. So he took them to his emergency clearing station. The mention of this roused us both, and after judicious inquiry we asked if he knew of an emergency clearing station that would take us on. He said of course he was going back to one soon and would be delighted to take us. So we are pretty well fixed up for exactly what we want. How kind my guardian angel is, although it does take roundabout ways to do things sometimes. Now I hope this plan comes off, because I simply can't go on in the *equipo* any longer and in a clearing station we would be nearer the front, have more work and the kind we like, dressing wounds, bandaging, giving injections. I really think our protector means to take us seriously. I hope so anyhow, because I am going to leave *equipo* Roldan whatever happens. Now that I have decided that, I feel as if I have been given a new lease of life and all my natural optimism and enjoyment of life has come back. This hospital is in the most awful state of confusion according to Consuelo, and, as neither the nurses nor nuns have come yet, Consuelo has offered her temporary services and has been gratefully accepted. So she will have plenty to keep her busy, looking after this hospital and ours, and me all at once. It is now 12 o'clock and she has gone off with the doctors, who have been here talking, to do a last round of the wards.

Wednesday, 10 June. We only spent one day in the new hospital in Iglesuela, because they could make no suggestion as to what I had, and my temperature went up to 39.8 degrees. So they agreed it would be best to get away to more civilized parts before I got worse.

Thursday, 11 June – Wednesday, 6 July. [*In Epila, resting.*] I was ill for exactly four weeks with paratyphoid 'A'. Carla was furious, I am told, because she only had 'B'. A few days after we arrived Princess Bee had to go off, as we had taken Castellón and she was head of the Canteen the Beneficiencia de Guerra sent there. After about a week she came back as Carla was leaving for Rome by air with Alvaro. I left Epila on 7 July and went home for five weeks' convalescence in England.

Friday, 19 August. We are off to Spain again. I am too tired to know what I feel about it. I am sorry to leave home and my family, as we all get on so well together, but I shall be glad to get back to work.

4

The Battle of the Ebro
July – November 1938

While Pip was convalescing in England the Republican armies mounted the greatest offensive of the war; the Battle of the Ebro. To relieve pressure on Valencia the Republicans crossed the Ebro on 24 July. The initial breakthrough achieved surprise but the offensive stalled with the failure to take Gandesa and Bot. The battle became a slogging match of 115 days as the Nationalists fought to regain the heights captured by the Republicans.

The Nationalists had total air supremacy with 300 planes – and heavy artillery and aerial bombardments preceded infantry attacks. The casualties were the heaviest in the war with perhaps 6,000 Nationalists killed. The major battle of the war, the Ebro, was an astonishing, if pointless achievement of an exhausted Republic. It was during the Ebro battle that the Czech crisis threatened a European war. Negrín, the Republican Prime Minister, believed a war would lead the democratic powers to come to the aid of the Republic; Franco feared it. The Munich settlement (1938) ended the immediate threat of war but revealed the weakness of the Western Democracies. Pip became very concerned at the prospect of war in Europe.

Pip arrived in Gibraltar on 23 August to pick up her new car. 'Lovely, very large and impressive, black with pale brown leather inside.' After a stay in Sanlucar and Epila she got back to her equipo in Calceite in late September.

Wednesday, 24 August. We did a lot of shopping for Princess Bee who was having her hair done. Then Mr Smith rang up to say everything was arranged about my car. He and Mr Imossi were both wonderful and fixed everything for me with the greatest rapidity, so that I was able to leave before lunch at the same time as Princess Bee.

I took Mr Smith and Consuelo went with Princess Bee, as theoretically the frontier is closed to Spanish people. We just missed each other in the customs and I was held up for about half an hour getting an entirely unnecessary visa for my passport.

Thursday, 25 August. [*To Sanlucar.*] I do love this place and am sorry not to stay here more than a day, but am overjoyed to be off to Epila so soon. Princess Bee has been the height of amiability all day as usual, and I have sat talking to her tonight till nearly 1.30. It was lovely and hot and sunny and I spent the day trotting around barefoot looking at the garden and the Botanico, where the trees are growing splendidly, the tennis court has been re-done a seductive pink and there is a gorgeous chicken farm with 250 Leghorns all numbered and tabulated. We fed them on over-ripe figs and they tried to eat my red toenails. The rest of the day we spent undoing and sorting parcels, mixing tea and packing. I went over to tea with the Duchess of Montemar, where I found Consuelo definitely morose and gloomy and a bit tired. I broke the news to them that I was not going to stay with them, as I was going to Epila with the Infanta. Anyhow, I left Consuelo my car, loaded with luggage to bring up to Epila next week. I hate leaving my car the day after I get it, but she drives well and is bound to drive it sooner or later. Anyhow, one should not be jealous of one's possessions.

Friday, 26 August. [*In Merida en route for Epila.*] Princess Bee and I are now sharing a room for the night at the *parador* in Merida. Last time I was here it was quite empty, but now the aviation had moved down here and the place is crammed full of aviators. We have a room belonging to a lieutenant-colonel who luckily is away for one night. He is a tidy man, thank goodness, so all his possessions do not get in our way, and the room is clean. It is already midnight and we are being called at 4 o'clock tomorrow morning, so we won't get much sleep tonight. This morning Consuelo came over to Sanlucar to bring me my suitcase which I had lent her. She stayed and talked to me until lunch time as I had nothing to do and Princess Bee was busy. I had already finished all my packing. Consuelo was moderately depressed and looked tired. Princess Bee and I finally left Sanlucar at 3 o'clock and arrived here at ten. It was very hot and we both sweated all the way. We talked and sang and enjoyed ourselves, at least I did. We

[107]

had two bottles of iced coffee in thermoses to slake our thirst, but it had frozen stiff and nothing would induce it to melt, so we had to scrape and scoop it out with a knitting-needle and a nail file. It was most refreshing when we finally got at it after liberally staining our clothes. All the way up here the country was parched yellow and dusty. All the first part of the journey was through the wine country, with masses of grapes hanging appetizingly along the edge of the road for miles on either side. I do love being back here. I adore seeing everyone in uniform and a vague atmosphere of war. At dinner there were stacks of young aviators looking very clean and attractive in their white uniforms. I kept catching all their eyes all over the patio, and I must say some of them were worth catching. It's a grand life and I'm so glad to be back.

Saturday, 27 August. We finally arrived at Salamanca at 10.30 and went to the Jefatura de Aire to ask for Prince Ali. There was only one young officer there and he told us that all the machines from Epila had arrived, and that Prince Ali and two others were expected at the aerodrome at any moment. So we drove out there and arrived on the aerodrome just as the planes appeared in the distance. There were already about twelve machines there being loaded up with petrol and 50-kilo bombs. An Airways machine from Seville came in and disgorged a quantity of smart civilians into the middle of all the officers and mechanics who were waiting for the machines to be ready to take off. We motored down to the end of the drome and collected Prince Ali from his plane. He was deaf and half silly from exhaustion. He is now a colonel and has been working hard organizing a new brigade. We stayed on the aerodrome sitting in the car till 2 o'clock, eating cold chicken and drinking fizzy water, while machines came and went on their bombing raids. It was fun to see all the aviators again. Ultano [*Kindelán*] has been wounded in the arm by a bit of anti-aircraft shell. He was in bed a week but is now alright, though still unhealed. It appeared after much commotion and inquiry that on the Estremadura front, where we have been advancing so well, the Reds counter-attacked and our men fled in terror.[1] So a frantic appeal has been sent for lots of aviation to improve the morale again. As the

1 General Rojo had long favoured an ambitious offensive in Estremadura in order to cut the Nationalist zone in two. This offensive was now carried out to relieve pressure on the Ebro.

order was only issued last night, no one really knows now how long it will be for, or if they will be staying here or going to Sevilla, but for the moment we are staying in Palacia Monterey with Ultano and Alfredo. We came here to drop our luggage after Prince Ali had taken off again in a cloud of dust. We both fell sound asleep for half an hour, then had to motor out to the San Fernando Aerodrome to pick up Prince Ali, as they were all landing there. We only left again at about seven, having to wait for Prince Ali who was busy with the telephone getting and giving tomorrow's orders. There have been lots of casualties in the Air Force while I have been away, but the only one I knew well was Kiki Mora, who disappeared fifteen days ago. No one knows what happened, as he was not seen to smash. He is either dead or a prisoner, which is much the same. Poor Kiki, he was lots of fun.

Sunday, 28 August. I got up at about nine this morning and spent until about two having ghastly stomach aches from my tiresome dysentery. It quite laid me out, and I just spent my time lying on my bed in a bathrobe, between wild dashes to and from the bathroom. Anyhow, it has made me take a grip on what I eat again. Ataulfo telephoned early this morning to tell Princess Bee he was rolling up with a German. We did not know when he would arrive and spent all afternoon waiting in the drawing-room watching all the cars that passed, and playing the gramophone. When he told Princess Bee he had fourteen days' leave and was going south I nearly died of desire to go too, but did not dare say anything. However, he asked me if I would like to go with them and Princess Bee said it was a very good idea, so off I am going. Oh, what fun life is! Ataulfo was pleased with all his presents. I gave Koch a six-coloured pencil too, as he looked so left out with everyone giving each other presents. Everyone wanted to hear all the news of London and admired all my possessions and clothes. All the aviators arrived back at about 7.30 and dinner was all war and economy talk. I am very tired after all my pains of today, but much too happy to mind that. How surprised Consuelo will be to see us arrive in Jerez.

Tuesday, 30 August. [*In Seville.*] I feel on top of the world today, undaunted and indomitable. I just know that whatever I do now will turn out splendidly. I have never been happier and crazier in my life, despite constant stomach aches which wake me nearly every morning. I lounged in bed this morning until 8.30 when Ataulfo phoned from his room to say good morning. Then I got up and was quite ready by the time he rang again to say that he was going down. So we three went down and breakfasted together. We spent the morning wandering about Sevilla in the car, buying bottles of ink, trying to buy cypress trees. Then we visited Casa Pilatos where the Mendinacelis live. We were finally allowed in by the porter and shown round. I had seen it before, but it is a fantastic house, all Moorish and old Roman and Greek statues. We saw Paz bathing in the garden, so she and her friend came and talked to us. Ataulfo and Paz discussed how they were supposed to be engaged, and if she was really engaged to Pepito Larios or not.[2] After dinner, we played cards. I told Ataulfo for the umpteenth time today that I was indomitable so I should obviously beat him, so we had a bet of a bracelet and ten cypress trees, which of course I won, although I must admit, only just. So now Ataulfo owes me two bracelets, as he had already promised me one as a present earlier in the day. I am so pleased with life that I don't know what to do with myself. It is fun to feel like this. It must be years since I last felt such an untroubled confidence in life. I love every moment of it and just know that it will all be fun. How lovely it would be if everyone else felt the same!

Saturday, 3 September. Yesterday we motored from Sevilla to Malaga or rather a village near it called Torremolinos, where we are staying in a lovely little hotel on the sea.[3] We lunched with Blanca in Algeçiras on the way, all feeling rather sleepy. Here we met Alvaro and Carla so are all together again, which is fun. Alvaro is rather ill and doing his captain's course and exams. This morning I awoke and was up by about eight. Ataulfo joined me on the verandah for breakfast at 9.15 and we chatted amiably then he said he wanted to go to Malaga, so I said I would go too. We wandered round Malaga, buying bracelets for me and cypress trees for him and drove back. I bathed and climbed about the rocks all morning. After lunch we

2 She was to marry Larios.
3 Torremolinos is no longer a village with one hotel, but one of the most ghastly tourist centres on the Costa del Sol. The one largish hotel was the Santa Clara, still the only hotel when my wife and I spent our honeymoon there in 1950.

played the gramophone and spent the rest of the day chatting on the verandah in the sun.

Sunday, 4 September. This place is ideal. Consuelo and I have two adjoining rooms which have no windows, only large doors opening straight out onto the patio on her side and the patio on mine. The bathing is lovely off the rocks with steps and paths paved in them. One walks straight down from the house and to the sea by a cobbled zigzag path down the cliff. There are about twelve people and innumerable children here, all very nice and almost all English. Carla, Consuelo, Ataulfo and I went to Mass at 10 o'clock in a horrid little church in the village. There was an ardent priest who delivered an incredibly theatrical sermon which reduced us all to hysterics. Ataulfo was next to me in his white uniform. He kept making stupid remarks to me all the time so I am sure church did us no good at all. It was more like a mothers' meeting than a service. Almost entirely female congregation with all their fans going strong and their children misbehaving. After that we all bathed until lunch time. Ataulfo found an octopus which they finally brought ashore minus two legs which went wriggling by themselves. No one could kill it and it writhed about in the most revolting manner. We went octopus hunting in a big cave but found none. After lunch they all played bridge so I came and lay on my bed and read till tea time. At tea we talked to an Englishman from Gibraltar who said that there was going to be a war between Germany and Czechoslovakia next Tuesday. He was quite convinced and very convincing; he told us how Gibraltar was arming; that groups of seaplanes had turned up; one battleship came in today and more due to arrive and that everyone was in a great state. I hope he is talking through his hat because one war is all I want and more. Everyone said I would be interned and they would come and feed me grapes through the bars. Before dinner I sat talking with all the other people here who feel just as angry with our fellow countrymen as I do. Ataulfo amused himself by trying to flirt with Consuelo who would not rise to it despite all the slushy records, and finally went to bed. At eleven I also retired, as one goes to bed very early here. Ataulfo says he is going to bathe before breakfast with me tomorrow as we both always wake too early.

Monday, 5 September. I got up early and bathed and at about 8.30

went to find Ataulfo. He was sound asleep but soon hopped out of bed and came down and bathed. It was lovely and sunny but rather cold and we did not stay in long. I tried to learn to dive and gave myself a headache. On the strength of our energy we ate a huge breakfast. Two Germans turned up, friends of Ataulfo's. They were both nice tall, pleasant-looking men. They told him that Koch and all the rest of his lot had been hastily recalled to Germany. So now he does not know who he has got in his group. However, it solves the problem of why Koch was recalled to Zaragoza, and Ataulfo is now less agitated about what has been going on. He went off to Malaga with the Germans and brought them back for lunch.[4]

Tuesday, 6 September. Today was our last day here in Torremolinos and most enjoyable. At about 7.30 Ataulfo came and called for me on his way down to bathe, so I joined him and we found ourselves the first people down. All my back has peeled off and I am red all over. I am very sorry to leave. It is a lovely place and a lovely life and I have enjoyed it immensely. I do wish it was peace-time and we could all stay here unworried. The King of Spain's eldest son, Alfonso Covadonga, has been killed in a motoring accident in Florida, which seems to me to be a good thing on the whole.[5] I wish we were not going away again.

Wednesday, 7 September. Tonight we are once more in a place we did not expect to be in. The Hotel Alvarez in Caceres. It is a beastly dirty hotel, sort of large low-class with bad food and the service done by grubby little boys. Consuelo and I have a decent room. We left Santa Clara at about eight after a large breakfast. We had a pleasant and uneventful journey to Sanlucar where we lunched. We joked and sang all the way and arrived at 1 o'clock, simply famished. After a good lunch we set off for Sevilla all in the best of form, stopping to see the Duchess of Montemar on the way. Pilar turned up in a dressing-gown with her eyes swimming in lakes of black grease. Arrived at Sevilla. We fetched my car from the garage and while I stored luggage in,

4 Koch was in the Condor Legion and a close friend of Ataulfo. The Legion was not withdrawn until May 1939.
5 This left the succession of Don Juan, Count of Barcelona, undisputed heir to the throne. If the eldest son, who had renounced his claims to the throne, had survived, intriguers might have revived his claims. Prince Ali was an enthusiastic supporter of Don Juan, as was General Kindelán.

Ataulfo went off to the Tablada aerodrome to fill up with petrol. He came back full of agitation to be off and said he was going back via Valladolid for some odd reason. However, we decided if we got left behind, to meet in Merida. Off we set, he in his car in front, Consuelo and I behind in mine with me driving. We kept up well and he waited for us to fill up with petrol. But about thirty kilometres from Merida one of my back tyres burst. Ataulfo was disappearing over the horizon so we set to work to change the wheel. The car being new meant that all the screws were so tight we had a terrible struggle getting them off. However, we finally did succeed and then a car-load of aviators stopped and helped us finish the job. So off we went again, hot and tired and covered with grease and oil. We met Ataulfo just before Merida waiting for us. He was furious at being kept waiting and asked where the hell we had been. I answered mildly that I was sorry to have kept him waiting, but we had had a puncture and had had to change the wheel. Instead of issuing sympathy he snorted with rage, and treated it as though we had done it on purpose. Then he told us there were no rooms at all in Merida so we would have to go on to Caceres. So off we went again. It was just getting dark so I switched on my lights, only to find that they did not work. When Ataulfo was stopped by the guard I sent Consuelo to tell him. She said he was quite furious. Anyhow, after a short discussion he said he was going on to Caceres and would see us in Epila tomorrow or the next day and no doubt someone would help me if I went and whined. So he left us with no word of apology or explanation and shot off in a hurry to Caceres, leaving us stranded in the dark with no lights and nowhere to sleep except the car. However, we recovered from our pained surprise and went off to the hotel, where a friendly mechanic fixed the lights again as it turned out to be something quite simple. So we set off in pursuit to Caceres. We arrived there tired and hungry at 10 o'clock to find Ataulfo not here. It did not surprise us as he seems to have gone odd temporarily. For him, the most well-mannered, thoughtful, chaperonish man I know to leave us stranded without even accompanying us to a garage or a hotel before leaving is most peculiar.

Thursday, 8 September. We set out from our gloomy hotel [*in Caceres*] at 8 o'clock after a filthy breakfast that made me feel sick, and only arrived here at Epila at 10.30 at night, dead tired

[113]

and bad-tempered. We had lots of small and tiresome adventures. Peculiar things always seem to happen to me in cars. At Plasencia we had to pick up two priests who wanted to go to Burgos and made us give them a lift to Valladolid. We wanted to refuse as the car was overflowing with luggage, but they would not take no for an answer; so we rearranged all the parcels and coats and suitcases and made room for one, and the other perched on a suitcase. About two hours later we suddenly became aware of an unpleasant stink, and then with one hell of a gurgle one of the priests was ill all over the car. Even the ceiling was bespattered. We pulled up, but it was too late. God only knows what that man ate for his breakfast but it certainly was a hearty one. He was soaked from head to toe and quite unable to cope with the mess. The rest of the journey he spent lying back with his eyes shut and green in the face, vomiting a bit from time to time. By the time we reached Salamanca it was raining, and the stench was so acute that we decided to rest a bit. We suggested the priests had better break their journey but they would have none of it, and after we had washed and eaten a few biscuits in the Grand Hotel we set off again for Valladolid with Consuelo driving. I was very selfish and drove all the time except for that one piece. I think Consuelo minded, as anyhow she is scared stiff of my driving. I hate hers too, but it nearly sends me off my head to have her their beside me being nervous all the time and telling me how badly and dangerously I drive.

Just before we reached Aranda de Duero we suddenly had another puncture. We had no spare tyre after yesterday's effort and no patches with which to mend it. However, we started removing the wheel when along came a car with three men in it. They were very amiable and fixed the whole thing for us. A beastly nail had run straight through the tyre. Yesterday's turned out to have exploded into small pieces so that mended the other and we put it back on. It rained hard into the bargain, but the driver of the other car was very friendly, although a bit cheeky. He asked us out to cocktails in Zaragoza and wanted to know our address so as to visit us. However, we were very vague and finally got going again. Consuelo swore the puncture was because I drove too fast, but I can't see that a nail would have gone in any less if I had been going slower.

Friday, 9 September. [*At Epila*] Consuelo was very odd this morning and sulky about everything. I got quite miserable, as she would say she didn't want to go to the front with me and was going on her own. As I woke up acutely depressed I took it all tragically and felt she did not like me, no one liked me and they all wanted to get rid of me and I would go away by myself and never see anyone again. In fact, I drove myself into such a state of self-pity I even had to pour all my woes out to Ataulfo at breakfast. He did not react at all and that made me feel worse. So by lunch time I was the gloomiest of souls having eaten a huge breakfast and biscuits all morning. However, after lunch we started fooling on the piano, playing Chopin waltzes with one hand each, by the end of which I had forgotten most of my sorrows and was in good form. Then suddenly the maid announced that the men who had arranged our puncture yesterday had called. There was nothing for it but to ask them in. Ataulfo retired hastily to his room, saying that he could not stand visits. So Mary Angel stayed and chaperoned us. Only two came. The leader and the fat, common Malagenio. He wanted me to go to Zaragoza for the evening with him which I firmly declined to do. He was full of beans and making an obvious pass at me. He talked and talked about whom he knew and where he had been. I could not decide what he was. He made himself out to be a rather influential diplomat attached to the secret service but it did not suit him somehow. They simply would not go.

During a jolly good tea of toast and lobster paste the man asked if we knew a friend of his called Goma. When we said, 'Yes – lives in the house', the man looked very startled. Ataulfo immediately rang Goma at the aerodrome so the man had to talk to him and wait for him to return. It was terribly funny because when they had gone at last we leapt on Goma to know who the hell he was, and discovered that he was a chauffeur attached to an embassy in Madrid. And to think of all the airs he was putting on and calling us Pip and Consuelito and talking to me as 'tu'. What is more, he is married, with a child, and was trying so hard to put himself over as a dashing unattached man. To think that the only conquests I can make are of chauffeurs! It made us all laugh a lot anyhow. Ataulfo was rung up by Princess Bee this evening. She is not arriving until the day after tomorrow and is at Aranda at the moment.

Saturday, 10 September. We breakfasted all together at 9.30. We had to go to Zaragoza and wanted Ataulfo to come to a cinema with us but he said he could not as he was in mourning for the King's son. Mary Angel decided to go to church instead of coming to the cinema, so we left her and went off to get the car which was parked outside a bar in the Plaza. At a table Consuelo spotted our ex-chemist Seminario. We were delighted to see him again and rushed up and said hello. He was equally pleased to see us, and we spent one and a half hours talking about old times and hearing all the gossip of the *equipo* since we left. Pepe Mirat has left more or less in disgrace for various bits of bad behaviour. Feli and Tomasita are as insupportable as ever, if not more so; Tomasita was apparently flirting with Mirat, and Feli has taken to going out in the evenings with strange young *alferezes*, and neither of them do any work. After we left, all the work fell on Pilar and serve her damn well right. She could not take it and left too, soon after. Roldan was ill and left Ramon in charge for some time. Everyone had quarrelled with everyone, and Roldan is hated by his superiors.

Monday, 12 September. Tonight for some unknown reason I am not only in the depths of gloom and depression but white as a sheet with dark circles round my eyes. It is more ridiculous, as I have been quite exceptionally gay most of today. Anyhow, I feel like a wet rag and a very sad one at that. I breakfasted at about ten this morning and spent the morning sitting about in my negligee talking and having a bath. When I turned up for lunch Ataulfo appeared with Princess Bee. I don't know when he arrived. All afternoon he, Princess Bee, Frau von Raben and I played cards and talked. Goma and Prince Ali were away at work and Mary Angel, Consuelo and Paz went to Zaragoza. So the day passed much as usual with no outstanding events. The news on the radio tonight was depressing. Hitler made a speech today over the radio which we listened to translated into French, Italian and bits in English. It was a very strong speech, saying pretty well that he was determined to get back the Sudeten Germans come what might, and that any trouble arising would be the fault of the Czechoslovaks, not his, as Germany was the rightful ruler of the Sudeten Germans. God knows how it will work out in the end. I still don't think there will be another war but must admit that the stage is absolutely set for one. There just can't be another. As though this one was not unpleasant enough without starting another. It would lead to such a lot of complications in all Europe. There is no doubt that the world is not all it might be. Just out to be unpleasant.

Wednesday, 14 September. Today was the day of the party. We spent all afternoon madly making canapés and sandwiches and every sort of thing while Princess Bee, Frau von Raben and Ataulfo prepared the drink. It was a delicious fruit cup of the very best. By 6 o'clock we were exhausted and everything was ready so we all went and changed. I dressed myself up in my new black dress and took immense trouble over my make-up and hair in the fruitless hope of making myself attractive for once and forgetting how fat I am. Prince Ali, Ataulfo and Goma were all dressed in their lovely white uniforms. Prince Ali looked so gorgeous in his that it is quite overwhelming and Ataulfo also looked pretty good. The only person who had come when I turned up was Lola Kindelán. We sat and waited a long time for the people to come but no one appeared. Of course, in the end it turned out that hardly anyone had told their people, so that of the thirty young officers only four came. Apart from them about fourteen older ones came who were to stay to dinner. While we were waiting for them to arrive Ataulfo played sentimental music and I sang, or rather tried to. By about eight the men arrived and a more unattractive, boring set of old geysers [sic] I have never seen. I was deeply disappointed, and anyhow knew none of them. Paz and Canuta were just as disgusted as we. After a time we finally pulled ourselves together and leapt into the fray in a brave effort to brighten things up, but it was pretty useless. However, I found Pilon whom I had met before and who was about the only good-looking man in the room apart from Prince Ali and Ataulfo. He is tall and dark with a small moustache and quite nice. I got on splendidly with him, aided by three glasses of the cup. I collected an old, fat lieutenant-colonel and an ugly major neither of whose names I know. The older man was really very nice and told me about how he escaped from Madrid. Quite à la Scarlet Pimpernel. He and three others were in hiding in Madrid and wanted to escape. They received a message from an unknown man to be in the café in the Plaza at 3 o'clock the next afternoon, so they went there and drank cognac, terrified that the police would recognize them. Then a stranger came in, sat down with them and passed revolvers under the table and told them to be at a certain place at a certain time. So they went there, and as they turned the corner a large car pulled up beside them and they jumped in. They were then taken to a house where another man came out and gave them each a carnet of the CNT with a false name.[6] Then the car drew in behind the car of a Red major. When they reached the guard at the outskirts of Madrid, the major in front of them was stopped. He made a great fuss and produced a paper saying that he was on urgent contra-espionage business. He got the guards thoroughly obsequious and then said the car behind was full of his luggage and ADCs and they were allowed through without a murmur. The same thing happened everywhere they passed a guard, until after a time they reached an inn where they stopped. There they found about fifteen others who had got out in various ways. The major asked them for their 'carnets' and said he would need them again for other people, wished them luck, turned round and went back to Madrid. The innkeeper provided them with food and cognac and they set off on foot, and after a day or two crossed the lines at night, exhausted but in safety. Evidently this man has a marvellous organization there and has got lots of people out. The other day he came over himself and was here as a simple *alferez* to talk with various people and has left again for Madrid today. I should love to know who it is but, of course, could not think of asking. We dined at about 9.30 or later, twenty-one of us. Consuelo sat at a small table with four of the aviators, two of whom sing too beautifully.

Friday, 16 September. We decided to leave on Monday for the front. God knows where, but any action or I shall go nuts.

Wednesday, 31 September. We left Epila this morning at 11.15. It was as doleful leaving as it usually is, if not more so, only at least this time we are going back soon. We are now in Castellón [*the air base near Zaragoza*] in a comfortable Hotel Suizo in a large, clean room with three beds; mine is a double bed, Consuelo's a large single and we have a small spare one. It is not at all what I had imagined it would be like. This place is full of luxury. A telephone, running water, electric light and perfectly good food. Not the sort of thing I call being at the front at all. There are even cinemas open. We drove straight down to Morella. Ataulfo's machines were all taking off as we passed his aerodrome so I expect he flew today. We stopped in

6 The CNT was the anarcho-syndicalist trade union.

Zaragoza to buy biscuits and some oil for the car, then went on non-stop down the foul Morella road which I know so well by now. We arrived there at four, having eaten boiled eggs and cold meat on the way which the Infanta had provided for us. We went to see dear old Silvestra, our ex-cook. She was delighted to see us and invited us into her house. Her husband, who is working at the hospital there, came over and gave us a packet of cigarettes, and the two elder daughters, Amelia and Antonia, beamed at us in silence. Old Silvestra insisted on bringing out their only bottle of wine which they had been treasuring for God knows how many years. It was very odd-looking and filled us with apprehension, but turned out to be very good. The cigarettes were foul but we smoked them manfully. Despite our assurances that we had already eaten and were not hungry we were pressed into taking some sticky hot chocolate and biscuits, followed by a huge glass of condensed milk. Not content with all that, when we left she made us an omlette and presented us with that and some ham inside a whole loaf of bread, also a box of fruit. I am sure the poor woman had nothing left in the house by the time she had finished. She is awfully sweet and kissed us fondly on both cheeks and almost wept to see us go. Her house was just exactly typical. A bare room with six chairs and a table with a bright linoleum cloth. On the walls four gaudy calendars, a Virgin and a picture of Franco.[7] Tomorrow we start exploring the hospital world.

Thursday, 22 September. We asked at both the hospitals of the Ejercito de Galicia before we could find anyone. Then we were told that Teniente Mirat was in the Hospital Instituto. So we went there to find that he had just gone out with his wife. We were just beginning to despair when we saw him come wandering across the Plaza plus an ugly little wife. He told us that Sebastian's *equipo* was also in the same hospital with the two Bayo girls. We went and paid them a visit. We found Marie Lou wandering down a passage knitting and looking very bored. We all stood and talked for a time. Fifi was not there and Angela has gone back to Malaga to recuperate from typhoid.

Marie told us her *equipo* was lousy and she did not advise us to try and join as the *capitan* is very unpleasant and they are going to leave

7 Javier Tussell tells of a similar juxtaposition of Franco and the Virgin Mary as an illustration of Franco's acceptance by Nationalists as a providential saviour of Catholic Spain (see J. Tussell, *Franco en la guerra civil*, Madrid 1992, p. 27).

it at Christmas and look for another. She seemed altogether fed up with both her *equipo* and Castellón. We got into the car and went off to the Hospital de los Carmelitos to find Roldan's *equipo*. We asked for Tomasa who came down after about ten minutes and seemed very surprised to see us. Tiresome though she is, it was quite fun to see her again. They have a nice hospital, very clean and spacious, built round a patio full of potted palms and nuns. In the operating room we found Feli, Roldan, his wife, Plaza and Ramon. Feli was not at all pleased to see us and Roldan did not even bother to get up to say 'How do you do?' He just looked up, grunted, and paid no more attention. Ramon and Plaza beamed greetings but were obviously embarrassed by the presence of Roldan. The wife is a small, cruel, hard-looking little woman with a black moustache. Finally, we asked Roldan for certificates of having been with his *equipo*, which he duly gave us with as bad a grace as he could. It was all just as usual. He was shouting and bawling at the orderlies and everyone going about in fear and trembling, hardly daring to talk to us. They all look very pale and ill, but whether that is from work, worries or merely dissipation of two months in Castellón, I don't know.

We went out shopping. Really, this town is pretty smart. There are a few bombed houses here and there and the streets are full of badly filled bomb holes, but for the most part it is quite decent and has lots of shops. We bought buttons and chocolate biscuits and then came back and slept till 6.30 as there was nothing else to do.

We were just going out when Tomasa turned up, so we took her along too. In the end we did not telephone and went to the hospital, where we met Marie Lou and Fifi in the passage with their arms full of cigarettes and fruit, no stockings, toeless sandals, white ribbons in their hair and a necklace of white flowers each like Hawaiian girls., which I must say smelt lovely, although it did look a bit odd in a hospital. They said they could come to dinner at nine, so Tomasa and Consuelo and I went to a cinema to pass the time. Then we dropped Tomasa back at her hospital and returned to our hotel just in time. We all agreed how dreadful *equipos* were on the whole and our respective ones especially, but what fun it would be if only one could get a nice one. We finally decided each to look for a new *equipo* and to let each other know when we find one so that we can still be together. It would be quite fun as five of us is a good number and we would get on well, as they three like the operating room and always work there and we like the wards. One thing is that, with Marie Lou and Fifi in the neighbourhood, I would certainly be spurred on to getting there.

Fifi told us a ridiculous story of a thing that happened to her. She was going to sit on the pot and misjudged the distance and sat down so hard she broke it. A great piece stuck into her and cut her badly. She called Marie Lou, who found her pouring blood all over the room. All the doctors came in to find her with her skirt over her head and smothered in blood. She had to be given three stitches and could not sit down for days and only walk with the greatest discomfort. I do wish I had seen her. She is awfully sweet and actually I like her better that Marie Lou, although she is not so good-looking. They are a handsome pair and both have the most lovely golden hair which looks quite natural. Marie Lou is a natural blonde but Fifi used to be so dark. I wish I knew what they use to make it so golden and shiny. Now it is 12.30 and I am sweating like a pig and the room is thick with smoke as a result of our party. I do hope we have more luck in finding an *equipo* tomorrow. I do so want to go back to work. I just can't wait.

Friday, 23 September. Tonight we are back at Epila again, so we were only away two days really, but we have done quite a lot although with no very great success. However, at least we decided where to go for the time being. I have enjoyed today enormously and am not at all tired. We left Castellón at nine and drove straight up to Calaceite near Gandesa without a pause except to give a lift to two soldiers. We arrived at Calaceite at about 1.30.

We found the hospital at once as it was right on the main road and the only big house in the village. It was lovely to pause after four hours of filthy, bumpy, dusty roads. Paco Uralso, who is the head of the hospital, was delighted to see us again and on hearing that we were in search of work immediately asked us to join him. We said we would tell him for sure after visiting Bot as, if we could not get into an *equipo* there, we would work with him temporarily. After a gay and badly cooked lunch we set off for Bot with one of the nurses who wanted to visit her sister in an *equipo* there. A large, beefy, horse-faced blonde, who seemed quite nice. Bot was three-quarters of an hour away over a very bad road. When we got there the other nurse went to see her sister while we went to see Lolita.

[121]

Bot is a filthy little tiny village and absolutely crammed with ambulances rushing in and out. There were always at least three passing through the Plaza at the same time. The whole *equipo* had been working like mad for four days and they are all exhausted and crazy. So after a time we realized they had no time to see us, so we wandered off to another hospital. We sat and talked to the nurses there for a time, between their dashes to and from the wards. There was much moaning and groaning going on from all the patients, which made me feel all squiggly inside despite the amount of it I have heard. But I have never got used to a whole-hearted bellow of anguish and never will. Later we went back to the other *equipo*. There we wandered into the operating room where Ley was operating a stomach on one table while the previous one was being bandaged up on another. We wandered in and out watching everything until the operation was over. It is a filthy little hospital in a dreadful mess. Wounded on stretchers were being dumped all over the entrance. After the operation, Ley talked to us and offered us cigarettes. He was very nice and amiable but said he was sorry he already has seven nurses, but if we came again later we could talk it over calmly. Then he showed us quickly round the hospital and we left. Roldan is to work with Ley, who can't keep up with the numbers of wounded. If only Roldan had been a bearable *equipo* how nice it would have been. I could have cried with jealousy to see everyone working and in the middle of things and to have to go away.

Gosh how I want to be back at the front! They have quite a lot of air raids in Bot and are only four kilometres from the front. At last, at about six, we got away from Bot and drove straight back to Epila, only stopping to drop the nurse in Calaceite with a message for Uralde to say we would arrive for work in five days' time. So at least we are fixed up with friendly people in a place where we can keep an eye on what is happening in the *equipos*, and grab the first opportunity to join one.

Saturday, 24 September. All morning I spent having a gorgeous bath while gossiping with Princess Bee, and lying on my bed. Ataulfo turned up during lunch. After lunch I went to Zaragoza with Paz, to go to the hairdresser. We did finally get our hair set and arrived back here at seven. Pepe Merito, his wife and the Marquesa of Almazan were here having come to tea. After dinner we just played patience until eleven, when Ataulfo went off to Zaragoza. Then we sliced peaches till 12.30 for the 'cup' for tomorrow's party when all the Germans are coming to a cocktail buffet dinner. It is lovely being back here.

Sunday, 25 September. All morning and afternoon we cooked and mixed and chopped and tasted all over the kitchen and dining room. The cup of apricots to drink, beetroot salad, lobster salad and cucumber salad. Paz made her hot cheese cakes, Mary Angel a very good meat mess and everyone helped everyone else. It was just as much fun as the party was. The total result was a banquet that might have been produced straight from Fortnum and Mason's – it was so luscious. At five we were all exhausted and dishevelled and dirty. I was covered in food, having used my skirt as a towel all day, with bare feet and my hair in curlers and no make-up.

Prince Ali coming back from the aerodrome got stuck on the flooded road and had to wade from his car to safety about waist deep in water with the parachute balanced on his head, while his chauffeur perched on the seat of the car and insisted on taking his trousers off as he did not want them to get spoilt. Prince Ali finally reached a telephone and was brought here, wet and barefoot but in excellent spirits. At eight the Germans had not yet arrived so Ataulfo came and asked if he could borrow my car to go and see if they had got stuck in the floods. As I was ready I went with him. We found them all just outside Epila but quite OK, so we led the way back. They had come in a huge diesel charabanc which could not get through the narrow streets, so they had to do the last lap on foot. They were quite a nice lot really, not vastly attractive but better than the last party we had. When we sat down to dinner I found myself between one of the ones I met in Malaga and a very young, shy, quite pleasant one. It was a 'grab-for-yourself' dinner and lots of people had to stand as the table was not big enough. After dinner we went into the next room and drank coffee and all stood about talking. Then I got my gramophone and records, and we set it going in the dining-room where we were soon joined by most of the people except the older and more important ones, who stayed talking seriously next door.

A German came up suddenly and asked me what 'frustration' meant. He admitted Ataulfo had told him to ask me. Rubio knew, so had to explain it in German. That started us off in good form and he asked me how I knew what it was. From then on the conversation was lewd and amusing. Ataulfo did nothing but drink to my frustration all night and encourage the innocent Germans who did not know what it meant to do likewise. Consuelo was permanently surrounded by six or seven palpitating officers which made me very jealous. Altogether it was a great success, but now I feel too low in spirits to be described.

Monday, 26 September. I woke up feeling fearfully gloomy and still do. If I started saying why or what about I would never stop so I won't try, but this is a lousy world!

Ataulfo came as usual and we all did nothing all day. We fed off the remains of the party and read our books and played a new patience. Tonight we listened to Hitler's speech which lasted two hours and was good and moderately disturbing. He definitely gives the Czechs till 1 October to hand over; if not, it is war. The European situation is hellish tense and is discussed all day to no avail. I won't let myself think about it, as if there is a big war I am completely sunk. I can't stay here and I won't fight with France against Germany, so God knows what I would do. If I stayed here I would never know if my family were killed, or vice versa.

Tuesday, 27 September. [*In Burgos.*] We got back at nine and stayed up quite late, then had a long discussion in Mary Angel's room with her and Carmelo about the European situation and the likelihood of a big war and its effects. It is awful to have it hanging over one. Anyhow, on Saturday we will know what is going to happen as that is Hitler's time limit. If there is a war I suppose I shall have to be on the other side and with no news of my friends out here. I do hope it won't happen. For all that I don't hold with worrying, I just can't help it now. There just can't be another war but it does look probable. Life is one long bother. And to cap it all, there may be a war. Hellish! Consuelo inoculated Mary Angel and me again for typhoid etc. tonight. Despite being up since five and motoring nine hours, I don't feel very tired tonight.

Wednesday, 28 September. [*In Zaragoza.*] Ataulfo decided he wanted to go to the cinema and arranged to meet us at the Grand Hotel at 3.30. He was very shocked at us visiting him, as the hotel is more or less a barracks with notices everywhere saying 'No Admittance', and women visitors are now not allowed. We lunched in the restaurant and gloomed about the forthcoming war. We did a spot of shopping, then retired to the hotel to wait for Ataulfo. He turned up looking pale and wan and wobbly. It is extraordinary how thin his face gets when he is ill. After sitting for about ten minutes, he began to feel so ill and have such a headache that he had to go back to bed again. He says he has to fly tomorrow, but I do hope they won't let him. It would be crazy. After dinner we listened to the English news which was interesting, as it gave exact details of all that had happened since last July with Germany and the Czechs as per Chamberlain's speech. Then all the orders for mobilizing and precautionary war measures. Evidently England is feeling pretty pessimistic as they are issuing gasmasks and digging trenches all over the country, etc. When we finally came to bed I had to do Consuelo's blood transfusion. As I had never tried to give an intravenous or take blood out, I was terrified, but got into the vein easily. Only the syringe was so stiff I had a terrible time getting the stuff out, and it insisted on congealing so quickly I could not get it all into her leg again. She giggled so much her vein shook like a jelly and we ended up with blood spattered all around and my hand dripping it.

Thursday, 29 September. We are now in Calaceite and have just got into bed. It is 12 o'clock and I am tired. My bed is hard and I have a candle balanced precariously on my knee. Our room is tiny but clean. There is no furniture except the two beds, but that does not matter as there is no room for any, anyhow. The only drawback is that the room has no window, so is quite dark. The situation about this war with Germany is preying on my mind to such an extent that I am worrying myself silly, which is most unusual for me, but it will be such hell if there is a European war. It will be the end of everything. And what am I to do if there is? Stand by my ideals and stay here and feel miserable at not helping my country and worry myself to death without any news of my family and friends, or go home and worry myself to death with no news of my friends here. Whatever I do will be hell, so I hope to God there is no war. I hate this place, I loathe the work and I don't like the other eleven nurses. As far as I can see, there are so far about a hundred patients, half ill with tummy aches or flu, and half wounded with a scratched finger or a stubbed toe. I have a feeling that I am not going to enjoy myself here at all and I hope we move soon. I would give one hell of a lot to be back at Epila again. I wish I could ever enjoy life nowadays. There is no news of the conference of Hitler, Mussolini, Chamberlain and Daladier. They have talked all day and will continue tomorrow. We hear the news in the car.

Friday, 30 September. I hate this place. It is not entirely the fault of the place, the people or the work, although I hate them all. But I feel so utterly miserable and lonely, with a painful feeling inside as if I want to burst with tears all the time. At least the awful fear of a European war is over as some arrangement has been come to about the Sudeten, and Czechoslovakia has agreed to give it up according to the arrangement. I could not make out the details as I can never get to the radio at the right moment, but I listened to the broadcast of Neville Chamberlain arriving back home and being received enthusiastically by cheering crowds. It was most emotion-making. It must be wonderful to do something great and be received by cheering crowds, knowing one deserves it. And he has been marvellous. To get back to the facts. We got up at 7.30, which is the general hour of rising here. It was pretty dismal rising by the light of a candle. The others were either up or getting up except Maruja, a beefy blonde, head of the nurses here, who had a bout of colitis and stayed in bed all day. We ambled off to the hospital in a state of gloom. Consuelo works in the upstairs wards where the diseases are, and I below with the wounded. It is mouldy not to work together, and I feel quite lost with no one to appeal to in English when I don't understand, or know something. We are in the same hospital, but quite separate. The day lasted interminably. It was mostly very boring. The usual temperature-taking and feeding. The dressings in the morning were all teeny unimportant wounds of no interest. In the afternoon we had all the people with abscesses. They all had to be given intravenous injections. I put in my first very badly, although I hit the vein straight off, which was not surprising, as I had never done it before. However, the doctor then showed me how it should be done, so I am improving. It was awfully shaming not to be able to, but I have never had a chance of learning, so I can't help it. My doctor is very nice. He is Lieutenant Magallon. A small, thin, kind man. I met him in Caspe before coming here, so we are old acquaintances. Most of today I spent sitting on a table in a room where we do the dressings, knitting a jersey and talking to Magallon. The hospital, as far as the nurses' work goes, is appalling. They amble about and never get anything done. I can't help thinking that if I had it all to myself, I would have the whole thing finished by twelve instead of trailing on through the afternoon. I must admit that there is a lot for me to learn here, which is pleasant but somehow I can't get up interest. I don't much care any longer where I am or what I do. I wish there could be so much work that I had no time to stop and not a moment to let my mind wander. I hate this place, God, how I loathe it. But I would hate anywhere else too I expect. I thought once I got away from Epila I should feel much better about life, but I feel even worse, if anything. The other nurses are a pretty gloomy lot. I don't like any of them very much, but at least the doctors are nice. Magallon quite agreed with me that they were hopelessly slow, and is evidently fed to the back teeth with them. Apart from being director of the hospital, he is censor of the post, so I must not write any rude letters about the people here in case he reads them. Today I have been thoroughly idle, getting my bearings and finding out the customs here.

Saturday, 1 October. I really must take a grip on my inferiority complex and grab this chance to prove I am of some use; I have proved to be a pretty big failure up till now, because I can't do intravenous injections, and I don't yet know where all the medicines and instruments are kept, and will never know their names. Also I suffer from the drawback of working with Maruja who is a professional nurse, and makes me feel like a lunatic worm. Marie had provided me with a list of what has to be done to everyone, and lengthy explanations about all the complications of filling in forms for everything, and they all have strange names I have never heard of, and all the habits in this hospital are most peculiar. Today I was in a desperately bad temper. I became so overwhelmed by my incompetence that I hardly dared move for fear of making an ass of myself. However, Magallon continues being very kind and helpful. This afternoon he did three small operations. The operating table consists of two ordinary wooden tables, with a sheet over them, and Maruja helped him. He removed a piece of shrapnel from a thigh, opened up a pussy amputated finger, and dressed a hand which had been shot through from close quarters, mucking it up considerably. There is another professional nurse here,

Mimi, who is typical: thin, pasty and bad tempered, and as old as the hills. Just one of those dried up, prudish spinsters, whose only joy is spoiling other people's fun. The doctors and nurses here absolutely hate each other which is a pity, but I don't blame the doctors. After dinner, when all the men had gone off to their various houses, we retired to bed, except a few who have gone upstairs to hear the radio which the Legionaries have there. They are all singing and playing. One of the soldiers has a perfectly beautiful voice which is fairly echoing down the stairs.

Sunday, 2 October. Tonight, for once, I feel quite happy, though I am vastly irritable. It has been fun today. It started badly by hearing that two of our machines were shot down yesterday. I got up at 7 so as to be first at the hospital, thus getting a flying start over my companions. I duly succeeded. My new companion, Paquita, is too fat and foolish for words, which is OK by me as it gives me opportunities to assert myself as boss instead of new girl. As Marie is not there, I had to take over all the work of the wards, Paquita being a useless nitwit. But I did not intend to be done out of the dressings, so I hurried and managed to do both by foisting all the boring writing work on the luckless Paquita, and she also gave all the abscess cases their intravenous injections. At 9.30 we had Mass in one of the upstairs wards. It was rather effective with all the men in bed around and us kneeling in the middle. The priest went round the beds giving Communion to the patients, which is a nice idea. I was busy all morning till 11.30 when everything was finished, which is not too bad with fifty-nine patients, even if we are four nurses. Just as I was going to go back to lunch, Maruja suddenly mysteriously called me outside, saying some friends of hers wanted to meet me as they were in need of nurses for an *equipo*. I was thrilled, but it turned out to be a flop as far as work was concerned, as they are just a group of lorry drivers etc. attached to the Maraqui who want a small *equipo* to patch up chauffeurs. However, they invited us to go with them to lunch not far away with a friend of theirs. So Maruja, Consuelo, Rosario and I went. They had an open car and I mine. We got lost, but finally found the place. They were all as mad as hatters and great fun. The major is crazy and makes all his officers stay up till three and forbids them to get up before ten. We finally arrived at our destination at three. We found lots of officers there and two girls. One a dark, quiet girl in

[128]

mourning and the other a pretty blonde with her hair all curled up, masses of lipstick and scarlet nails. There was a hugely fat major and I thought she was his girl friend, but she turned out to be aged seventeen and the wife of a fellow officer who was not present. She talked in the oddest, most affected way, and got rather tight. Everyone was quite mad, and we sat for half an hour round a table in the garden eating clams and asparagus and drinking wine, while waiting for lunch. We were all famished but only sat down to lunch at 3.30. It was a splendid meal. I sat between the two majors and opposite the strange girl. There were twenty of us at a long, narrow table. All through the meal everyone sang and threw plates, food and glasses about. They just played ball with them up and down the table. One man sang beautifully and never stopped. We stayed there till 5.30 behaving like lunatics. Some excellent brandy was produced and we all ended singing at the tops of our voices, while dancing round the table holding hands. At last we had to go, to our great sadness, as it really was a gorgeous party. However we agreed to lunch with them again in Caspe on Thursday. When we arrived back at the hospital at six there was a terrible row, because no one had taken the temperatures upstairs. They all bolted. The doctors were rude to the nurses and the nurses ruder still to the doctors. It went on right up till dinner time, with the result that another change of nurses is to be made. One of us, Katerina, goes upstairs and instead Mimi comes down. She is a nasty, dried up old spinster and very snooty. Everyone dislikes her heartily, with reason. I shall be most embarrassed working with three other nurses all aged between thirty-five and forty, and two of them professionals. Vastly alarming, but I ought to be able to learn a lot from them. Our friends of lunch turned up again from time to time during the evening. An orderly of the Roldan *equipo* paid us a short visit on his way back from leave. We operated a man to extract shrapnel, but could not get it out, as it was behind the femoral artery. It was terrifying to see the artery just sitting there exposed to view. At dinner we were all very merry and I was made to yodel. Magallon was very nervous about it. Afterwards I put on my dressing-gown and joined the others on the verandah to play the gramophone as it was a lovely night. There, despite our neighbours from above looking on, I danced rumbas for hours on end, on my own in the moonlight. At about twelve we decided to go to bed. First I had to transfuse Consuelo's blood for her. Last night I had to do it in our room, with no table and the light of one candle. Tonight I did it a bit better, as I used a table and two candles, but I can't do it quick enough to stop blood congealing at all. I made a bit of a mess but am improving. Anyhow, a candle is no light to inject veins by.

Monday, 3 October. It is even more difficult to do the interesting work now that Mimi has joined us. However, I spent a pleasant and not entirely idle day with the usual work. I am gradually learning my stuff here. Consuelo has got a temperature of 38 tonight, and has to stay up all night and does not get any rest tomorrow, so I hope it wears off. She is terrified she has caught typhoid, as one of her patients is dying of typhoid. I sincerely hope she has not. For once in my life I am not the youngest here, as there are two nurses younger than me, one of nineteen and one of twenty. This evening, while Magallon was operating an ankle, Maruja, who was assisting, was called to the telephone. It was difficult to hear, but the opinion seemed to be that it was Tomasita ringing up for Roldan to ask Maruja to join their *equipo* and would Consuelo and I return. I can't believe it is true that he would ask us to go back. Anyhow, we could not and would not, so what of it?

Tuesday, 4 October. Today and tonight I am on duty in the hospital, which means that I can't leave the building at all, even to go home and wash my teeth. Tonight I sleep on a mattress on the floor in the linen room. My makeshift bed is very comfortable but the room is thick with flies, and I suspect a lot of lice, although I can't see any around. My companion on duty is Magallon who is sleeping next door in the doctors' room. The day was pleasant. I am beginning to get much more at home here and have a vague idea of what I have to do and why. All sorts of strange soldiers and people come in in the afternoons to be cured. Magallon pays no attention and one copes on one's own, unless it is complicated, then one applies to him for advice. Personally I nearly always apply for advice, because I don't know what all the various pots and tubes really do and am not used to opening abscesses, boils and other growths. Wounds are more my form. Consuelo is feeling even iller today with quite a high temperature, but nothing will induce her to go to bed and stay here, or even take any small precautions. I lunched here in the hospital with Magallon. The meals to the doctor and nurse on duty are served in the doctors' room. For 6 o'clock on Mimi and I rushed madly about trying to give help at operations, do the cupping, give hot compresses, give medicines and feed them all, all at once. It was really great fun. At last it was all finished and everyone went home, leaving Magallon and me in charge. We had a pleasant dinner and sat talking till 11 o'clock. Magallon is a nice man and an ideal doctor to work with, as he is always willing to teach and is very patient. We talked of everything under the sun, mostly of the war and nursing. He explained at great length all about the interesting wounds we have and why they are interesting.

Wednesday, 5 October. I woke up at six. When the others turned up, I decided to go home directly I had finished the temperatures, as I was filthy and wanted to wash my face and comb my hair. But just as I finished the temperatures, three blood-soaked men were brought in. Some bomb or other had accidentally exploded, puncturing them all over. So we set to work to patch them up and put injections, then it was time to do all the dressings, so in the end I only came home at lunch time, having been twenty-nine hours in the hospital without moving outside the door. Some of us had meant to drive out into the country with the gramophone and some brandy after lunch, but it did not come off because it rained instead of being sunny, and we lunched pretty late, as nine new wounded arrived just when we had finished everything. So we just sat on the verandah and played the gramophone till 5 o'clock, when we had to return to work. After the usual dressings of outside patients, Magallon did two little operations. One was a calf of a leg which was all swollen and bloated from an old wound. He opened it up in three places. The third unluckily had not been anaesthetized, and the man bellowed and yelled and kicked in the most awful manner. The second was removing a tiny piece of shrapnel from inside a lip. That also had to be done even without a local anaesthetic, but the man was terribly brave. Finally, after serving the dinners at nine, we were all finished and came home to eat. It was a lovely moonlit night and we sat on the verandah playing the gramophone and admiring the moon, which was in full splendour. Now I am pie-eyed from sleepiness and it is 12.30. It is quite possible that very soon we might have to move from here. There have been dozens of lorries roaring through today. Evidently the Reds have had a spirited and successful attack on the

Castellón front, so now men from the Ebro have been moved back to protect. The whole thing is infuriating as it will slow this war up again. I can't write any more because my eyes won't stay open any longer.

Thursday, 6 October. Today has been thoroughly enjoyable on the whole, and tonight I feel as mad as a hatter. I woke feeling like hell and very tired. However, the morning, once started was enjoyable. Maruja has gone off to Bot with two wounded. They were men who shot themselves through the hand so as to be sent home and not have to be at the front. It is a crime punished by being shot, so they are not only cowards but fools to try it. But even though they will ultimately be shot they have to be looked after now, and here Magallon has no instruments to do a proper operation, but it is forbidden to send them elsewhere. So off they went to be operated in Bot with Maruja. That left Mimi and me to do all the dressings, which was nice as Magallon always lets me do anything interesting. He is awfully kind to me and when we finally get into another *equipo* I shall frankly be sorry not to have him to work under any more. There was an awful row in our part of the hospital today after lunch. I have to serve it, which I loathe, as not only is it boring to stand ladling food out for about half an hour, but it is such chaos remembering out of fifty-nine patients who eats what and getting it. Anyhow, today I mucked it, and Mimi, Paquita and Marie-Carmen all stood round me shouting and yelling at each other and at me, because there were four fish missing. After lunch Magallon, the chemist Margarita and I went for a walk to a little chapel on a neighbouring hill. It has been burnt and wrecked by the Reds, with an opened tomb full of old bones, but it has charm, as it is perched right on top of the hill, surrounded by cypress trees. From there we ambled to the next hill where there was another tiny chapel and the remains of a Roman town which looked singularly boring to me. The chapel was scribbled all over with rude remarks and filthy pictures by the Reds. We sat on the rocks there for some time looking at the world below us which is lovely, with a long row of shaggy blue mountains on the horizon. There were lots of aeroplanes flying about there, as it is the front. This evening I went with Mimi and put the intravenous injections. I was scared pink, as she let the poor patients who were to be injected know that I could not do it and she and Marie-Carmen stood on either side of me, watching. The result was that out of the four I did, not one was really good, and one I failed entirely as it was a difficult vein.

Dinner was a riot. I don't know what the jokes were, but we four [*Consuelo, Margarita, Uralde and Pip*] and Magallon, who was next to us, never stopped laughing for a moment. We were awfully stupid and rowdy and shocked all the others deeply. I was made to yodel during dinner, which made me feel rather stupid. But after was far worse. When everyone had gone, the others insisted that I should dance a rumba for the benefit of Maruja's sister. I tried to get out of it, but it was no use and I had to go through with it. The result was exactly what I expected; it fell as flat as a pancake, because they would take it seriously and I was not feeling like dancing anyhow. I was never more embarrassed except putting those intravenous injections. Evidently the Reds' attack on the Castellón front must have been pretty strong, because the troops are roaring through here in lorries on their way from this front and that one. Everyone here teases me all day about being so fat, and about my Spanish. I must say that I am the size of a house now and can hardly do up my uniform.

Friday, 7 October. It is always the same, quite busy, but not a bit hectic. I am getting to like it more and more as I get used to it and begin to know what to do, and learn what all the medicines, greases, injections, etc. are called and their various uses. Today during our morning's pause two soldiers suddenly came in with a poor little child covered in bloody bandages and yelling its head off. It was only four years old, a well-built little boy. He had been playing with a hand grenade as usual and it blew up. It was a dreadful sight. Quite one of the most horrible things I have ever seen. His face was absolutely destroyed, he had neither eyes nor nose nor any sign of where they had once been. It was just a mass of raw flesh and dirt with a slit for the mouth. One arm was blown off just below the elbow and the other wounded all over with the fingers in ribbons. Both legs were also full of holes and his chest too. In fact, there was very little left. There was nothing to be done, so we just cleaned him up a bit and bandaged it all up again as it was. He stayed in the surgery on the table moaning and rolling about all the rest of the morning, while we waited for the ambulance to come and take him away to Alcaniz to be operated. Just before lunch the poor mother

[133]

turned up. A little ugly peasant woman with tears streaming down her face. Mimi took control and took her to the child and went with them both to Alcaniz. Luckily the boy died there before they even got the bandages off. It was the best thing that could happen. Mimi took him back to his home and prepared him to be buried, and consoled the mother. The sort of thing I loathe to have to do.

Magallon has promised that in future with unimportant operations I shall take it in turns with Maruja to help. I am delighted, as I long to learn how. It is only a matter of practice, like everything else. Magallon is a heavenly doctor to work under. He helps and teaches me all the time and is always good-tempered. We laugh and joke and sing all the time, whether working or not. He teases me mercilessly about my size, and I am enormously fat now. I tease him about his, as he is very small. Much smaller than me.

Saturday, 8 October. I never seem to get to bed early here. Tonight it is already 2.30 in the morning and I am pining to go to sleep but must write this first. I have no pen as I have lost it, and my light is a candle balanced on my bed. This morning went by splendidly. I did most of the important dressings and my day was made by the fact that not only did I overhear Magallon telling Consuelo that he was delighted with me as I did the dressings so well, but also most of the wounded said with relief how glad they were that I was doing it instead of Maruja, as I hurt far less. She is so brutal. I may take longer, but there is no frantic hurry, so I don't see why one should hurt them unnecessarily. Also I put an absolutely perfect intravenous injection. We had our usual break at eleven, to eat mushrooms and biscuits and have a glass of wine and a cigarette. Magallon operated an ingrowing toe-nail, removing the nail and various bits underneath and around. He let me help instead of Maruja. It was the first time I had helped at an operation and even though it was a tiny one, I was quite frightened of doing the wrong thing. However, it went off beautifully, especially as I had read up the operation in one of Magallon's books during the morning, so was all prepared. There was one bad moment, when I suddenly realized that I did not know how to thread a needle, but luckily he did it himself. Maruja showed me how afterwards, so at least I know that now. It is grand to work with someone who takes an interest in teaching one, because I learn lots every day. Maruja too is very nice to me, and does not resent my butting in on her territory at all.

[134]

Wednesday, 12 October. My leg hurts quite a lot so I spent all the afternoon and evening sitting in the surgery putting hot fomentations on it as my whole ankle is swollen and red. After lunch, before returning to the hospital, I went out into the country with Magallon in the car to blow off the two hand grenades he had. They exploded beautifully and we nearly killed a partridge with one. At lunch time we went to watch the village people trying to select a few bulls for their fight in a few days' time. It was quite ridiculous. About ten men with coats were trying to attract the attention of one wretched thin bull. They ran round and round him in circles till he was so bored he would do nothing. Consuelo is terribly tired tonight after being on duty yesterday. She looks dead. One of her patients died last night which has upset her a lot. I was supposed to be on duty tonight but Maruja is doing it for me. She is not altogether bothered about my leg and driving to Zaragoza tomorrow and the next day, because her big hero De Torijos is also on duty tonight, otherwise I would not have accepted her kind offer with such alacrity. The other day I got a fantastic letter from one of the soldiers I met in Bot the other night. It was simply glorious, complete with poems and all. Now Magallon is writing one too, which is a hoot. He started it yesterday, and it is progressing in luscious poetic instalments. Tonight I must go to bed early as we are leaving for Zaragoza tomorrow at 9.30 and must get most of the work of the hospital done before then. We are going to get up at six, and God only knows what time we will get back here again.

Thursday 13 October. We stopped in Alcaniz for petrol and in Zaragoza for tickets for the bullfight. We arrived at Epila at 1.30 to find that Princess Bee and Ataulfo are in Sanlucar having left about ten days ago. I broke all records by going from Epila to Zaragoza (50 kms.) in twenty-five minutes. I went over 140 kph which is nearly 80 mph!! The *corrida* was definitely lots better than the other one I saw, but I can't say I really awfully like it although parts of it are fascinating. Ortega was a great disappointment and did nothing, but Belmonte Junior was good and had distinct style although he is only a beginner. I can't bear the picadors. It makes me ill to see the poor horses being ripped to pieces by the bull. One of them was as good as killed and had to be finished off by a dagger in the back of his neck. The man killing him missed at least ten times while the poor thing struggled feebly on the ground. Then he was covered with an old sack and no more attention was paid to his corpse.

Friday, 14 October. We had set the alarm clock for 8.30 but were so tired we never even heard it and only woke up at ten. We both felt thoroughly fed up with Zaragoza and hoped we would not have to go again. I was terribly sleepy and bad-tempered. When we got to the hospital we found everyone in a stew. Uralde was in a rage at us having thought him tight (which he was) and was very offended that we had been ashamed of him. He refused to go to Zaragoza again today. Magallon, complete with four tickets for the *corrida*, was determined to go but angry that Uralde would not go. Margarita and Marie had decided not to go. In fact nobody knew who was going. Then Consuelo said she would not go as she would not leave Margarita to do all the work again. Then I got furious and turned on her and everyone. Finally, in a temper, we went and got dressed, and at 11.30 at last we set forth, Consuelo, Magallon, the chemist and I. We stopped for lunch at the chemist's house with stacks of maize all over the floor. His mother, a fat, kind peasant woman, gave us lunch with excellent ham, sardines, fried eggs and apples and we set off again for Zaragoza. We were pretty late so I drove like mad. Poor Magallon who was sitting in front with me was terrified as he hates going fast. As it was we arrived just a bit late for the *corrida*. It was better than yesterday but I am coming to the conclusion that I don't really awfully like bullfights. The poor horses make me sick. To sit cold-bloodedly watching a bull ripping the guts out of a terrified defenceless horse is not my idea of fun. Ortega was fighting again. He got a wonderful bull, but because he did nothing very showy the crowd booed and shouted at him so much that he lost his temper and killed it which made everyone furious. The bull was dragged round the ring to cheers and the man who bred it came out and bowed while poor Ortega was booed every time he showed his face.

Rafelito mucked his first one but his last was lovely and really worth watching. After the fight we drove all round Zaragoza, then retired to a bar where I had tea with two glasses of cider and some clams. Then we went to see the virgin Pilar. It was lovely with all her candles and the organ playing. After that Magallon went to see his mother, the chemist to see his aunt and we to buy quantities of food and drink and to fill up with petrol. Then we all joined up again and

[136]

went off to the fair which was gorgeous fun. We wandered around the sideshows showing strange foods and watching the people on swings, etc. I tried to shoot at one of the booths but failed entirely to hit anything. I was wearing a spotted handkerchief on my head to hide my curlers. It evidently attracted as lewd comments followed me all around the fair. We dined at the restaurant. Soon after us a *requeté* arrived who was completely sozzled. He was terribly funny. He danced and sang and talked to everyone. Finally he sat down at the table next to us with three fat women who were the owners of various brothels in the town. When they got up to go he rushed after them and asked them loudly if they had paid, at which the whole restaurant burst into laughter. He offered us cigarettes and insisted we throw away the ones we were already smoking. He kept on making signs at me but was very frightened of Magallon or at least pretended to be. After dinner we went to the Fronton to watch people playing Pelota which is a lovely game.[8] It enthralled me and was much more fun than the bullfight. Everyone gambles at it a lot but we didn't much. Finally at 1.30 we set off home. I drove all the way back as I was far less tired than last night. By dint of singing and talking I kept quite awake and got to bed tired and with a very painful and swollen leg at 4.30.

Saturday, 15 October. I spent all day in a stinking temper probably because I was tired. But somehow everyone annoyed me. Magallon went round telling everyone that I drove too fast and was very dangerous which made me livid. Then Consuelo became tiresome and I got sulky. It is foolish the way I suddenly get offended when I am teased. All through lunch she teased me and I got worse and worse tempered. There were three tiresome soldiers lunching who want us to lunch with them at their post at the front on Monday. Also the father and mother of one of the nurses. Finally Consuelo started to persuade me to let her do my night duty tomorrow for me so that I could go to the bullfight here. In the end I gave in because she would have been hurt otherwise, but it is quite stupid because I really don't want to see the bullfight anyhow. I was very sleepy all day so we went to bed at about 8 o'clock before dinner despite the lieutenant-colonel turning up. We tried to shoot with Magallon's pistol after lunch but it

8 Pelota is the Basque game *par excellence*. It consists of hurling a ball at great speed against walls from a basket strapped to the player's hand.

bust so it was no good. It was lovely to get to bed early and think of the long sleep I could have for once.

Sunday, 16 October. I am in one of my spasms of woe at the moment with the result that I am gloomy, irritable and depressed. The work was as usual. I was left to cure a woman with an abscess or something on her chest. She is feeding her sixth child and has a chest like an old rag. Naturally I had no idea how to cope with a woman's chest. I did my best and had a great time. Now I am tired and bad-tempered and can't be bothered to write any more. The bullfight was a farce. The bulls were miserable, thin bullocks who were bored stiff and the men cowards and idiots. They could neither pass the bulls nor kill them. Had I been in a good temper no doubt I would have laughed myself silly as the bulls butted everyone. They knocked down five or six people. The second one was a little calf with false horns who galloped about like a frisky lamb.

Monday, 17 October. This morning two lieutenant-colonels came to see round the hospital, one stayed to lunch. He looked like an orangutan and I thought he would never leave. This evening Magallon had to do three small operations. The third was a hoot. I laughed myself silly. Maruja had gone off to do something else, so I aided the operation which was opening the back of a man's hand. It was all destroyed. Mimi and I were both shoving gauze in the wound for all we were worth, arguing as to what to catch first with only one pair of pincers. Finally I dug out two more quite unsterilized, huge and clumsy pairs and, with their aid, we fixed it all. Magallon was also laughing like mad. It really is awful the way one treats things. The poor man with only a local anaesthetic sits there pale and moaning with pain while we all peer over each other's shoulders and poke the wound and have it explained to us at great length as though he were a piece of dead meat not a live and vastly suffering man. Anyhow they say that all those twenty-four we have of hand wounds who have shot themselves from fright are to be executed. I feel very sorry for them. One this morning who is only eighteen sat all through his dressing crying like a child and saying he wished he had never done it, and was ashamed of himself etc. Another faints away without uttering a sound every time we dress his wound. It is all a mess but such is life in a war. Consuelo has

[138]

been crazy all day and is in the depths of depression about life too. We are a cheery pair of nitwits.

Tuesday, 18 October. A lieutenant and a *guardia civil* sat for hours in the surgery seeing the men who had shot themselves and writing down their signed statements of how it happened. I can't help feeling terribly sorry for them as unless their stories can be proved true they will be shot. I am certain that some of them are perfectly innocent. One, for instance, is only twenty and has been twenty-one months at the front. His hand is all shot to bits by an explosive bullet. He says he picked up a Red's gun instead of his own during a battle and it exploded in his hand. There is another of eighteen who sits and sobs all day. At about 7 o'clock I went with Magallon to do his rounds in the village. It was the greatest fun. We walked by the light of his torch up and down innumerable little dark, cobbled streets. Firstly we visited a fat old man in bed, then a thin, watery-eyed one with a bad heart. Then a tiny baby of only a few months old who had chronic bronchitis. To my great alarm, I had to give it an intramuscular injection. I don't mind plugging things into great toughs but a intramuscular baby is quite different. However, all went well. It was such an adorable baby, I hope it gets better but I would not bet on it. Then we visited an old grandmother who was in bed with a bad eye. One of those tough, bald, scraggy old hags of about a hundred. The whole house was full of fruit from floor to ceiling, apples, grenadines, etc. The smell was wonderful. Old Grandma was in bed in the middle of mounds of fruit. They offered us all sorts. We finally left with two apples which we ate all the way up the street. We arrived at our last house still chewing apples. It was rather more high class. At first I could not make out if the patient was male or female as it had a large, black moustache. It turned out to be a woman. Her daughter is a plump, peroxide, frizzy blonde with greasy black eyelids and pencilled eyebrows. She is a sister of Magallon's girl friend and a frisky piece. Tonight we have electric light at last. Whoever would have thought the day would come when I was doing the rounds as a nurse in a poor Spanish village. I enjoyed it enormously. I wish everyone was not so depressed tonight, it is catching.

Wednesday, 19 October – Friday, 28 October. Since the 19th I have been ill with some tiresome intestinal infection. I have been up for the last three days but only from just before lunch till before dinner as I now have an attack of liver which has made me go bright yellow all over with completely yellow eyes.

Magallon turned up at about 10 o'clock also with a splitting headache. We dosed ourselves with pills, and I spent the rest of the morning working and sweating together. During our little tête à tête lunch I got colder and colder till Magallon made me hop into bed with three blankets on top. I lay in bed all afternoon frozen stiff with my temperature going up. By the evening it was obvious that it was not going to pass off and as my temperature was nearly 40 degrees it was decided that I must stay where I was in the doctor's room, and I went properly to bed in a furious rage at being ill again. All next morning I felt too miserable for words and could not stop crying as my temperature was very high which demoralized me completely. Somehow Magallon found out I had been crying although I never noticed anyone come in. I can't help it if sometimes I feel I just can't go on with this beastly life any longer, and I was certainly not going to explain to Magallon why I was crying. He can think what he likes. Maruja came dashing in before lunch and did not at all approve of my being in the doctor's room. So I had to get dressed and move back to our dark, unventilated room at home. She offered me hers but as everyone going to the bathroom has to pass through it, I declined the offer. I prefer peace in the dark. The next day I had less temperature so got up to wash in the bathroom. I was just wandering back in my overcoat when Consuelo appeared with the three officers of the wounded who had come to visit having sent me messages all day. Unluckily I had only sat talking to them for a few moments when I suddenly began to feel terribly ill. I went back to bed almost fainting and feeling very sick when I was attacked by the most ghastly pain in my stomach. I have never suffered so much in my life. I writhed all over the bed to Consuelo's alarm and I think I lost consciousness. She shot out to fetch something to stop the pain and met Uralde who came in to see me and sent her for morphia and camphorated oil. By the time we got it my pains had gone and, thank God, did not come back again, but they left me a wreck. I never want to suffer so again. After two or three days at home I was still with a high temperature so they decided to transfer me back to my original room in the hospital as our room is so very depressing and unhygienic. Life has been full of complications during the last few days. First of all Consuelo has been feeling ill but would not admit it. She has been moved to the new hospital with Paquita which is pretty mouldy for her. But the idea was to get us out of the way. Apparently, according to Magallon, one of the nurses, backed up by Maruja, told the lieutenant-colonel a pack of lies about how we behaved badly, smoked in front of the wounded, drank, etc., that Consuelo had been tight in the wards one day and had done this that and the other. In fact the lieutenant-colonel was filled with virtuous rage and was deeply impressed by the correctness and sense of the ones who had told him. He came down like a ton of bricks on poor Magallon who, of course, had heard nothing about it. The result is that we may well be slung out on our ears for something that never happened. There are dozens of rows of that sort going on which I can't be bothered to write about. The whole thing boiled down to the fact that Maruja and Torrijos are in love. He is a fool and she is clever and ambitious. So she pushes him forward in everything to do with the lieutenant-colonel with the ultimate intention of ousting Magallon and putting Torrijos as director of the hospital. I don't think she will succeed, but one never knows and she will stop at nothing to do it. Anyhow I am fed to the back teeth with the rows and complications. To hell with them all. Today it is bitterly cold and I am moving home again as I am better.

Saturday, 29 October. Now I have a snorting cold in my head and look even better with a thin yellow face, yellow swollen eyes with dark circles under them and a red nose. A gorgeous sight. Today I have not moved out of the house as it is bitterly cold. I have returned to my same old winter skirt and jersey (my last year's nightdress) and my overcoat. It is a joy not to be dressed in uniform. I got up just before lunch. I ate a splendid meal prepared by Consuelo of chicken broth and two huge boiled onions, not to mention two potato rolls filled with minced meat. All afternoon I talked to Magallon about nothing. Despite my face he continues to be keen on me. I don't want complications in my life here but I expect I will get them. Already my fellow nurses are beginning to blah about injustice in a meaning way because he never gives me a row. Maruja said to Consuelo that it was a disgrace that everything I did was all right just because he was keen on me, but she would put up with it now because very soon things around here were going to change! I am evidently right as to her intentions. Charming friends one always has. I have had a small temperature all day and now my left leg has got infected and it hurts a lot. It has begun to swell a bit but I hope won't be anything as I have dressed it with real gusto. I hate the continual undercurrent of rows and complications here. Yesterday we had an air raid but as they only dropped one bomb on the village I hardly noticed it.

Sunday, 30 October. Franco passed through here today to direct personally the new offensive on the front which began today.[9] All day aviation has been roaring over and I am told that we have advanced a lot, taking the hill which has been holding us up for months. The tanks have all left here in a hurry, for Gandesa, and everyone is feeling optimistic. Maruja had to play the harmonica for the first Communion of the village children. We could hear them chanting outside in the Plaza.

Monday 31 October. At last I am back at work and in a new hospital with a new room to live in. I am working in the new hospital with Consuelo. Just the two of us in sole control. It is fun to be in our own hospital at last, even though the work is not as much fun as in the big one where one is always curing strange things. At the moment we have one top ward almost full of wounded, about forty and only four downstairs. The downstairs ward used to be a theatre and has the stalls full of beds, the stage is the dining-room and the gallery is divided into store rooms and one bit partitioned off, which is our room. As it is much nicer than the room in our house we have moved there. It is teeny-wee, all made of badly fitted planks except the outside wall with a window in it. There is just room for our two beds and a table, two chairs, and a basin squeezed into a corner. But it is very cosy. I can't really say I like being back at work again. I feel gaga with my cold and being rather weak and I get furious about everything. This evening Magallon pulled out one of Consuelo's back teeth which was rotten. It hurt her quite a lot but was very funny. She was scarlet in the face, clutching her chair with Mimi clasping her head, we lighting the operations with a torch and Magallon heaving and tugging for all he was worth. It was very firmly fixed and took a packet of work to get out.

9 Franco's final offensive of the Republican lines in the Ebro began on 30 October. After a heavy bombardment by artillery and aircraft the Nationalists took the heights which commanded the whole battlefield. On 1-2 November the Nationalists stormed the only remaining height and advanced to the Ebro.

Tuesday, 1 November. Today I have been thoroughly idle. Theoretically, I am on duty but I have been out of the hospital all afternoon and am now comfortably tucked in bed. Last night at about 4.30 Consuelo had to get up as twenty-five sick arrived. Five more wounded arrived this evening while I was not here but they all turned out to have a beastly, itchy, catching skin disease. All morning after Mass in the hospital, we dressed the wounds except for when Magallon came to pass his visit. By the end of the morning I was dead tired and with all the muddle of the food for the new ones we served lunch very late. I would willingly have sat down and cried by then. This afternoon I drove Magallon and Marie Carmen along the Gandesa road to look for a better place for the women to wash the hospital clothes. We duly found a splendid place quite near. While we were wandering about inspecting, Franco roared past in a posse of about nine or ten smart cars. He saluted us to our great pleasure as he shot by. When we got back I took one of our wounded over to the other hospital to have his arm opened. When I got there I found Paquita waiting to be operated. She had her ingrowing toenail removed which includes delicate cutting and replacing of the surrounding skin. The poor girl had her toenail in an awful mess and her knee which she fell on is all red and swollen. Now she will be in bed for days and unable to walk for two weeks. She was very brave about it all. By the time her operation was done, and my man was opened up, and I had gone home, fetched my car and taken Paquita home in it and returned to the base hospital it was 7.30. Magallon arrived at our hospital with me to do his visit at 7.45. Consuelo was hectically serving dinner in a bad temper so I went round with him. He prescribed all sorts of things that I had never heard of. I dressed one of the new ones and gave an intravenous injection and Consuelo gave two more and at last our work was over. She would not come to dinner so I went up alone and ate my spinach and ham. I am sick to death of being ill. Now that my liver is getting better, my dysentery is getting worse because, of course, the food for each is the exact opposite and what cures one is poison to the other. Now it is 12.15 and I am terribly sleepy so I shall go to sleep, and I do hope I don't have to get up in the middle of the night.

Wednesday, 2 November. I have bogged an injection today. I had to put six intravenous injections in and one of them must have slipped out of the vein because the man's arm swelled up in a big lump and looked suspiciously as if it would turn into an abscess. Most shameful behaviour. I am disgusted with myself. Magallon turned up here at 9.30 to see all the dressings today. Of course the hospital was in a mess. It was just the one morning when no one had turned up and something had gone wrong with the breakfast which should have been served at 8 o'clock but was actually still being given at 9.30, with the result that none of the temperatures were yet taken. I am so easily tired nowadays. By the end of the morning I feel I shall die if I have to do another thing, and ditto at dinner time.

This afternoon I went with Magallon in the car to the river. We left the car and walked about half a mile accompanied by an orderly. Then Magallon slung a hand grenade as the easiest way to go fishing. Unluckily there were very few fish. We waited a bit until slowly the dead or stunned fish began to come to the surface. Marie and the orderly crossed to the other side barelegged to fish out the corpses. Our total catch was three fair sized trout and about a dozen little tiddlers like whitebait. In the end, to get them, the orderly, who had been clambering over the rocks, waded in. He still could not reach one of the big ones and ended up by taking off all his clothes, except his underpants, and swimming, to our great amusement. So today I had fresh fish for dinner. My diet was the excuse for the whole thing.

Friday, 4 November. This morning by the time Magallon came to do his rounds we had finished everything. He stayed and watched lunch served and of course it all went wrong. There was too little food, too few spoons and hundreds of quarrels. serving the meals drives me crazy. As Consuelo was on duty today, after lunch I went with Magallon, Rosario and the batman Manolo to fish with hand grenades. We drove to the river about fourteen kilometres away in my car then sat out to walk along the edge to look for a good place. We scrambled for miles over rocks and boulders. We took off our shoes and stockings and waded in the river which was bitterly cold. Manolo was carrying three hand grenades and Magallon's rifle. Suddenly the strap of the rifle broke, and it fell to the ground and blew itself off. I don't know where the bullet went but we were jolly lucky it did not hit any of us. We threw one hand grenade but caught nothing as there were evidently no fish there.

Saturday, 5 November. This afternoon Magallon came to put the intravenous injection to the man with the peculiar veins. I am so glad to discover that he really has got almost impossible veins because he is the one I mucked. The ones I put were all a great success today. This evening Magallon told me I was beginning to be tubercular because of my cough. Imagine me with consumption! What an idea. Consuelo is so worried about my health that she keeps threatening to write and tell Mama to come and fetch me as I am ill. Just because I am ill, have a bad cough and infections on my legs.

Sunday, 5 November. Yesterday I teased Consuelo by telling her she interfered in my ward. The blasted girl got offended and this morning refused to help me dress the wounds into the bargain; what with Mass and Magallon's round I only started at 10.30 so had to hurry like mad. I was furious but swallowed my pride enough to ask her three times to help me but she would not. The result was that for once my patience left me and I got offended too and thought, very well, she shan't ever touch anything to do with my forty-seven wounded again. Then there was too little lunch and Marie Carmen got furious as usual. In fact by the end of the morning I was in a foul temper. Then Consuelo cured all my personal infections which are getting more and more numerous. After we had lunched I came back to the hospital in a fit of sulks to do all the injections but finally we apologized to each other and made friends again. So all afternoon I slept and then at about 6 o'clock went over to the other hospital with Paquita and one of our wounded who had an injured wrist which hurt him a lot. When he was being dealt with (he was not operated after all) he suddenly got a peculiar fit and went pale green and panting. I can't find out what it was, some sort of intestinal chill I think. Anyhow he collapsed and was fed on wine to pull him together. After lunch Consuelo went to ask Maruja something and found the door of the doctor's room locked. After a bit Maruja came out saying she had shut the door as she had a headache and wanted to rest, but Consuelo saw Torrijos legging it down the stairs out of the corner of her eye. Romance in the hospital between a jellified skeleton and a prize sow.

Monday, 7 November. This evening while waiting for dinner I wandered out and sat on the balcony by myself in the moonlight for about half an hour thinking about life and how mouldy it is. It appears that everyone was waiting for dinner because Magallon was missing and by bad luck so was I. The obvious result was they thought we were together. And by bad luck when Consuelo fetched me in, he arrived at the same moment. I could not make out what was going on. Consuelo came shooting out and when she found me on the verandah was furious and mysterious and would not say why. All through dinner she kept talking nonsense and telling awful lies. I could not make out what it was all about. How was I to know she had explained I was in the hospital putting fomentations to one of the sick men, and was trying to prove tactfully that Magallon had not been there? How tiresome those old cats are. Nasty-minded old buzzards. To think one can't even sit on the verandah without being accused of all sorts of things.

Now I expect they will tell the lieutenant-colonel that I am having an affair with Magallon in the hope of getting not only us but him also thrown out. Hypocritical old cows.

Tuesday, 8 November. I missed the news from England on the radio, so went to eat ham in the kitchen where I found Magallon being assaulted by five women begging to be allowed to go to Castellón in the lorry tomorrow. He operated a leg today, just opening it to let out the pus. It was quite incredible. It came out like a fountain and did not stop for about ten minutes. I guess Consuelo's muddle is really only because she is feeling ill. In fact neither of us is worth a farthing. Poor old us.

Wednesday, 9 November. Today has been dreadful. This afternoon at about 4 o'clock we were both in the hospital working when Margarita came to tell us that Mercedes Milá had come and would we go up to the house at once. Mercedes M. leapt on us in a fury and asked what on earth we were doing here. She maintained that when we went to see her in Burgos she had not told us we would come here. Then in front of them all she ticked us off soundly and said we would have to leave.

I was livid as it was all rot. We definitely told her we wanted to come here till we found an *equipo* and she definitely said 'OK'. However, later it turned out that there was more to it than met the eye. She went off into a corner for a long chat with Maruja in which

Maruja did most of the talking. Then she took Consuelo aside and started to talk to her, obviously a row. After a bit I went and joined them to find Consuelo furious and Mercedes Milá telling her that I could stay but she must go. It was all about the beastly tales that have been made up about us, since we came here. Maruja had either written to tell her or told her today that we behaved badly and that Consuelo was a drunkard etc. We begged to be allowed to stay and swore it was all absolutely untrue. We told her to ask any of the doctors or ask the nurses to repeat in front of us. We also told her about Maruja having told it to the lieutenant-colonel without telling the director of the hospital, which shook her a bit. I don't know how I resisted coming out with Maruja living with Torrijos. Anyhow after a long and painful conversation she told us we could stay but not before she had been damn rude. At least I was glad to see that before she left she ticked off the others for having danced and said – looking straight at Maruja – that we could not go out to any lunches or dinners in uniform and the usual about smoking. God, what a swine Maruja is. Later, talking with Magallon, Consuelo discovered that when these rows first started Maruja said to Magallon that she gave him twenty hours to get us out of the hospital and if not, beware. Why she had taken against us so much I can't understand except that Consuelo was tactless enough at first to say that she thought Torrijos was pretty much of a wet rag, which he is, and of course, people are inclined to think that I am a spy. Anyhow, she is dead set on getting rid of us and has made two attempts now. Filthy swine. She must be damn disappointed to find us still here tonight. God, I am tired of the rows and complications. Why can't I murder Maruja painfully? And why, oh why did I ever come here? Won't life ever be fun again, however hard one tries to enjoy it? God, I hate wars and all they entail.

Saturday, 12 November. Peace has descended on the world again. I am now the possessor of eleven abscesses on my legs and feet. The rest of me is covered with bites, spots and young growths. An unattractive sight and uncomfortable.

Sunday, 13 November. I am very tired tonight, which is not surprising as the last twenty-four hours have been pretty busy. Last night twenty-one sick patients arrived about 10.30. Consuelo put them all in bed downstairs in her ward, and we continued to go to bed ourselves. We had just got settled at about 12.30 when awful moans and groans suddenly penetrated to our room. The orderly told us that an Italian had just been brought in. We both leapt out of bed, and dressed in haste expecting, by the noise he was making, to find a dreadfully mutilated corpse. The wretched man had nothing wrong at all except shock and bruises from a bad motor accident. We put him to bed in my ward. He moaned and shouted as if he was dying. Despite putting him an injection of dope he kept up his row all night. All day he has lain in bed surrounded by Italians and girls, with his eyes shut, making pathetic gestures. His companions have swathed his head in bandages because he has one little scratch on his cheek. During the morning while I was still doing the dressings Uralde sent three of the new patients from downstairs up to my ward. One has a strained knee, another a swollen ankle bone. The third has a large swelling on his balls and penis and suspicious spots. Uralde asked him all sorts of questions about when he had last been on leave and if he had a fiancée, which made Consuelo quite hysterical. However, Magallon seems to think it is some ordinary infection so maybe I won't get syphilis yet. When we arrived at our house for lunch we were informed that our new head nurse, Isabel, had arrived. We were quivering in our shoes as to what she would be like. She turned up a tall, fattish, oldish woman, whom Consuelo had known all her life and who is a great friend of her mother's and all the Montemar family. So at least we have a useful friend and Maruja can't get her claws on us any longer. We are safe as houses at last. She is a nice woman, and was a nurse in France all through the Great War. This afternoon I had a bath while Consuelo drove herself mad collecting all the clothes to be sent to the wash. Each man has to put all his clothes in a bag and we have to mark the bag and each thing in it with the number of his bed and the name of ward. With thirty-two new patients, it means about a hundred and fifty marks or more, which is the devil; terribly boring and filthy as the clothes are revoltingly dirty. My bath was heaven and badly needed, but alas, marking clothes all evening afterwards soon spoilt my clean feeling. This evening was hectic. We marked and marked until the bell went to serve dinner. At that moment Magallon came to go round the ward. There were nine new ones who had come at lunch time, all ill instead of wounded. They all had complicated prescriptions and diets and treatments, so that I filled pages with instructions and words that I did not understand. Then a rush to serve dinner, then dash up to the chemist's to write out my book of things wanted for our hospital today: it filled pages too. Then rush downstairs again to dress a leg of one of the new ones, and at last hop off to dinner.

Five more arrived at about eleven tonight, so now we have the hospital full, with eighty-three beds and one hell of a lot of things to do. The day thirty-nine patients arrive within twenty-four hours one is swamped with boring work. Now it is twelve and I must go to sleep. I have got the radio here now which is pleasant.

Monday, 14 November. My last day of being twenty-one, and I can't say on the whole it has been a vastly successful year in my life, although it has been adventurous and full of events. We still have a lot of work at the hospital. We sent six away this morning, and six new ones arrived at dinner time, so we are still full up. I coughed all night and did not sleep a wink but now Magallon has given me some medicines which I hope will stop it tonight, otherwise I shall get terribly tired.

Going round the ward this morning Magallon was in a very bad temper and blew off at everyone. He ended with a stinking row with the chemists about not sending out medicines quickly enough. So then they all said it was my fault for going round the ward too late. So we all got angry and shouted. However, now I am friends with everyone again. Tomorrow I shall be twenty-two.

Wednesday, 16 November. Not a letter, not a telegram. No one has remembered my birthday except Mama. Into the bargain, today has ended badly. It seems that in a hospital one must be a nun. Isabel is very nice but devilishly old-fashioned. She objects to everything. This morning she led me aside for about half an hour to ask me where I had worked, how long for, what exams I had taken, when etc. and if I was happy here and got on with everyone, and a long sermon about being correct with the doctors, get up when they come in, talk to them as 'usted' instead of 'tu' etc.[10] I stayed in the hospital all afternoon doing one or two things. Magallon came at five to see the patients as he had not come during the morning. Later I took one down to have shrapnel taken out of his leg. I was supposed to take

10 'Usted' is the polite form of address, 'tu' the familiar.

two of them, but the second was so tight he could hardly stand up so I had to leave him. However, I have put him under arrest for tomorrow as punishment and to stop it happening again. Magallon let me take out the shrapnel this time as it was very easy, being near the surface. Consuelo, who has spent the evening frantically marking clothes, stayed here for dinner but I went home, complete with my bottle of Carlos III. Isabel was terribly shocked that I drank brandy: she said she had never drunk it in her life. I tried to explain it away by saying that it was quite usual in England but I could see that she was mortally pained. She said I could not go back to the hospital alone so Magallon said he said he would send his batman with me. After a bit we set off, Rosario and Magallon to her hospital and Manuel and I to mine. But once outside the door they said why didn't I go with them, so I left Manuel to take my knitting to my hospital and went with them. At Rosario's hospital we found the orderly entirely failing to give a saline injection, so we stayed there a bit to help. When we went out again it had begun to rain. On the way Magallon stopped to fetch the sister of the girl in the house where he lives. Then he said why didn't I come back to his house for a bit, so I, like a goop, went and spent a pleasant ten minutes sitting round the log fire in the kitchen with all the family. Then I went back to the hospital. He accompanied me to the door and in I romped to find Consuelo pretending to be asleep, having left me a note to say that if I must be such a fool she was going to leave, etc. and don't try to give any explanations.

It appears that Isabel came here after dinner and was pained that I was not here yet and curious to know where I was. Consuelo was furious with me and when I explained exactly what I had done she said it was very stupid if it were true. In other words, even she had to think nasty thoughts about me, so I guess she is right. Because if she can't believe in me what can I expect of the others? But all the row and unpleasantness just because I suddenly wanted to sit round a log fire like at home and forgot I was a nurse. I hate life!

Every small pleasure one can invent to lessen the boredom of one's life is a crime. I can't smoke, I can't hardly drink anything, I must hardly talk to a man, must never let slip any slang.[11] In fact I might as well be a nun and it is not my form. I can't help having been brought up to a lot of liberty and it drives me mad to be spied on and followed about and treated like either a child or a bloody tart who

11 It must be remembered that nuns are often hospital nurses in Spain.

must be reformed. I am quite willing to behave like a nun in the hospital from eight in the morning till nine at night, but at least I might have some enjoyment afterwards. I suppose it is just that I am spoilt, but I can't help wanting to forget I am a nurse sometimes. The work is interesting and I like it, but oh my God – how I hate the life!

Somehow my twenty-second year does not seem to be starting very well, and I am trying so hard to be happy but people just won't let me. I am sick of life and its pettiness.

Thursday, 17 November. Such a lot happened today of no importance, but it seems important here, where life is always the same. We had just finished all our work for the morning when the electrician came in and told us that two ladies and a lieutenant were waiting to see us up at the house. We dashed up there and found the Infanta, Frau von Raben and Ataulfo. It was grand to see them again, it hardly seemed real. At lunch I sat between the Infanta and Ataulfo and we all talked and laughed and joked for the first time for nearly two months; it was a real pleasure to be alive. They brought us all sorts of things: ham, cheese, chocolates, and three telegrams. After lunch, we came and sat in our room for a bit and talked. As the Infanta is going to England I wrote a hasty note to Mama and a list of things I want her to send me, and a list of surgical instruments I want the Infanta to buy for me. Finally, we showed them the hospital and then they had to leave, so we went back to the house to see them off. It seemed a short visit.

Unluckily I lost my voice almost completely, and can only croak today, which was rather embarrassing. Tonight all my growths are infected and painful and Consuelo nearly burnt my chest off with a hot compress. I am uncomfortable and miserable. How silly one is to be miserable just because one gets a glimpse of the gorgeous outer world. Princess Bee says she is going to organize a flying *equipo* to go hurriedly wherever there is a lot of work to lend temporary aid to the hospitals and *equipos*.

She asked if we would join, which we said we would. Of course, it is not fixed yet and may never be, but it would be fun. Now it is nearly 1 o'clock and I am tired, my throat hurts, my chest burns, and my legs and feet ache.

Friday, 18 November. Today started badly. I was feeling pretty glum anyhow and foolish, and pie-eyed from my cold, so I only got up at about nine. I was half dressed when Isabel came in. Luckily Consuelo had got up early to go to Confession so was trotting around the hospital taking temperatures. Isabel started saying I must stay in bed with my cough and we would have to move out of our room here so she could send others to replace us. I got very angry and said I would not go to bed and was perfectly all right. We were still arguing when the orderly announced that Magallon was waiting upstairs. I flung on my remaining clothes and rushed up breakfastless and angry at his turning up so early. He was in a filthy temper and was very rude to me. We had a heated argument – he saying I had been rude to him on purpose yesterday by talking English in front of him. I got furious at his being so rude about something so stupid. Finally, he said I could go away if I wanted as he could visit the ward perfectly well without me. By that time I was getting done down at nearly an hour's arguing before breakfast after coughing all night, and I very nearly lost my temper.

He evidently noticed how upset I had got, because when I left the room and went to the kitchen, he followed me, offering a cigarette and trying to make conversation. I meant to be silent, offended and aloof, but I felt so miserable at having quarrelled that we made friends again. Unluckily I got a violent fit of coughing and choking with tears streaming down my cheeks and wishing I was dead.

During the morning, the batman brought me a note saying if it was not a bother would I go to the other hospital to see Magallon before lunch. I could not think what it was about but it turned out to be that all the nurses had to go to Gandesa this afternoon to see Franco present the Medalla Militar to the remains of the 1st Division of the Brigada de Navarra, which is what I have always been attached to.

The march past was splendid. It took place on a large flat space outside Gandesa.[12] Franco did not appear after all and General Avila gave the medal and took the salute instead. We had a splendid view right in front with all the important folk. Lots of our fellow nurses from *equipos* there. It was very different from a peacetime march past. All the soldiers dirty, unshaven and bedraggled in various strange garments, the flags shot to rags. It was very impressive to see them and know all they have been through in the last few days. Now

12 The outskirts of Gandesa was the furthest point the Republicans reached in the Ebro battle. The Republicans had been ordered by Rojo to 'dig in and hold at all costs'.

they are to have a few days' rest which they certainly deserve. Gandesa has been shot to bits since I was last there.

Magallon told me that a captain has arrived here now as director of the hospital, so now Magallon is no longer the director. It should be much better because he was not a born organizer. Isabel sent me to bed for dinner, which made me furious. All day she does nothing but tell me to put on my cape in case I catch cold, to shut the windows, to change my apron, to go to bed etc. as if I were a child of twelve. It drives me off my head, she is very nice and kind, but quite maddening.

Saturday, 19 November. I am dead tired with a headache I have had nearly all day, or rather an eyebrow ache. It must be my sinus again. Consuelo got a coughing fit at 4.30 this morning and coughed without stopping till 6.30 when, with an injection of mild dope, she finally went to sleep. Her coughing fits are terrible. She just goes on and on coughing and vomiting without a pause. I was so sleepy it took me an hour to wake after she started and even then I was as if I were drugged. However, I got up at 7.30 and roared round the hospital taking temperatures and various oddments. I started the morning unable to do more than whisper, but am now back at croaking again. Consuelo slept till nine as a result of her injection, and has looked like hell all day. I am sure she is really ill but it would not be much use trying to find out as she would never admit it.

I had a shocking row today as I found out that my car had been used to carry all the clothes and linen from one hospital to another, all full of lice I expect. It was not the fact that I minded, but that no one had either asked my permission to use it or told me afterwards even. I asked the chauffeur who had given the order and he said 'Torrijos', so when Torrijos turned up at the end of lunch with the new director, I was icily politely rude about it. He was aghast and assured me he had never given such an order. In the end he came later and explained that one of the orderlies had asked him while he was talking to a general who was visiting the hospital and he said, 'All right, do as you like' without even hearing the question. The wretched orderly has been arrested for fifteen days as a result of Torrijos's carelessness, which makes me feel very uncomfortable and is very unfair.

Sunday, 20 November. As usual I woke up at four with a coughing fit, and after an hour Consuelo gave me an injection as I could not stop.

We heard all the Italians setting off at 5 o'clock and then my dope sent me straight to sleep for once.

We had a colossal row because a legionary in my ward went out for a walk with nothing on except his bandage and an overcoat. He got sozzled and went about lifting up his coat for the edification of all the girls he saw until he was arrested by a *guardia civil* and brought back unconscious from drink. Two who were with him were also tight. One was just tiresome and later sick all over the floor, the other was swearing and trying to fight with everyone. I had to order him to bed with great gusto. In fact I spent the day ordering people about and arresting them. The drunks have all had their clothes taken away and are kept in bed as punishment.

Monday, 21 November. Consuelo is ill tonight. I don't know how ill, because she won't let me take her temperature or anything, but I think she has quite a lot of fever, as she is red in the face and behaves oddly. I wish there was some way of curing her cough. Every night she coughs till she sicks up all her dinner and most of the night she coughs and vomits. However, now she seems to be asleep.

I have given her drops and an injection of dope, so hope she will sleep all night and be all right tomorrow. Lieutenant-Colonel Isasi came to lunch today, bringing us the news that we will be moving from here in a week or two's time. This hospital is to be shut down tomorrow and the sixty-five patients we still have are to be divided amongst the other two hospitals. Five of the nurses are going on leave tomorrow. We do not yet know where we will be moving to, but the general opinion says northwards as the lieutenant-colonel said it would be a cold place. Also, we are going up to the front so as not to be left too far behind when our troops advance. I think we are going to Lerida. The others think Fraga, which is near Lerida. Anyhow, we will see when we get there. It is fun to be moving and to be going up to the front again. Perhaps we will have more adventures. I hope we will be able to make a good start there and be rid of all the rows and troubles. Magallon says he is going to ask Isabel to get rid of Mimi, and I think she is the cause of all the trouble. Maruja apologized to Consuelo this morning for everything she had against us and has promised to tell all the people to whom she told it that it is all untrue. She says she did not invent any of the stories but did back them up. I think Mimi invented them. She is a soured old spinster who is out to hurt the world and everyone in it.

In a way I shall be sorry to leave this hospital; it means Consuelo and I can't be together any more and it was such fun being able to organize it just as we liked and being friends of all the patients. They are so sweet and nice on the whole. Even the drunken *legionario* yesterday did just what I told him, saying he had never had a mother and he would do anything I asked him. It really is awfully nice to be able to do things for people and them to be grateful, even if I do lose my temper with them often. I like being relied on for everything. Whatever bothers them, they ask me. Sometimes it is something to do with their wound or illness, sometimes clothes, sometimes a quarrel which I automatically have to decide for them, sometimes I am a go-between to get them leave to visit relations or friends. In fact, I pretty nearly am their mother, though God forbid I ever have forty-seven children.

Tuesday, 22 November. It is 7 o'clock and I am pretty tired, as I have had a very busy day and got up at seven. Canuta has been ill in bed all day minus a voice plus a bit of temperature and a cough. I had to do all the dressings and injections before lunch, as all the wounded and ill were to be evacuated to the other hospitals after lunch so as to leave this one empty and shut it down. Actually, there are still twenty-one patients here tonight as there were not enough empty beds to move them all. I am pretty tired, as it has been lots of work today. But I got everything done in time which is the main point. I can't be bothered to write much. I have been in a bad temper most of the day through things of no importance.

Sunday, 27 November. I don't know how much longer I shall be able to stand this place. Everyone thinks I am so calm and unemotional; that I don't mind all the rows and muddles there are, but it is driving me potty. Only seeing everyone else in such a state makes me pretend to be even calmer than I would normally appear. Mimi and Helena are still hard at work against us, despite the temporary absence of the other swine. Every day there is some small trouble, never a moment's peace, one unpleasantness after another. Always with one's nerves on edge, waiting to see what they will do next. Today they have written again to the Head of the Nurses, complaining of Consuelo and me, though what it is this time, God knows. Why must some people always be out to harm? They are against Magallon, Consuelo and me and yet not one of us has done anything against them, even without meaning to. I have got into such a state that in the last few days twice I have burst into tears for no reason and got almost hysterical. To hell with the bitches!

Tomorrow we are off to a country house somewhere north of Lerida. I hope to God it brings me better luck than Calaceite. I can't stand much more.

Monday, 28 November. What a day! I am exhausted, but in a splendid temper. The house we are in is a huge building called Monte Julia, on the top of a rise where one can see for miles all around, dry, empty, deserted hills, and far away in the distance the snow-capped Pyrenees. Although there are stacks of little villages all around, not a house in sight and we seem to be cut off from the world.

I was called at 6 o'clock this morning in the hospital where I was sleeping soundly on a bed made of two tables in the surgery. I shot off home in the dark and icy cold early hours, to find Consuelo in bed fully dressed even down to hobnailed shoes, and the whole room littered with suitcases, rugs, packing cases and hundreds of oddments. We packed frantically, while the orderly carried the luggage out to the car. I went to get Helena's, and found her sound asleep, quite unaware that she was supposed to leave early in the morning. Finally, after driving back and forth from the hospital with luggage, and packing, and stuffing the car with all the fragile things like bottles which weigh a ton, we finally got off at 8.30. Isabel, Consuelo and Katalina behind; Helena, Magallon and myself in front. It took us four and a half hours to get there, as the roads were moderate and we did not hurry. All the way the country was hideous, dry and arid, all red and yellow like a desert with no houses, no cultivation and no animals. A few hideous poor villages so exactly the same colour as the land that one hardly noticed them.

About half way we had to stop as a bridge of boats had broken and we had to wait while they mended it.

On arriving there, we immediately set to work to explore our new abode and find our rooms. We two wanted to live apart but it could not be managed, and we are all together in the two top floors of one of the towers. There will be eighteen of us when the new ones and the ones on leave arrive!!

Isabel nearly drove us mad all afternoon fussing over one thing and another, changing her mind about everything and making us climb up and down the interminable stairs over and over again. We lunched out in the open air off anything we could find. I fed on cold meat in my fingers and cheese. All afternoon and evening the lorries were unloading, but there was nothing for us to do except accompany Isabel on her useless journeys up and down the stairs, and as a respite sit on the luggage outside and gossip.

General Melendez turned up at about four and snorted round the house in a bad temper, calling for his usual bicarbonate. Then I took Magallon in the car to the nearby village to find women to char this place tomorrow. When we arrived there we went to the mayor; he sent us on to the major of the *guardia civil*; he sent us to an *alferez* of the general staff, who in turn sent us to the *alferez* of *intendencia*, who sent us to the sergeant of *intendencia*, who finally arranged it for us. And after all our peregrinations, the sergeant lived in the house in front of which I had parked the car!

We got back here at about 6.30 and by seven were all eating dinner. Now it is nearly ten and all the others are asleep. Isabel has finally retired, after bothering us all to have rugs or hot water bottles. As the people who loaded the lorries forgot to put in any blankets or sheets, we are all sleeping as we can under coats and capes thrown over us. I have lines under my eyes and am too tired to do anything.

Tuesday, 29 November. Today has been pretty hectic and a mixture of the greatest fun and infuriatingly irritating and depressing. I really rather like this place and would be delighted with everything if only it was not for the thought of eighteen nurses and the rows there will be.

We did not get up till nine, which was a God-sent rest although I slept very badly as I coughed all night and it was bitterly cold. Somehow, with all the cold and the fact that it had rained all night and everything was damp and overcast, this seemed a less attractive place. I started the day by being sent to the village followed by a lorry to fetch the women to clean the hospital as they had not arrived. I went to the *intendencia* in search of the sergeant. It was crammed with soldiers who made silly remarks and shoved me about. When I finally found my man, he said the women had left a few minutes before, and in fact I passed them on the way back. All morning was spent putting up beds and running about counting how many would go where and shouting and arguing. Isabel continued all day as tiresome as usual. In the middle of lunch the first ambulance arrived with all the wounded and we had to rush off and put them in their wards. All day continued the same muddle and rush. Before lunch I drove over to another house three kilometres away to see if it would do to live in. It was no good for that but would make a lovely hospital, but unluckily the chiefs don't approve. Anyhow it is full of furniture which we are all going to steal for our rooms. I am too tired to write any more. It is 11.30 and I have not started to go to bed as the ambulance with two new nurses only arrived an hour ago and we have been gossiping and making their beds etc. Consuelo and I are to work with Magallon. We have the second floor and at the moment thirty-nine patients. Here we have no girls to help as there is no village near, so we will have much more tiresome work, like having to get up early so as to give the breakfast and being continually in the wards to fetch bedpans or glasses of water, etc. All the bitches are being sent away together with Torrijos and the skin diseases. God, how angry they will be. Mimi is furious already but we are all pleased. The two new girls are dark and young and seem very nice. Poor things, they are sleeping in the passage tonight. They will freeze.

Wednesday, 30 November. God, how cold it is in this house, and the people here say the cold has not begun yet. As usual I am so tired that I can't think how to write this beastly diary. I wish I did not get tired so easily. This morning we got up at 6.30. It was a very lucky thing we did because I went down to the kitchen at 7 o'clock and discovered there was no water with which to make coffee for the patients. The complications to get some were colossal. I shouted at everyone and no one would go. The lorries were all cold and would not start up and then were taken away from us, etc. Finally Katalina turned up and took it over while we went and started to arrange the surgery, which was still all in packing cases. All the time people kept popping in and out with muddles and bothers and Magallon cosily in bed in his room next door giving orders. Men have got a cheek. What with all those muddles, no women to clean the floors, no girls to make the beds and the surgery unready, we only finished the dressings at 12.30 and had to rush to serve lunch. One of the new girls,

Nucha, is working with us and seems quite nice, although they are both a bit 'uppish', complaining about their room, their blankets, the work. They both speak very good English. Now Consuelo and I are the proud possessors of a table, two chairs, a mirror and a chest of drawers. The work of turning this into a hospital progresses slowly. Our floor is nearly done now, at least we have all the beds put together and made. We got a new patient today. A man with a very deep cut over his eye and a lot of haemorrhage and swelling. It turned out, on further inquiry, that he cut himself three days ago and had not been injected with anti-tetanus or anything. Tonight he has a high fever and it is a moot point if we are going to have a case of tetanus on our hands or not. I hope not as it is a horrible disease. Consuelo is like a maniac tonight with her new furniture and madly tidying everything. At lunch today Mimi was intolerable and ended by telling Magallon, in front of all the officers, that her dog had more sense and education than him. She said it in such a bloody rude way that everyone was livid and later Isabel made her apologize.

Thursday, 1 December. I am going to buy myself a chauffeur's uniform and give up being a nurse. All I seem to do is drive my car. The afternoon I spent the whole time driving. First to take five of the nurses over to the other house to look for furniture, then to take Isabel to a distant village to look for a servant for us. I am sorry all the nurses on leave have come back but I must say that I have not noticed them much yet.

As I am to take Isabel tomorrow to Alcaniz to fetch some things the *capitan* has decided that Helena is to come too to be looked at in the hospital. She always feels ill in cars and it is at least four hours away. She says she won't go and I feel there will be a splendid row tomorrow. I must say that for once I agree with her. It is a crazy idea to send her so far for nothing.

Wednesday, 7 December. Due to one thing and another (mostly that I am always dead tired in the evenings) I have not written this for days. Now I am sitting in bed waiting for Consuelo to come and give me a hot compress, theoretically to cure my sore throat, actually to burn my front off. The journey to and from Alcaniz was pretty boring. We spent the day trying to locate a new nurse who was to come here. We did not find her as she had gone back to Zaragoza. On Saturday

Mimi got a telegram telling her to go immediately to the *equipo* of Pruneda. This was the result of our hard work. So after all we win the first round. She deserves everything she gets because she is a foul bitch, but I can't help feeling sorry for her. She suffers so terribly from the cold and will have to live very uncomfortably, also Pruneda treats his nurses very badly so that he can never keep them for more than a week or so. At the moment, as usual, he has none. Poor Mimi – what a punishment, but she has asked for it. So on Monday Consuelo and I went to Zaragoza to leave Mimi and collect Paquita back from leave. Isabel decided we should stay the night there. When we arrived at Zaragoza at 1 o'clock (after dressing all the wounds and a hurried change out of uniform) we went to telephone to Epila and when at last I got on at 2.30 I found Ataulfo was there all by himself. So we roared off in the car to join him. He seemed quite pleased to see us, though not enthusiastic due to a hangover. He produced us some lunch and then we sat and talked and he played the piano. I was unable to speak because my voice had gone completely as usual and I felt ill and depressed. Everyone told me I was looking pretty moderate and very much thinner. I am getting thinner every day, although I eat a lot, and am very pale and always tired. It is sheer nerves as there is nothing wrong with me except my lack of voice, and my boils. I suppose I must be run down, although I can't think why, except that I can never sleep well.

The next day (yesterday) we breakfasted with Alvaro and Prince Ali at 9.30, then packed up our things and went to Zaragoza to go shopping. We were terrified driving there as the wretched chauffeur had arranged the brakes so that they were terribly strong and the car shot to one side. Madly dangerous. However, after a lot of trouble we got it arranged in Zaragoza after lunch. We lunched in the restaurant with our three fellow nurses. We were all very hearty and laughed our heads off. We ended by stealing all the fruit as it looked delicious and it seemed a pity to leave it there. As I was feeling depressed I merely wanted to murder them all but I don't think they were aware of the fact.

Friday, 9 December. Rumour has it that we will be going to Tremp.[13] The divisional post office has disappeared plus all the troops in our

13 Tremp, in the Pyrenees, was captured in April 1938. Its hydro-electric plants supplied Barcelona with electricity.

Army Corps in that direction, nobody quite knows where. All around here is now full of Italians. We have a battery of Italian anti-aircraft up on the next door hill, all mounted on lorries; it will be fun if they start blowing off one day as they are only one kilometre away. Last night I was on duty until 3 o'clock when someone else took over. There were two very seriously ill men downstairs so from time to time I visited them, then retired again to the surgery. This morning Consuelo and I only woke up at 9.15 so shot down to do the dressings. We breakfasted when we had finished just after 10 o'clock and the rest of the morning I spent doing the highly unpleasant job of collecting the dirty washing from all the wounded and sorting and writing it all down. This afternoon at about 4 o'clock I took Magallon and Fernando the engineer to the town. We arrived there, only thirteen kilometres away, just as it got dark. Magallon shot off to visit a friend. We three accompanied Fernando. He insisted on going into the bar to drink. We said we could not go in uniform, but as every time he left us we got surrounded by an unpleasant crowd of rude soldiers, we decided that the lesser of the two evils was to go into the bar. So we sat at a little table drinking beer with the place crowded with solders making remarks about us. Fernando is as mad as a hatter and appears to be permanently drunk. Actually it is just his manner but it is very funny. He has oodles of charm. We all got back here at about 6.30. On the way back Fernando sat in the back of the car with the two nurses and evidently they had a spirited time because the whole journey was accompanied by scuffling, fighting, shouting, etc. God knows what the three of them were doing. As it was dark I could not see. Tonight Consuelo is ill. I don't know what is wrong with her. She says she just has a headache, but she has been looking pale and red-eyed all day and has eaten neither lunch nor dinner. I hope she is not really ill again. She usually manages to recuperate in quick time. She went to bed for dinner, which was a gloomy meal.

At last we have got water laid on here, and tomorrow can start to wash if we want to. Personally I don't want to at all. I think it is a very unnecessary pastime needing a lot of energy and a waste of time. I am a bit tired tonight so will go to sleep.

Saturday, 10 December. Tonight Consuelo has got her headache again. She has been up all day feeling 'illish' and is now in bed being sick and coughing. I thoroughly lost my temper with her tonight. She went to bed for dinner and when I had finished mine I brought her up some coffee but forgot her water. I trotted down to get it whereupon she came galloping after me in her pyjamas with her cape flowing out behind her. I told her to go back to bed and she would not. We had a furious argument on the stairs and I threw away the coffee cup in my temper and it smashed down below with the most awful noise. To my fury everyone popped out to see what it was. I can't think why I got so angry except that Consuelo always does the same thing of getting up when she is ill and dashing about in her pyjamas and it makes me furious. Either she is well and can come down to dinner or fetch her coffee, or she is ill and should let me do it. But she has to ask me to fetch something and then when I am halfway there to come prancing after me. Magallon is ill today with fever and strange spasmodic pains. This morning he was sure he was going to die. Isabel has been very tiresome today. She has been told by someone that I spent my night on duty in Magallon's room, whereas I was in the surgery. She thinks the worst and was only scared off ticking me off and so on by Consuelo, who said I was as innocent as a babe and would be so disgusted at her ideas that I would certainly leave the hospital and go home, furious with the Spanish. What is more, I really am just as offended as Consuelo said. I wonder who invented it. Anyhow she has passed on her nasty suspicions to most of the nurses who stood up for me and has said nothing to me. Tiresome old hag. Consuelo, Nucha, Magallon and I laughed ourselves silly about her ridiculous suspicions. The Red aviation dropped three bombs somewhere around here this morning, but very far off. I only heard one of them, which made a splendid bang about two kilometres away.

Sunday, 11 December. At lunch we decided to go to the cinema in Binefar. To our great surprise, Isabel and the *capitan* both gave us permission. So tonight at 8 o'clock, Consuelo, six others and I all set off in my car. We arrived at Binefar in the pouring rain to discover that the cinema was reserved for the Italians today as they are staying there tonight. So we went to Monzon. It also was full of Italians but we got seats. As we had half an hour to wait we stopped the car on the side of the road and played the radio and talked. We were all as mad as hatters at the joy of being away from our school and school mistress. The cinema was American and quite fun. We were almost the only women and Margot was pinched all through the film by the Italians, entirely her fault for giggling, but I believe she enjoyed it. We arrived back here at about 12 o'clock full of spirit. It really was great fun and a God-sent relief from the usual form here. The school atmosphere is driving us all dotty.

Monday, 12 December. I am fed up to the back teeth with life, with Spain and mostly with that damn, filthy-minded Isabel. I have been frothing against her all day and most of yesterday, and I am damned if I will have her trotting around spying on me and thinking I am misbehaving all the time. And if she does think so, why the hell can't she just come and talk to me about it instead of telling everyone else. This morning going down to breakfast we met her on the stairs. She asked me why I was in uniform and I said it was because Consuelo was going to Zaragoza instead of me. She asked my why, so I told her because Consuelo wanted to and I did not. So she looked at me with a nasty glare and said, 'Ah! I see! You want to stay and keep Magallon company.' I said she was crazy to which she answered, 'Well, nothing would surprise me now.' I was livid, especially as for all I know everyone may have heard as they were all passing. It makes me furious because I sat all that night on duty in complete silence knitting, but nothing will ever induce anyone to believe it. And what right has she got to think the worst of me. Anyhow tomorrow I am going to have it out with her whether she likes it or not.

Evidently Mercedes Milá has received another letter from here informing her of our bad behaviour. My God, what filthy swine people are. It is a good thing the ideals for which I came out here are not as high and romantic as they might have been or I would have gone home disgusted with the people here long ago. Magallon himself, the cause of all the trouble, is worse today, and, despite constant aspirin, has been delirious on and off most of the afternoon. He is miserable about all this row and gets himself into a state bothering about it. Now Isabel has forbidden us to go into his room. I think it is damn mean when a man is ill and likes company, to forbid us to see him when we have to sit in the next door room all day anyhow. I am so fed up with all this that I really think I am going to ask to be moved. I don't like the work here anyhow, and since it has turned into a school and a reformatory I loathe it. I have spent all

[163]

day gossiping with Nucha, who is most awfully nice. She also is fed to the back teeth with Isabel and bored stiff. Anyhow at least rumour has it that within a very short time we will be moving to somewhere near Tremp. That, at least, will be a change.

Tuesday, 13 December. Today has been full of action. I started the morning by oversleeping and being found by Isabel at 10 o'clock still dressing. She never ticks one off but just says things in a roundabout gentle way which drives us all crazy. When we had finished our work I decided to have things out with her. So I removed her to our room and burst out with a flow of explanations. We argued for about half an hour but she is impossible. Nasty old hypocrite.

As I did not want her to know Consuelo and Katalina had been repeating what she had said, there were a lot of things I could not say. I tried to draw her out to say them to my face, but she remained placid and smiling and said nothing. She continues with her facetious idea that I am dominated by Magallon which makes me livid. It is impossible to describe the whole row but it was very unsatisfactory and I am sure she remains under the idea that I am dominated and a silly child who does not realize the danger of life, etc. I would like to strangle her. At lunch we decided to go to Fraga to see if Prince Ali had arrived. Twelve kilometres from the front and crammed with soldiers, lorries, mud, noise and filth. We found the headquarters of aviation. We were just getting up to go when Prince Ali walked in looking handsome as always. He was surprised to see us but too distracted by things and people to talk to us much. However, we have invited ourselves to dine there on Friday, if nothing unexpected happens. After ten minutes he went off to visit a general and we said goodbye and set off to find petrol. The road back was filled with lorries going in both directions and it was a beastly drive and very narrow with the flooded river on one side and a deep muddy ditch on the other. However, we arrived back safely at 7.30 and Isabel was so relieved to see us safe that she forgot to be annoyed. Escariot says the new offensive is to start the day after tomorrow if it does not rain.

5
The Final Offensive, Catalonia
December 1938 – March 1939

After driving the Republican armies back over the Ebro, Franco turned against Catalonia on 23 December.

The Republican resistance, as in the Aragon offensive, collapsed. 'It was a rout,' wrote Rojo and Pip's entries reveal the lack of any signs of resistance and the few casualties.

The Nationalists entered Barcelona on 25 January 1939, and Pip the day after. It fell, as Rojo remarked bitterly, 'without glory'. His last ambitious 'Plan B' was a vain attempt to halt the advance in Catalonia by an offensive in Estremadura. The Catalan offensive had been planned for 10 December; postponed, it started on 23 December. From Pip's last entry for 13 December it is obvious that the rumours were circulating before the start of the campaign.

The Republican offensive in Estremadura achieved nothing in spite of capturing considerable territory. As a result of this offensive, Pip spent a brief period near Merida. For most of the time she was working in hospitals on the Catalan coast or searching for a friendly equipo; she also worked with the Infanta Beatrice who was in Catalonia at this time.

Wednesday, 14 December. I have just found out something which is devastating. Consuelo has been in a strange rebellious mood ever since she got back from Zaragoza the day before yesterday, and at last I know why. Evidently the reason why Isabel went to Zaragoza in such a hurry was that she had received a letter from Mercedes Milá saying that she had had a letter with more complaints about us and that Consuelo was to leave the hospital within twenty-four hours. So at the moment Consuelo is officially not here, and only here in fact on Isabel's responsibility. Much as I hate the old trout she does mean very well. If only she had a tiny bit more moral courage she might have made everything all right for us. The worst of it is that I think the letter must have been from Mimi saying about my supposed flirtation with Magallon, only saying it was Consuelo instead of me. God, what filthy swine people are. It takes a long time to make one realize the full filth of humanity. And if she is thrown out she will never be sent anywhere else and we can't be together any longer and she can't be a nurse any more and everything is a mess. She is in a thorough state although she does not say much. And all this just because she is a really good, honest, trustworthy person, so the bad ones hate her, and bad people always win. Well, if she is thrown out or not I am going to leave this stinking hospital. I think I have been more thoroughly miserable here than anywhere else in my life, but I don't suppose I shall ever get sent to a front line *equipo* again, which is what I like, because Mercedes Milá has taken against us. And to think of all the petty illusions of heroism and justice with which I came to this filthy country. I suppose it is a good idea to have one's silly illusions smashed, but I wish it did not have to be at Consuelo's expense. How I wish we had never come to this hospital, although it would probably have been the same anywhere else too. The unfairness of life makes me writhe, and there is not a thing that one can do about it. Consuelo is too sensitive and will never get over this row. And even if she does not have to go we can't stay on here now, but where will Mercedes Milá send us? God damn the idiotic woman. News of the hospital this morning was that we were moving on a few days to a huge convent near Balaguer only twelve kilometres from the front. But then Fernando came to lunch with the news that we were not to move after all and are to stay here merely as a resting place for the wounded evacuated from the *equipos*. So we are all furious and bored stiff. I want to work again. Every day I think more about giving up the whole thing and going home. Why should I go on helping such a set of swine at the cost of feeling continually ill and tired and being covered in boils and lice? And yet I know if I go home and have no worries I shall worry so much about the war that it will be worse, and I am too much in all this war to be able to walk out and leave it flat for good.

Thursday, 15 December. I am supposed to be on duty tonight but Isabel has sent me to bed as she says I am run down. I think really it is that she does not trust me a yard, but who cares. Now I can sleep all night.

So far we have no news of whether the new offensive has begun or not except some Italians who say we have advanced. It will be rather fun if they send us all the wounded from the *equipos* as it will mean lots of work as they will be very ill. Back to our old form again of moans and groans, and saving people's lives. I quite wake up from my present coma at the thought. We had a tea party in our room today by candlelight as the electricity had failed. Only ten days till Christmas now!

Friday, 16 December. This evening Consuelo, Nucha, Blanca and I went to dine with Prince Ali in Fraga. We set off at 5 o'clock and although it is only forty kilometres away, we took three hours. The first hour we wasted as we had to go to Binefar for petrol and back. As usual I discovered at the last moment that the car was empty, so was the tank here and the chauffeur had gone off in the ambulance with all the permits. However, we did finally get some, by which time Consuelo was in a bad temper at so much waste of time. She was in the heartiest form at lunch and started by flicking a spoonful of soup in my eye which drenched my apron. She followed that up by a glass of wine which soaked my sleeves and neck, and a cigarette end which nearly burnt a hole in my back. But by the time we set off she was as glum as anything. It was a grim journey of rain and mud, crawling behind long convoys of lorries and continual stops to let other convoys pass on the narrow parts. However, at last at 8 o'clock we arrived famished at the headquarters of *aviacion*. We found Prince Ali, Escariot and Matas waiting for us. Prince Ali was in grand form and told us that a cousin of Escariot's and Ataulfo were also coming to dinner. I was delighted, but although the cousin (a very shy but nice *alferez* of Regulares) came, Ataulfo failed entirely to turn up.[1] We did not dine till 9.30. We all sat drinking and talking while Consuelo and Escariot went to the kitchen to cook dinner. When it did come it was good. Asparagus soup, fried eggs and potatoes, and meat, cheese, jam, figs, wine and liqueurs. Prince Ali told us the offensive had not yet begun after all and would not begin tomorrow either as the weather was still too bad. Matas talked the whole time without stopping and was very taken by Nucha, who is definitely attractive. I was once more told that I was getting thinner every day, which pleased me, but is not surprising as I hardly eat at

1 The Regulares were native Moroccans officered by Spaniards.

all. Everything I eat makes me feel ill. I would like to give it up altogether, especially as I am never hungry. At 11.30 I said we had to go so we set off on the homeward journey, which took us two hours although there were far fewer lorries. It was foggy the last bit. When we arrived back we called on Isabel to tell her we were safe and sound. She said she had been terribly worried and had not slept a wink, which seemed a pity and very silly to me. So at 1.30 we retired to bed. I personally have quite enjoyed myself and am very tired.

Saturday, 17 December. Today I was feeling very lazy and thinking of going to bed for dinner, but when we got up from lunch at 2.30 Isabel and the *capitan* took me aside and asked me if I could take him to Zaragoza this afternoon. I was vastly put out but of course said I could. When we arrived in Zaragoza I took him to the place he wanted to go, and he told me to wait and he would only be a few minutes. Actually it was the offices of General Melendez and the general was there, so he took an hour while I sat and froze in the car thinking of all the things I wanted to do in Zaragoza but would not have time for. At last at 9 o'clock he appeared, very apologetic and said he must go to the Hospital Militar. At 9.45 at last the *capitan* had finished his business but it was too late for me to do anything, so we decided to eat at the restaurant. We were neither of us hungry so ate very little and at 10.30 set off back. It took us three and a half hours, during which I got very tired and had a headache which got worse and worse. We had a long patch of thick fog near Huseca which slowed us up a lot. At 2 o'clock we arrived back here. I popped in to tell Isabel who said I could stay in bed tomorrow as I had had two late nights.

Sunday, 18 December. Isabel told me she had had a long chat with Magallon about me. He had made her shut the door and had been very mysterious about it and quite ridiculous giving rumours such importance. She also said that Maruja had a long talk with her in which she was very repentant and said she was going to swallow her pride and start afresh. Consuelo and I immediately wondered what new dirty trick she has played on us.

Monday, 19 December. I have gone to bed for dinner as I am now starting on a serious campaign of improving my health. I am getting thinner and thinner, which would be perfectly splendid if I was not thoroughly run down at the same time. I can't eat anything because I am never hungry and eating makes me feel sick. I have headaches, palpitations from walking up the stairs, I am always tired and lazy and irritable, I sleep badly, I have boils, and a slight temperature nearly every day. All of which comes from nerves and depression, but must be cured because the worse I get the more depressed I become, and the more depressed I become the worse I get. How nice it would be if I could stay asleep for a year; waking every morning is such a terribly depressing thing to have to do. Three of the nurses have gone to Zaragoza today to buy things for the hospital for Christmas and to fetch Magallon's wife, Mercedes, who is going to stay here for a time. They have not got back yet. Magallon is up and about again today, very thin and pale and quiet. He came and had tea with us in our room, invited by Isabel!

Wednesday, 21 December. Magallon's wife, Mercedes, is perfectly sweet. She is small and dark and quite pretty and well dressed and awfully nice and madly in love with him. We have decided to go to Zaragoza tomorrow instead of on Friday so we have a lot of shopping to do for Christmas because no one has done anything about it yet. The sermon was as boring as all sermons and just like being at school.[2] All the girls in uniform seated at desks with which they have fitted out the chapel.

Friday, 23 December. Today I am miserable and feel like a swine as I have let myself be persuaded by Consuelo and Mary Angel to stay here for Christmas and not go back to the hospital for a week. Now poor, good Consuelo has to go back alone to a miserable Christmas in the hospital. A bloody poor friend I am, I am disgusted with myself for such low down, weak-minded behaviour and have a horribly guilty conscience about Consuelo going back alone. I am a swine.

Saturday, 24 December. Christmas Eve! My second one out here. It is now 2 o'clock in the morning and I am freezing to death alone in my room. Everyone is pleased because the advance, which started yesterday by breaking the Catalonian front in four places, has continued today, about fifteen kilometres, despite the bad weather. The Infanta arrived for Christmas at Epila.

2 Isabel arranged for a daily sermon to prepare for Christmas.

Sunday, 25 December. Another Christmas at Epila is over and it did not feel a bit like Christmas Day although we had a tree, turkey, plum pudding, champagne and too many sweets. The only thing that makes me realize it is Christmas is that I have eaten too much and feel sick.

Dinner was very Christmassy with turkey and Christmas pudding and champagne and the table decorated with holly and pine. Afterwards we played cards and lit the candles of the Christmas tree and played cat's cradle until everyone wandered off to bed. Now it is 1 o'clock and my fingers are freezing still so that I can hardly hold my pen and am suffering acutely. The advance continues successfully.

Monday, 26 December. The Infanta and Ataulfo were in the drawing room. We sat and talked for a long time until we decided to see if the water was hot enough to bath. Then I went and dressed. When I came back there to my surprise was Consuelo. She had got leave for both of us until 2 January so we have another six days here. She has not been to bed since she left here the day before yesterday. Her Christmas was evidently pretty grim and Lili got furious because the nurses all danced. She has written a long letter to Mercedes Milá, which I suppose is complaining about it, which Consuelo was to deliver. All the others played bridge. Prince Ali left again for Fraga this afternoon. A *capitan* of aviation came to dinner, very attractive and spruce. Afterwards everyone played bridge or Mus, a Spanish card game. As I can't play one or the other I just watched the bridge.

Wednesday, 28 December. Dia de Inocentes! In other words the equivalent of April Fool's Day.

At lunch we were given rissoles made of cotton wool. It was very funny as Consuelo had made them very well and for a time no one realized. Princess Bee was laboriously trying to cut hers with a knife while Carla was chewing happily. When we all realized we started to laugh and Carla kept on chewing and asking what the joke was. She nearly swallowed it, cotton wool and all.

Thursday, 29 December. This morning the Infanta, Ataulfo, Consuelo and I, who are the only people who get up at all, played bridge until 12 o'clock. Then Consuelo went and had a bath. All afternoon they all played bridge and I watched until at about 5 o'clock the chauffeur arrived from San Sebastian with all the parcels for everyone brought by the Infanta. We all leapt on the parcels which were put on the dining-room table. There were stacks of them, books, flying clothes, gloves, chocolates, gardening tools, lamps and God knows what. Ataulfo amongst other things got a box of twenty-five new records. Mama had sent me lots of magazines, a pair of clips and earrings, pencils, various Christmas cards, lovely gloves which are of leather with a furlined finger cover, which is either a fur gauntlet or folds over and snaps shut like ski gloves. Also three fountain pens, of which I have given one to Consuelo and one to Ataulfo in exchange for his old one which he does not like. All evening we sat on the sofa playing the new records and reading the magazines.

Saturday, 31 December. I think tonight was one of the happiest New Year's Eves I have ever spent and I wish I could believe the year was going to continue in the same spirit, but alas it won't be very probable. We were just tucking into the Christmas pudding when Ataulfo turned up again. Everyone was glad to see him back as all the family were there except him, Prince Ali having come from Fraga for the night. Ataulfo was sleepy which he said was due to too much beer. Evidently his people had done four flights today with a lot of anti-aircraft and were exhausted and nervous wrecks and had decided that New Year could see itself in as they were going to bed. After dinner we played cards until a quarter to twelve, when the Infanta, who was looking pale and ill, produced a huge bowl of punch which was delicious, like a mixture of turtle soup and black currant lozenges. By 12 o'clock we had all drunk a glass and heard very good war news on the radio and were feeling cheerful. We did all the right things of drinking our healths in punch and opening the window to let the New Year and a lot of cold air in.

We switched on some dance music on the radio and lit the Christmas tree and turned out all the lights. Ataulfo started to dance with me and the others followed our example. We danced and talked and laughed and had a lovely time. I have not danced since I was in Seville on 1 September, four months ago. I finally went to my bed at about 2.30 feeling tired and sick with a headache but quite happy.

Monday, 2 January 1939. What a perfectly loathsome day! Here we are back at Monte Julia. I feel just like coming back to school after the Christmas holidays, only the holidays were very short this year. But still, they were ten of the most enjoyable days that I have had for a long time. Everyone here is terribly friendly and good-tempered at the moment, but within a minute of arriving we were told the latest row. Evidently Mercedes Milá turned up here the other day and made the most fearful fuss about the dance on Christmas Eve and almost threw out Maruja for her affair with Torrijos and said that one more misbehaviour and she would send every one of us home. Evidently she ramped and roared and raged and stormed and everyone was in a state and Isabel said she was leaving and God knows what more. Anyhow we were all out of it.

Tuesday, 3 January. This morning Consuelo was feeling ill and it appears that she has congestion of the lungs; she says she caught it on Christmas Eve and felt like hell in Epila with a temperature every day but would not say anything as she felt the Infanta would have found it awkward. She is terrified that she is getting pneumonia and says she is going to die. What a pessimist Consuelo is. I don't think she will get pneumonia and I sincerely hope not. The problem of food in this hospital is very tiresome. There was no coffee for breakfast and lunch was appalling and very stingy. I did not have dinner but I believe it was worse still. I went down to the surgery this morning at 10 o'clock but there was no one else about so I went and talked to Isabel, who has decided to go and talk to Mercedes Milá about us in a few days' time. I met Fernando downstairs who asked if he could visit Consuelo, so I brought him up. He was as mad as ever and teasing everyone. Isabel came in and nearly died at seeing him here and took him hastily out into the passage. She really is old-fashioned. Afterwards she leapt on me saying how could I let him come into the room and a girl in bed should never be seen by a man. I told her not to be so silly and I had not let him come in, I had brought him in myself and did not see anything wrong with it at all. Finally when I was backed up by the others she cooled off and said maybe it was all right but that it was not done in her day.

Thursday, 5 January. Last night Consuelo was quite delirious until about 2.30. She was terrified and shouted with fright, which nearly scared me pink as it was 12 o'clock and I was just dozing off to sleep. When I realized she was not just dreaming I put on the light and sat on the edge of her bed holding her hand and trying to soothe her. She was terribly nervous and kept suddenly jumping up saying the devil was under her bed or pulling her hair. However, I finally persuaded her I had chased him away. Then the windows began to rattle and she was sure he was trying to get in there. It struck her as funny that he should be out there in the cold and she roared with laughter. I kept telling her to go to sleep but she was sure it was daytime and begged me to bring her lunch and get the other girls to come and play bridge as if she went to sleep now she would not be able to sleep at night. However, at last she dozed off for half an hour and woke up at 2.30 more or less sensible again, so I was able to get to bed after all. Today she is much better, although she vomits everything and is pale green and very weak.

This evening Consuelo was very excited so I gave her an injection of dope which I hope will make her sleep, as otherwise she will work herself up again all night. I have felt ill all day and we are almost without food here. I ate a little rice for lunch and a few beans for dinner. There was nothing else except tripe. We will get thin.

Friday, 6 January. Today has been idle and peaceful. I have done nothing all day except the dressings this morning and three injections this evening. Such is our colossal work here. I hope we go to Artesa soon where we ought to have lots of work. A small child with a swollen knee was brought to cure today. The dressing took half an hour as Magallon took out the pus with a hypodermic. The child never stopped screaming for one moment, poor little thing. I plied her with chocolates, but it was all no use. I hate having to hurt children, it seems so unfair somehow. Grown-ups understand that it just has to be done. One new man we have cries like a child every day. Great tears rolling down his cheeks at the mere sight of me.

Sunday, 8 January. I have lost all interest in this hospital since there is no work and simply cannot make myself do the little there is any longer. Today I have not even been down to the wards all day and have just left the others to it. Bloody cheek and lazy but I just haven't got any energy at all. This afternoon Consuelo was up and we played bridge. The others were just as bad as me, which was a pleasant surprise. It appears that we are not going to move to Artesa after all as the house we were to go to there has been knocked flat, so we are still stuck here. But I don't care any longer as soon, I hope, the Infanta will call us for her *equipo*. The day after tomorrow I have to go to Zaragoza again.

Wednesday, 11 January. I am terribly sleepy and wonderfully comfortable which is really a fatal complication when it comes to trying to write this wretched diary. I am ensconced in bed in Epila with a hot water bottle and a cigarette. If only I had my radio on the bed table, life would be nearly perfect. Princess Bee, before I went, asked me if I would come back for two days to help her pack everything up and move to Monzon. So I said yes I would love to and asked for leave. I picked up the priest, Magallon and Mercedes in Zaragoza and we went to the market to buy fish and to the food shop to pick up parcels. Then at 10 o'clock we went to the convent to fetch two of the nurses who had given me a pretty bracelet. We dropped Mercedes and with the car stacked to the ceiling with parcels and stinking of fish, set off back to the hospital where were arrived at 1 o'clock, nicely in time for lunch. I asked for leave, explaining that the Infanta was ill. It was granted me, so at 3.30 I set off once more leaving a sad and lonely Consuelo behind. Consuelo at lunch was as mad as a hatter. She and three others had a contest to see who could eat most, with the result that no sooner was lunch over than there was a dash for the door and they all fled to be sick in various bathrooms. Quite crazy. I arrived here [*at Epila*] at 6 o'clock. God what a joy it was to be away from it. If the truth be told I am dead tired of hospitals, and everything to do with this war and would give almost anything to drop the whole show and go away if it were not the fact that I know full well that within a few weeks I should be back in a flurry of nerves with no news and pining to come back. Anyhow now it is 2 o'clock and I must sleep.

Thursday, 12 January. This morning I had a lovely long bath in which I soaked for hours reading my book. The rest of the morning I spent setting my hair in the most frightfully complicated way with a mass of curls on the top of my head and a roll tight down the middle of the back. Actually it turned out very well and was much admired.

Friday, 13 January. Here I am back at Monte Julia, but only for two nights I hope. I feel mouldy, tired and cold all day. It was sad leaving Epila. I don't think that we will ever go back to live there again.

[174]

Saturday, 14 January. I was furious this morning, and all day for that matter. At 10 o'clock I turned up in the surgery to start work, when in popped the *capitan* to say could I take him to Alcaniz. I looked as disgusted and distressed as I could and said I had promised to go to Monzon after lunch, but it was no good, he insisted, saying we would be back before 5 o'clock and I could go to Monzon then. So there was nothing to be done and I fetched the car and at 10.30 we set off. We bumped eighty kilometres over bad roads to the bridge over the Ebro. But alas, the bridge of boats was conspicuous by its absence as the river had risen. We inquired as to where there was another, to find to our horror that our only way was via Zaragoza. Nine hours' driving just because the *capitan* wanted to see his old friends! I am still foaming with disgust as I find nine hours a lot for one day where there is no need and with someone who bores me. I arrived back and was greeted by Consuelo and Nucha, who informed me that Magallon has at last slung Consuelo and me out of his wards. But as no one will take our places Consuelo will have to go back. He is being thoroughly rude and foul to her and she is in a state, so I hope she is not made to work with him or there will be fireworks. The news of the war today was stupendous and our advance is simply shooting along to Zaragoza; each day is better than the other. Most cheering after months of inactivity.

Sunday, 15 January. Tonight I am in Mora de Ebro. It is nearly 1 o'clock and I am writing by the light of a candle sitting up in my white hospital bed in a palatial room, the only one in the house that has remained whole.

The village is absolutely knocked to bits by aviation. All one side of it is flat and there is not one whole house here as far as I can see. The hospital belongs to Capitan Zerolo, who speaks perfect English, as he was educated there. It is one of the nicest, best-run *equipos* I have ever seen. The organization is beautiful and everyone charming. We all sat and talked and drank *oporto*. Everyone was thrilled with the news that we have taken both Tarragona and Reus and are already eight kilometres the other side of Tarragona.[3]

While we were having dinner the *capitan* was called away to see

3 Tarragona was taken by the Nationalists on 14 January. Hugh Thomas writes 'the first mass in two and a half years was held in the Cathedral, while the proscription began in the city!'

his lieutenant-colonel, who told him that he was to leave for Reus tomorrow, but that tonight he would be sent lots of wounded. They were all thrilled as they have been here for weeks on end with nothing to do and only have two wounded. We had not quite finished dinner when the first ambulance arrived. It was heaven to be back in the atmosphere of work again.

We went and changed into uniform and stayed till twelve watching Zerolo operate. He operated one stomach from which he removed about a yard of intestine, and one head. Next door the second doctor was also operating slightly less important things. We just stood and watched. The only thing I did was to give saline to the stomach all during the operation. It seemed quite like the good old days of work and adventures to be in the operating room again. I was in heaven and really enjoyed myself. Tomorrow we are going to help the *equipo* to move to Reus, and also visit Tarragona. I am terribly tired but in much too good a temper to mind. It really is wonderful how quickly this advance in Catalonia is going. The amount of prisoners taken daily is colossal and there is hardly any fighting and very few wounded, especially down here. The Reds must be very demoralized or they would fight instead of giving themselves up. Anyhow, their situation is pretty tense because we calculated before the Ebro battle that on this front they had about 140,000 men, and in the Ebro they lost 90,000 casualties.[4] Now they have called up everyone of both sexes from the ages of fifteen to fifty-five. It is ridiculous and shows their need.

Monday, 16 January. The drive to Reus was lovely over highish mountains with bright red earth and little villages hidden in the valleys. Not a sign of the fact that all the country was taken during the last week.[5] Everywhere were growing miles of hazel-nuts and occasional olive and almond trees just beginning to blossom. Reus itself is hideous and completely peaceful and unhurt, despite having been taken yesterday afternoon.

We stopped here at a factory. The poor owner, who is a charming man and speaks excellent English, was received by all his workmen and servants with the most wonderful pleasure. They all embraced

4 An exaggeration. The Republicans, at the most, lost 15,000 dead and their total casualties were around 50,000.
5 A sign of the relative lack of resistance to the Nationalist advance.

him and the women burst into tears, they were so ecstatic with joy to see him again after two years that they lost all control.[6] He was thrilled to be back too, but very sad as he has had his eldest son killed and the second one has a leg blown off. The only signs of the war here are that the roof and windows of one of the big sheds have fallen in during an air raid and that there are six dead Reds beside the drive. They were killed yesterday evening – so far quite harmless, as they don't smell or anything. We had a splendid lunch here; the people produced us eggs and meat and wine, apart from the cold meat and tinned tunny that we had brought with us. After lunch we hurriedly cast a glance at Tarragona, which seems a nice town and more or less intact, and returned to Reus to find out from the lieutenant-colonel about the *equipo* Zerolo. He was not yet decided where to put them and sent us to see the lunatic asylum where two other *equipos* are already installed. There we found Mercedes Milá. Mercedes was in a dither as she had just found an aunt who was supposed to have been killed. The only thing she said to me was that I must wear stockings with my uniform, and was very put out when I told her I was wearing them but that they were good ones. Then we followed the lieutenant-colonel to Tarragona. The road from Reus to Tarragona was simply covered in soldiers, marching to Tarragona and out along the main Barcelona road. In groups of about fifty, each with its flag, hundreds and hundreds, dirty, unshaven, carrying guns with their pack and blankets tied round them, all terribly tired, as they had averaged thirty kilometres per day for three days.

It is fun to see newly taken big towns. Auxilio Social distributing bread from lorries, men sticking up anti-Red and Up-with-Franco posters everywhere, people clearing up the debris in the streets, putting down telephone wires, looking for houses, for hospitals and offices, and dozens of simple sightseers.[7] Unluckily the fun of a frantically pleased population waving flags and making whoopee was missing, as the Catalans are Red, so don't look on us much as heroic liberators.[8]

6 In many of the smaller Catalan enterprises which had been collectivized (i.e. by the establishment of workers or Union control) in the early months of the war the workers remained loyal to their old employers.

7 The Auxilio Social was the welfare branch of the Falange. To a semi-starving population the prospect of 'Franco'd bread' weakened resolve. It was distributed after a town was taken.

8 An interesting comment on the hostility of the Catalans.

Altogether life is fun and interesting. I hate the war and I am sick to death of it, but at least I am seeing the most amusing part at the moment.

Wednesday, 18 January. My plans have suddenly changed and I have arranged for Consuelo and me to join an *equipo* of the Army Corps of Morocco, which is at the moment in Reus under a Capitan Parachi. In a way I am delighted to be going to an *equipo* again at last, although I am not sure if my health is good enough to stand the strain. But I am terribly sorry to have to desert the Infanta, as she wanted to have us with her. But I can see that the nursing plan will never get properly organized, and I would like no work except as companion to the Infanta which, liking her as I do, would definitely be far more enjoyable than working. But, after all, I came here to work and can do nothing in the atmosphere of older women who are incapable of organizing anything. If they would leave things to the Infanta it would be all right, but they very respectfully won't let her get within sniffing distance of any work at the moment, so what is one to do? I could just be companion, which I would love, as it would mean always trotting round the front. But I mean to work if I can. Altogether a conflict, especially as I think the Infanta thinks my leaving her disgusting too, and unappreciative behaviour. But what can I do if her plan of work simply does not and never will exist here?

Parachi appears charming and pleased to have us. He has three nurses; one was in bed, the other two seemed nice. They were all overworked and tired, having operated all night. Tomorrow morning I am going to fix up definitely about the *equipo*, and I am determined that this time we are going to make a success of it. Third time lucky maybe. Anyhow it seems a nice *equipo*, and I hope Consuelo will be pleased, as that is what she wants.

Thursday, 19 January. It appears that Parachi, our maybe future chief, has already had a colossal row with Mercedes Milá as his three nurses are friends of his who came without Mercedes knowing, and two of them have no nurse's certificate at all. Naturally she was furious, as she had brought him two very good nurses whom he refused to take. So now that he has asked for us it is going to put us in a sticky situation. So directly I can I am going to see Mercedes Milá and, quite innocent about the complications, say that he has asked us to join his *equipo* and may we go. So if she is not pleased, he will get the row, not us.

All afternoon there were quantities of aviation going over, and we could hear the bombing and artillery easily, although the front is now fifteen kilometres away. We were shown round the factory by our host; it is surrounded by bomb holes but not hit. Then to Tarragona and the *equipo* Zerolo, but as he was operating we went to Reus to the canteen again, which was just closing after having served 800 people. Back to Tarragona to the canteen there, where we drank coffee and talked to the people of Frentes y Hospitales. Back home to the canteen, where we met Don Luis and Commandante Urzaiz, and drank more coffee and talked more bilge. Then back to Zerolo, where we watched him operating a stomach on one table, while his assistant sewed up a mangled penis on the other. We gave saline injections and poured alcohol about. If only people here would talk less and do more it would all be so much easier. Tomorrow our plan is to spend all day with Zerolo actually working, but I don't really believe it. We may spend all day there but I don't expect we will work. The Infanta is driven just as mad as I am by not having any real work, which makes everyone feel even guiltier about leaving her. Anyhow, on the whole, I am enjoying my trip.

Friday, 20 January. I can't think why, but I am dead tired tonight. The Infanta and I went to *equipo* Zerolo at nine and stayed there until six. It was peaceful and pleasant. There was very little to do. We heard Mass and then watched about four operations and talked and watched a blood transfusion. There were hardly any wounded today, although I believe we have advanced quite a lot. One wounded was an old, old man who had bumped into a hand grenade. He had the whole of his nose and between his eyes smashed, and died a few hours later; another this evening was also a hand grenade, a boy of fifteen with four perforations of the intestine and his hands wrecked. A surface head wound came and a broken femur with gangrene, and an *alferez* with leg wounds. We lunched with the *equipo* Zerolo at 3.30 and at last everything is arranged for us to leave at ten tomorrow. I will be sorry to leave here, as on the whole it has been most enjoyable. It is such lovely warm weather that we breakfast and lunch out of doors in the sun; our host and companions are really very nice, and Zerolo is one of the nicest *equipos* I know. I only wish I could have the luck to get into one as nice. Our room is decorated with a lovely spray of almond blossom which we picked in the orchard here. Funny to have sun and flowers. This time last year I was frozen stiff with all my winter clothes on, not more than 500 kilometres from here.

Saturday, 21 January. Here I am back in our odious hospital in Monte Julia again, but thank God it is the last night that I shall sleep here, as we leave for good tomorrow. What a joy to get away from all this, but alas things are not as bright as they should be, but I insist on feeling optimistic. This morning we saw Capitan Parachi and he said he had seen Mercedes Milá yesterday and told her about Consuelo and me. She had said that he could only take one of us and as I had seen him it must be me and not Consuelo. The old bitch! She has no right to listen to the filthy gossip and catty letters of our fellow nurses. Poor Parachi was very embarrassed at having to tell me, and terribly upset about how depressed it made me; I have been miserable about it all day, but at last my innate optimism is reviving. God knows that I don't want to go all alone to a new *equipo* miles from the Infanta and her family, where I know no one and there is no one who can speak a word of English or has anything even distantly to do with my previous life. It is all very well for Spanish people because they always find they went to the same school or have a communal cousin or friend, but I have no connection. I think I shall be terribly lonely. Apart from that I think most of the work is being edged on to me, as none of them know anything about *equipo* work, and if I have lots of work I know my health won't stand it. I am so far from strong these days and am always tired and feeling sick and have pains.

However, no doubt it won't be as bad as all that once I get going. Consuelo is going to live with the Infanta and accompany her to the front until this thing gets fixed, and she either finds another *equipo* or we can bully Mercedes Milá into letting her come with me after all. Maybe it will all turn out for the best, but I don't see how yet.

Monday, 23 January. This time tomorrow I will be all on my own in my new *equipo* and probably very miserable, and this time last year I was wildly excited that at last I was off to the front. God, how sick I have got of the war in that time. It really does seem that the war should be over this year. I sincerely hope so, because if I have to spend another wartime Christmas here I shall die of depression and worries and illnesses. The war continues well. We are now within thirty kilometres of Barcelona on the coast, and have taken Manresa more to the north. I have arranged, as I shall be separated from everyone, that the day after the taking of Barcelona is announced we all meet for lunch at the Ford factory there if I can get away. I have done nothing here all day. I meant to have a bath but the water was cold so I set my hair instead. This afternoon we went over to Monte Julia to get our carnets signed and certificates of good work and behaviour from the director. We said goodbye to everyone we saw and Torrijos and Maruja both bade us farewell, apologizing humbly for how beastly they had been to us. How I hate having to go to work again tomorrow. How will it turn out this time? My other two attempts have been dismal, and if this follows their example of beastly stinkingness I shall give up all hope of striking lucky. God knows, it is starting badly enough with all these worries and bothers and having to go alone. But sometimes the worst beginnings lead to the best ends. Anyhow, I am depressed and miserable and feel that I really can't put up with very much more. If only the war would be over so that I could stop worrying and go away somewhere and never move, speak or think for a month. I am tired out and ill, both morally and physically. If only I did not always feel so ill and tired nowadays.

Tuesday, 24 January. Tonight I am in my new *equipo* [*the Parachi equipo*] in a huge hotel in Sitges which appears to have been the fashionable bathing place of Barcelona, as it has a long beach about two kilometres in length overlooked by handsome houses with gardens. Our hotel is also on the esplanade overlooking the sea. It must have been very luxurious. The ward is in the ballroom, which is big enough for fifty well-spaced beds and has huge glass chandeliers. We have a vast selection of bedrooms. The other three nurses all sleep together in one big one while I have a nice large one all to myself with cupboards and mirrors and a private bathroom. We have running water and electric light. The *equipo* seem nice and friendly, but how frightening it is to arrive alone to live with them.

When I arrived there was only one patient here, an inoperable stomach wound, a Red who will die tonight I expect. But just as we were about to go to bed an ambulance arrived. I don't know how many it brought, as I allowed myself to be persuaded to bed as I was so tired, not in uniform and with a foul stomach ache. I hope there were not many, or I shall feel very guilty tomorrow.

Wednesday, 25 January. This place is really heaven, with the sun shining and the sea looking lovely. At about nine the lieutenant-colonel turned up and said we might move to some dim village today or we might not, but in any case we were to let in no wounded until he let us know. Half an hour later two lorries turned up saying they had been sent as we are moving. As we still had no order they were told to wait, which they did all day. Our only patient died this morning, so we have a large and lovely empty hospital. Occasionally a few clean sheets turned up and we folded them and put them away. That was the only thing there was to do in the whole day. Lots of aviation came over at intervals, all very low. At dinner time the lieutenant-colonel's ADC turned up with the news that our troops were in the outskirts of Barcelona, and this *equipo* would almost certainly be sent there tomorrow. What fun to one of the first to enter Barcelona. How right I was to maintain that there would not be very much resistance. Of course it is true that we have not taken it yet, but still, we will soon do that. As for my new companions, I neither like nor dislike them. Isabel is more or less boss of us females, and fat and giggly. Victoria is tall and thin, sister of one of the doctors, and slightly hysterical, while Lola is half French, thin and elegant, and rolls her 'r's and seems to be one of the foolishest women I have ever met. She and I are to work together on the wards. Isabel is operating room, and Victoria does the food. I don't think she is a nurse at all. Tomorrow we are to get up early and pack up everything in case we move.

Thursday, 26 January. The news was that the Maroccah, our Army Corps, has been told not to enter Barcelona until the others also reach it, so that we were to go to a nearby village and wait some four or five days for the rest of the troops to arrive. We were all very depressed as we wanted to go there today. We breakfasted at 9.30 and just as we were finishing three wounded turned up. All three were very bad. The stomach was inoperable and died before lunch. The head was operated but it is hopeless and he will die in a few days, and the chest will probably die tonight, also inoperable. So I dashed round putting injections and salines, and thoroughly enjoying myself. My companion in the wards, Lola, is quite hopeless, so I have decided, despite her being over thirty and me only twenty-two and new here, to take over command, which I am doing with great gusto. All afternoon we spent idly collecting and packing things up. As wounded had come and no lorries, and no news, we took it that we were not going to move after all. Then came rumours that we would be leaving tonight, but no one knew where, then that we were to go to Barcelona, but no one knew when. And so on all day. At eleven we received the news that Barcelona was definitely ours, and the lorries would be here to fetch us tomorrow morning at seven.[9] So at last we know when and where we are going. For the first time for ages I don't feel ill and tired, and am excited about something. My grim apathy has almost left me and I hope it won't come back. They say we will have lots of work there, as the Reds have probably left all their hospitals full of wounded. Anyhow, I am willing to take on anything. This *equipo* needs a lot of taking on. Now I have seen them at work I am confirmed in my opinion that it is so badly organized. No one knows what to do or where anything is, and fuss madly over details and forget everything important.

Friday, 27 January. What a crazy day! We had a hurried cup of coffee and at 9 o'clock the lorries were loaded and I set off in my car to Barcelona. Except for a few dreadful patches the road was good, but due to blown up bridges we had to go a long way round and finally arrived at 10.30. Barcelona is a lovely big spacious town and quite unharmed though very dirty. We drove madly all round it. The port is a shambles due to the hard work of the aviation. The streets were crowded with people showing considerable enthusiasm. Everyone shouting and cheering, and all the girls parading up the street with flags. The troops marching through were surrounded by cheering crowds, and everyone was in splendid form. And yet as soon as one was out of the main streets, where all the fun was going on, the people looked surly, and as though there had never been a war.[10] Walking

9 There was no resistance to the entry of Nationalist troops; Catalan resistance had been undermined by the Negrín government's attacks on the powers of the Catalan Generalitat which represented Catalan enthusiasm for the Statute of Autonomy and by the Communist offensive against the POUM so eloquently described in George Orwell's *Homage to Catalonia.*
10 Since most commentators make much of the enthusiastic welcome accorded to the Nationalist troops, this is an interesting observation.

about to their jobs with their dispatch cases or shopping bags. Lots of smart people quite well dressed, and apart from a total lack of bread there has not been a colossal lack of food. Lately, yes, but only in the last few months.

Our intended hospital was the Civil Hospital, huge and quite filthy, with all the wounded on the floor. We were told not to unload anything and to await further orders, as we were probably to move on to the other side of Barcelona and up the coast. However, later our orders came, which were to return today to Sitges, as our Army Corps has finished its work in this attack and is not advancing any further. Nice as this place is, I am very sorry as it is fun to follow the advance. We lunched in the car off tins of sardines, tunny and jam, in the Exposition which is dilapidated and deserted,[11] and then after a lot of aimless motoring to and fro, we set off back to Sitges, where we all arrived dead tired at about 7 o'clock to find everything filthy and upside down. We had no food and no beds, and the lorries did not arrive. Finally, at about nine, after we had dined off a tin of sardines and water, one lorry appeared, but not the one with beds. By 10.30 we gave up hope and all retired to sleep on the floor. Luckily we had blankets, so we had the important things as we also had a mattress each and the beds of the four men.

I don't know why the men automatically have to live best, but they seem to mind discomfort so much. Anyhow, I am just as happy on the floor as in a bed, and dead tired.

Saturday, 28 January. I have been very hard-working today. I meant to sleep late but as I woke up I was up by nine, just as the lorries arrived, having lost their way and spent the night stuck on the road without petrol. No one was up except me, so I organized the unloading and dug out coffee, milk and bread for breakfast and ran up and down getting out cups and plates, etc. and laying the table and sweeping the floor and dusting, as everything was filthy. So when Parachi and Isabel and the priest turned up for breakfast at 10.30, for once it was all ready. All morning I spent frantically sorting and piling broken and not broken beds, and clean, torn or dirty mattresses and pillows, and disentangling all the linen and blankets. Everything was in a dreadful mess, and I am determined to start everything new with a general overhaul of having everything mended,

11 The exhibition of 1929.

washed and counted. All day I have worked sorting linen until I am covered in lice and quite tired. At two, just as we were going to lay the table for lunch, a general and three well-fed big-bugs appeared asking if they could lunch here. Everything is in a mess; I was filthy and nothing unpacked. So while Isabel, who was clean and tidy, played hostess, I rushed up and down unearthing cutlery, plates, glasses, etc., washing and drying everything and producing the drinks and soup and God knows how many things. It was a dreadful muddle as there was nothing ready and I could not find the things. I was quite right about this *equipo*. All the work is left to me. Isabel does everything of her own job, which is the operating room, and consequently very little trouble when there are no wounded. Victoria does solely hers, and singularly little of that, which is *intendencia*. She produces the food, but I lay the table, clean the plates, get up early to see to breakfast and sweep the dining room, while Lola does nothing except sleep and make suggestions. The result of our visitors was that we did not lunch until nearly four. The strange thing is that work and eating tinned food at odd hours agrees with me so well that I feel far better than I have felt for months and have no aches or pains, and eat like a horse. This life agrees with me evidently.

Sunday, 29 January. Parachi, Lola and I left Sitges at 10.30 after having breakfast and hearing Mass. We meant to leave much earlier, but as usual did not succeed. On the way we were held up over and over again by huge lorries which could not get round the corners. The last time was the worst. It has been raining a lot, and the path over the river has become a bog in which a large lorry was firmly and irretrievably stuck. We had to wait over an hour while the other cars and lorries went one by one, either for about ten miles along the railway lines or down a boggy lane and through the river. We chose the latter, as the least dangerous of the two, but it was grim. I did not think we would get through. The mud in the lane was about a foot deep and then a steep hill and a muddy corner where we skidded and slid, but just made it. We only arrived in Barcelona at 12.30. We went up to the hospital, and there was the car with Consuelo in it and a little way away the Infanta and Mercedes Milá sitting down to a good old row. Milá was being extremely rude, bellowing like God knows what and shouting the Infanta down. I don't know how the Infanta did not get up and smite her. In the end she gave no satisfactory explanations, but said she absolutely refused to allow Consuelo to go to my *equipo*. Poor Consuelo was crying like anything by the end, so we sent her to sit in the car. The Infanta was livid and so was I, and so was Parachi, who wanted Consuelo to come to his *equipo*. The Milá roared off, still shouting for all she was worth, and being very offensive. How I should like to be able to tell her just what I think of her. But as I am a nurse I can't say a thing. So now Consuelo will stay with the Infanta permanently, and me in my *equipo* ditto. Such is life, and I suppose as there is no more to be done we must just put up with it and make the best of it, as things are. I lent Parachi my car and went with the Infanta and Consuelo and lunched with them. They live in a very smart little flat belonging to a Catalan couple of great elegance. They produced for me my surgical instruments from England at last, letters and newspapers. Papa has gone to Kenya with my sister Bronwen and her husband, my sister Rosemary is in Paris and Mama has gone to Ceylon, Java and Singapore.

Tuesday, 31 January. I did not get to Barcelona after all, and am still in Monzon. I set off at about 11.30 to Lerida, leaving Carla all alone and very lonely and bored. As usual Prince Ali and Alvaro had gone off to work and as usual she was to spend the day all alone, which she hates, poor thing. When I reached Lerida I set about looking for Ataulfo, as it seems to me the best way to find anyone is to look for them. None of the *guardias* very helpful as to where the Condor Legion lived but after going about three times around the grubby little town I located them in the Hotel de España. On the way I stopped for petrol and met Zerolo and Piri his wife on their way to San Sebastian on leave. Lola Kindelán roared past in a huge car and we waved at each other. In the hotel, after asking various hopeless Germans, I finally met the doctor who told me Ataulfo was living there but was at the moment on the aerodrome. So I asked if I could ring him up. He got me on in a moment. Ataulfo was surprised to hear me on the 'phone and said he was afraid he could not leave the field. So I asked him if I could pay him a visit there, which he thought was a good idea.

Of course Ataulfo's instructions had been all wrong, and it took me ages to get there along a maze of little lanes. I finally arrived at about 2.30. Ataulfo came galloping down the hill from the sheds to meet me, very grubby and good-tempered, and we stood and talked for a long time. I told him his family was very worried as to where he had got to, and he said that if they had any sense they would have rung up the Legion Condor and asked.

He explained that he could not visit them as his car was bust. He then told me that it was impossible at the moment to get to Barcelona via Cervera, and anyhow it was too late to go now as the roads near there were dangerous at night. So I said I would go back to Monzon for the night. We finally decided that I should pick him up at his hotel at five and take him to Monzon. He was a vision in a brand new grey uniform with all his lovely real gold aviation buttons and his wings and stars and *escudo de Navarra* beautifully embroidered in gold and surmounted with large proper imperial crowns, not the nasty flat little crowns they put on nowadays. Also two stars as lieutenant at last. In fact very chic.

Wednesday, 1 February. Back in Barcelona. I actually got there today. I gave a lift to a sergeant of infantry from Lerida to a few miles from Barcelona. A tiresome Andalusian, who as usual did nothing but show me photos of his family and talk about vegetables. I nearly came to grief on a bridge. There was a lorry coming towards me very fast so I clung to my side of the bridge, failing to notice that the edge was full of holes the Reds had prepared for dynamiting. I hit a hole with a frightening bang, missed going over the edge by a whisker and thought I must have wrecked the car, but the only thing that happened was that the jerk made my wheel caps fly off. They landed down in the valley, from where we retrieved them, and continued on our way. I arrived here at about 2.30 and could not find the Infanta. As it was then 4.30 and I had had no lunch, someone produced me a tin of *foie gras* and bread and coffee and I sat and talked to Consuelo, who seems depressed about life and is mysterious about more enemies and spies in our late hospital. I must say the subject no longer interests me. It is past and over and I hate them all, so why worry. There is no way of remedying the harm they have done to Consuelo and no point in revenging it, so I shall ignore the whole subject instead. The Infanta finally turned up delighted to hear news of her family and very pleased with three dozen eggs, ham, cheese, sugar, cocoa and meat I had brought. She gave it to her hostess, who was ecstatic with excitement.

Thursday, 2 February. I should be back in my hospital at Sitges tonight, but I am still in Barcelona, because I was going to leave this evening to be back for dinner but at the last moment the Infanta said she would rather I did not travel at night as an order had been issued today that all the Reds are to give themselves up or they will be arrested, so there will be a lot of frantic men trying to get out of Barcelona, and it is just possible that one of them might force me drive them to Zaragoza, or steal my car or knock me on the head or something if they saw a girl travelling alone. So I shall go tomorrow morning. We started today by going up to the English Hospital to see Mr and Mrs Park and her sister. They are wonderful people. They have been distributing milk, biscuits, chocolate, etc. to the starving ever since this war began, and have never missed a day distributing between the three of them some 1,000 rations daily in a garage opposite the hospital. Mrs Park, poor woman, has had a stroke from over-strain and has got both arms paralyzed, but still goes on working the same. She has seen countless untold horrors visiting the prisons, etc., and has lived in constant danger of death, as helping the refugees was a terrible offence. She talked very little of all she had been through, but told us one or two cases of, for instance, one woman having both her sons killed in front of her and their eyes gouged out and their faces skinned, of people who had gone mad or whose relations had been tortured to death in the famous Checas, which are the Communist torture chambers. Later in the day the Infanta went with the Corps Diplomatique to see the Checas, and came back quite faint and ill with disgust. It would interest me a lot to see them, not out of morbidity but so as to be able to say that I can swear to their existence, having seen them with my own eyes. It appears that they are a series of rooms especially made with every kind of refinement to send people mad. The floors are constructed so that one's feet would just not fit in any way by a complicated series of T-shaped bricks, the walls built in such shapes that one could neither sit or lean, and painted with strange circles and squares most calculated to hurt one's sight.

The prisoners had their hands tied and their eyes propped open with rough kind of monocles, and were faced by a powerful lamp. Others had dripping water and continual sound of bells or rollers: others were fixed into one uncomfortable position, again with the light. Naturally the instruments with which they pulled people's nails off and gouged their eyes out, etc. were not there, although there are plenty of people who have seen it done. It does seem incredible that in these days people really do go on doing those sort of things and that civilized governments like the English one will close their eyes to it and send money and help to the instigators. Evidently the British vice-consul was so disgusted he said he would never go back to England, which continued to side with these people, and was going to throw up his job. The Swiss consul lived almost alongside the Checas and said that often all night there would be such awful screams from there that he use to leave the lorries out in the street with all their engines running to try and drown the sounds. And that is the 'government' which my fellow countrymen respect, aid and recognize. They make me sick.

All the torturing was an official government thing, as all the buildings and cells had the Spanish arms on them. However, enough of horrors, of which God knows there have been too many during this war.[12] Never a day passes that one does not come into contact with some horror or misery. Today passed much as usual. Everyone talked a lot and did very little. We lunched in the officers' dining room and dined in a restaurant. This afternoon, while the Infanta visited the Checas, Consuelo and I went out shopping. We only went into one big store, but it was full of things, and we bought two teeny little suitcases to make into First Aid cases. I bought some gorgeous dark red thick satin with which to make myself what one calls here 'air raid pyjamas' and some pearl grey satin, because I could not resist it, with which I shall make a sort of dinner-dress-cum-dressing-gown. Then we came home and our hostess started to show us hesitantly some of the smart clothes she used to wear before the war. We all became so excited at the unaccustomed sight of lovely clothes that we were trying them on in secret, like small children doing something forbidden. It seemed so funny to put on an evening dress and fur cape, and we laughed ourselves silly. She had lovely things and gorgeous underwear too.

Friday, 3 February. Today for the first time in my life I really assisted an operation. Scrubbed and sterilized, in overall and gloves, I hung onto pincers and chased after veins etc. It was a strangulated rupture on one side and a plain one on the other. As everyone was either on

12 How much of this description represents the facts and how much the horrors were the creation of Nationalist propaganda is impossible to discern.

leave or in Barcelona, there were only Parachi, Lola and I in the hospital. I was not a bit alarmed, as I have watched so many operations that I knew I could not go far wrong, although a rupture actually oddly enough was one I had never seen. However, it all went off all right and Parachi was very patient and nice, as I must have been a great bore, but he always told me exactly what to do when, so it was easy. I left Barcelona at 8.30 after breakfast.

Saturday, 4 February. Tonight I am in a loony bin in San Zandillo de Libregati! Why we have been moved here I cannot imagine, but still, here we are. We consist solely of the Alferez Cabals and I, the cook and the orderlies. The rest are away on leave. I have the money and accounts of *intendencia*, the key of the chemist. In fact the whole hospital is solely mine. Zerolo's *equipo* is also here, but we are going to live separately to avoid any trouble.

Sunday, 5 February. I like my new hospital and it is frightfully funny being quite alone. Just Cabals and I and a dentist friend of his who is also in this house. He lives and eats with us, of which I am glad, as he acts as a sort of chaperon. One girl and two men is somehow better than a man and a girl alone. I got up at 8.30 and prepared breakfast, and started putting up the ward. Of course neither the orderlies nor the cook were up when I went down, and I had to rout them all out of bed. So the kitchen was not lit and we did not have breakfast till ten. Then, while they all went to Mass, I made beds, etc. Then we went to see the mayor about sending us women to clean the hospital, but he was not there. We ran out of petrol and had to wait a long time till a kind lorry gave us enough to get us to Barcelona to fill up. The result was we arrived back just in time for lunch. After lunch I finished the ward, which is now very elegant and spacious, as I have only put up fifteen beds each with a little white bed-table, on which I am going to put vases of white flowers. Then I went to the hospital in Barcelona to visit the Infanta and Consuelo. I found them both working like blacks, as they are in sole charge of a pavilion in which they have over 200 wounded. They made me put some intravenous injections, which, after driving and with the Infanta and Cabals watching, I did pretty badly, to my great disgust. We arrived back here in time to prepare and have dinner, then I went down to beg bread off the *equipo* Zerolo on the floor below, as we have none left for tomorrow's breakfast, and also to pay them a visit, as despite being in the same building I had hardly seen them all day. I found them just finishing dinner round a huge table with four guests. There must have been about twenty of them, with brilliant light from two petromax hanging from the chandelier, vases of flowers, and my gramophone, which I had lent them this morning. The comparison with our dark and solitary meal was funny. I talked and laughed for a long time and thoroughly enjoyed it.

Monday, 6 February. I have a companion now as I have fetched Carola from Barcelona. She is ugly, but seems most awfully nice. My ideas about her seem to have been quite right. She is definitely all set to reorganize and boss the *equipo*, but as I got my say in first it is all right. I started right for the beginning telling her how hopelessly badly run the *equipo* is, and that I am determined to change it all and hoped she was going to help me. That we could start with *intendencia* and the lines and do this, that and the other, etc. etc. So all she could do was agree enthusiastically. I have also told her all the bad luck and rows Consuelo and I have had and what it was really about, as I am sure that Mercedes Milá has sent her here partly as a spy to see how I behave. I was not surprised to find that she already knew all the rows of our late hospital and everyone's name. She professes to despise and dislike Mercedes Milá which, if true, will be an asset. Anyhow, it appears that she is a nice, sensible, energetic female, and we have made firm friends despite my being twenty-two and she must be over forty. This morning after breakfast I went to see the *commandante militar* of this village about sending us women to scrub and clean. As usual neither he nor the mayor was there, and the only person we could find in the offices was a man who could only speak Catalan and could neither read nor write. This afternoon I went into Barcelona with Bustamante, our perfumed dentist, and three of Zerolo's nurses. There we picked up Carola, went to the Jefatura, left my materials with the Infanta's hostess, as they were getting filthy in the car, and to the hospital to see the Infanta and Consuelo, who were less rushed and pleased to see us. The Infanta was called to a man they said was having an epileptic fit. He writhed and fought in spasms on the floor and cried and screamed not to be put in the chair, scared to death. It certainly was not epileptic. In my opinion it was one of two things, and I watched him very carefully; either it was entirely put on because he is a drug fiend and wanted a dose of morphia, or else he is mad as a result of probably some sort of torture associated with a chair which the Reds may have inflicted on him in the Checas. Consuelo and I seem to be rising in the world. She is head of her pavilion of 200 wounded, and I in my little way am unrecognized head of my *equipo* if Carola does not boot me out. I have got fleas again, which is very tiresome. I think this house is full of them.

Eugenia, the cook, came running up to me and said, 'Thank goodness you have come back, Senorita Pip, because I can't stand that other nurse another moment.' Then Cabals called me to his room and said for God's sake do something, because Carola had been making rows about the food saying the orderlies ate too much and were only to have beans, that we drank too much condensed milk, and in future our coffee was to be mixed in the kitchen with one tin per so many people, that the orderlies were all to be up at eight and report to her for orders every day, and anyone who was late would go without breakfast. She had also complained that the orderlies did not help her to work and threatened to send them to the trenches if they did not obey her orders better, etc. Total result of one morning that the cook was leaving at once and the orderlies all complaining and saying if she was going to go on like that they would like to be sent somewhere else as they were delighted to help everyone who asked but did not like to be treated like small children. So I rushed off to the cook and soothed her down as best I could, which was only a partial success. She said she was not used to being treated like that and was going to leave if it went on, so I assured her that it had all been a misunderstanding as Carola came from a large military hospital where everything was run quite differently and everyone strictly rationed, and that she had not realized this was different but I would explain it all to her (quite imaginary, but the only thing I could think of on the spur of the moment); to the orderlies I just smiled and said it was all right and I would fix it. Then I took Carola aside and explained the result of her morning's work and said that of course I was sure it was all a misunderstanding, but the cook was very sensitive and although I agreed entirely that the *equipo* needed organizing perhaps we had better set about it a little more gently, especially as the food was really Victoria's job, and although I had taken it over temporarily perhaps it would not be tactful to make any radical changes until she came back. I then snaffled the key of the store room and assured everyone it was all quite right and that was that. But what an afternoon Carola made me go through. If she keeps this up, God knows what will happen. Why can't I ever be left in peace? Now rows will start again and then everyone will say wherever I go there are rows, and all I do is to be tactful and soothe ruffled feelings wherever I go. Blast Carola.

The news of the war continues stupendous. Azaña is already over the Swiss frontier and inundated with Reds.[13]

England and France want a pause to talk over an armistice, and rumour has it that Miaja is contemplating giving in.[14] I don't think he will, but even if we go on to the bitter end it can't be very far off now. Rumour also has it that we are to be moved from this charming place in the near future, but no one seems to have the least idea where or why. It is too bad that I can't stay away more than one night, but I am damned if I am going to have Carola butting in and ordering all over the *equipo*. Tactless, blundering old cow: she should practise patience.

Wednesday, 8 February. Cripes what a day! Fifteen hours solid driving the car! I left at six this morning and arrived here in Barcelona at 11.30 tonight. It is not 1.30 and instead of feeling dead I am in the best of spirits, although jolly glad to be in a comfy bed. To start from the beginning, Cabal called me at 5.30. It was cold and dark, and it was only with great effort that I managed to hoof myself out of bed. We set off, Cabal and I in the front, and Alphonso, the orderly, behind with the luggage. It was bitterly cold and I thought my hands would freeze off despite my huge fur gloves. The sun rose as we were passing the montain of Monserrat, which looked gorgeous, all pink and purple, with its strange lava projections. All the almond blossom was like pink cotton-wool. We ate chocolate and biscuits all the way to Lerida, where we arrived at ten. From there onwards there was a thick fog which slowed us up a lot. I loathe driving in fogs. In Lerida I went and asked for Ataulfo and was told that he was in Sadabell, a village near Barcelona.[15] So then we breakfasted off coffee and bread in a dirty little coffee-stall near the station, bought two omelettes, sandwiched in loaves of bread, and set off again. I had hoped the long climb up

13 Anzaña was President of the Republic who crossed to France on 5 February. He did not go to Switzerland.
14 Miaja commanded what was left of the Republican army in the centre of Spain.
15 Sadabell was an important textile town.

from Fraga would take us out of the fog, but it only got thicker, until we thought there was no chance of catching the 2 o'clock train. But through dangerously fast driving in the fog and a few free patches we arrived in Zaragoza just before one. After dropping the orderly, buying a few oddments, sending telegrams and inquiring about the train, which did not leave until 3.30, we fetched Cabal's brother and a friend from the hospital where they work and all went and lunched in a restaurant, and had coffee at the 'café' opposite. I then dropped Cabal at the station, his friend in the town, bought more food supplies, and set off for Monzon at 3.30. It took me three hours to get to Monzon, as I had to drive very slowly as I was suddenly so dead tired that I did not think I could go any further. I gave lifts to various soldiers, and to a sweet old blind man and a little boy, who were walking some sixty miles from Huesca to Monzon. I arrived in the flat there to find it empty. The servant told me Prince Ali was in the Brigada and the Principes were in Barcelona. So I asked him for some toast and coffee and went over to see Prince Ali who was in confab. with all the officers. I only stayed a minute as I did not want to disturb them. Prince Ali had no views on whether I ought to stay or go on, so I decided to go straight on to Barcelona, as anyhow my room was no longer available, as the owner has returned. So I drank my coffee, collected six or seven letters addressed to me, and lots for the Infanta, a package of partridge for the Infanta and some telegrams and set off at 6.30 in the dark. I immediately ran into thick fog. For three hours I drove all alone through the fog. I very nearly turned back, but left it too late to be worth the trouble. I got more and more despairing and tired until I really felt it could not go on any longer and I would just sit down in the car and cry. However, I crawled slowly on, scared pink and hardly able to see the edge of the road, telling myself that it could not go on for ever, and sooner or later I must come out of it again. At last I did, and the rest of the journey I achieved in peace. I found the Infanta, Consuelo and Ataulfo here when I arrived. I was looking terrible, with a filthy uniform, my hair straight and lank, and no make up. We sat and talked and laughed and told each other all our news until past 1 o'clock. Consuelo and I are sleeping together in one room, Ataulfo is sleeping with the Infanta next door, and there are no more rooms. I have had a bath and I have lots of fleas, which the Infanta objected to.

Thursday, 9 February. The war is as good as over. We have reached the French frontier, Minorca has risen and defeated the Reds and is now ours, and rumour, supported strongly by the French radio, says Madrid and Valencia are ready to give in. Official orders have been issued everywhere for the illuminations to be prepared for when the war stops, and great preparations are going on in all the big towns.

The lieutenant-colonel turned up during the afternoon to tell us that within three or four days we would leave for Estremadura between Caceres and Merida! Of all the beastly places to be sent to. Miles away from anywhere and very dull, ugly country.[16]

Sunday, 12 February. I woke up at 7.30 with the sun streaming in at the window, and played the radio in bed till eight, when I had to go downstairs to get out the coffee, bread and milk, and make breakfast. My flowers, alas, are almost all dead now, which removes surprisingly the charm of my little attic. Also, no one will leave me alone for five minutes, as it is much the cosiest of the rooms and they all sit in here in turns or at once. The worst is the crazy-perfumed-*legionario*-dentist, Bustamante, who sits here all day. I do hope he is not going to start trying to flirt or anything like that. I am even taking pains to look as unattractive as possible, which goes hard against the grain as one instinctively wants to encourage surreptitiously. However, I never comb my hair, which hangs dankly down my neck. I don't make up, but then I never did, and I look grubby and shoddy, in fact I don't think even weeks of being cooped up together could make a man take any interest in me, anyhow I hope not, as it really is too tiresome.

In the afternoon I lay on my bed trying to read while Bustamante sat on a stool alternately writing and talking to me. I paid no attention to him so he kept trying to tear my book away and make me entertaining. He is as mad as a hatter. When the electricity was switched on he played the radio and started dancing *pasadobles* all over the room. Pepe got up this morning but returned to bed again after lunch feeling very low. I gave him an injection for his cough.

Monday, 13 February. I spent the afternoon ironing and writing letters till five. I went to Barcelona with Bustamante, where I bought a purse and a nailbrush. Then we drove round till we found a cinema

16 In a last desperate attempt to relieve pressure on the Catalan front, Rojo had launched an offensive in Estremadura. As the offensive was over Pip laments 'We don't have anything to do when we get there.'

with a film we had not seen. It was full of people and we had to sit right in the front, getting a crick in the neck and seeing everything lop-sided. There was a very old Janet Gaynor film and a Betty Boop cartoon and then a lovely Spanish film of a story in a peasant village near Zaragoza. I loved it. It was so typical, the accent almost unintelligible, peasant clothes, singing, dancing, donkeys, and the life and conversation just what I have lived with so much here. Somehow on the films it looked like a fairy tale, the sort of thing one sees and says, 'What a pity it isn't like that any longer nowadays.' But it is exactly like that, which is the fascinating thing about this lovely country. It somehow made me feel how much I love Spain, despite how miserable it has made me. It is really funny that my two childish passions were Spain and aeroplanes, and my ambition to be a surgeon, and here I am in Spain being a surgical nurse.

Tuesday, 14 February. Consuelo rang up from Monzon this evening, but I was in Barcelona, where I saw five films in quick succession. The films this afternoon were fun. One gorgeous flying one and one heavenly spy one with Gary Cooper, whom I dote on.

Wednesday, 15 February. Last night I woke up at God knows what hour to find a torch shining in my face. I could vaguely discern a pair of pants behind the glare and my dirty mind immediately made me sit up with a bang wondering who in hell it was. What was my surprise to find myself confronted with a very embarrassed priest, Padro Santa Cruz, who was looking for an orderly because something had gone wrong with the waterworks and they were all being drowned in their beds on the floor below and he could not find the main to turn it off.

After my usual idle morning, reading and ironing in my dressing-gown, we lunched and then all set off in the car, except Carola, who is still ill in bed. I dropped Pepe, Bustamante and Lola in Barcelona and set off for Reus with the priest, Matute, who is a dreadful bore and can't see a car without getting into it. He always wants to go somewhere. We stopped in Villanueva y Geltru for petrol and my car was immediately surrounded by children as always. To my surprise, the priest, who had alighted, leaps forward and starts to deal blows all round with his rolled up newspaper. The little crowd dispersed in a moment. I was furious, as I thought it very unnecessary, as they were doing no harm.

Also hardly the right behaviour for a priest. However, I said nothing and we drove on to Calepel, where he wanted to visit someone, then on to Reus, where the little crowd appeared again and was once more dispersed. This time I complained to the priest and said to leave them, as they were doing no harm and only wanted to hear the radio. So he went off to find Eugenia and do some shopping while I gave the children a concert. They were sweet, all peering in through the windows and hushing each other and dancing and pretending to play the violin. When the priest appeared they began to melt but he, wishing to make amends, asked them if they had learnt the Falange song, and made them sing it. Then he gave them a long sermon, explaining the words and telling them to be brave and believe in God etc. I was convulsed with unmaidenly mirth as they only stayed from a mixture of fear and a bribe of sweets.

Thursday, 16 February. Another day spent in the car. I wonder what percentage of my life I spend in my car nowadays? Today the *capitan* and I set off at 9.30 for Barcelona, where he had to fetch some spare parts for his car.

From Manresa to Solsona there were some dreadful patches of road, avoiding blown up bridges. Awfully muddy little paths so narrow one almost scraped both sides, and with huge ruts, holes and stones. I really don't know how I got the car through unharmed. At least three times I thought we were done for. The rest of the drive was lovely. Mile upon mile of beautiful road through pine forest, all over the foothills of the Pyrenees, with never a house in sight, nothing but pines for miles and miles on either side, with occasional glimpses of the snow-capped mountains looming up not far away.

Saturday, 18 February. Heavens what a strenuous life one does lead when one has nothing to do! Yesterday I drove four and a half hours to Monzon and talked till two in the morning. Today I drove back, getting up at 7.30; tomorrow back to Monzon, the next day Zaragoza and Epila, the day after to Sanlucar; about fifteen hours' driving! I shall arrive there dead. I am tired already. I have ten days' leave starting from tomorrow which I intend to enjoy one way or another.

Tuesday, 21 February. [*At Sanlucar.*] It is now 1 o'clock in the morning and more than forty hours since I was last in bed, so very naturally I have no great urge to waste precious time writing this diary, but it must be done. Mama has sent me everything I asked for: 500 bed covers, which I have left there till I can get a lorry to transport them, white material, cloaks, boots, stockings, peach brandy, and last, by certainly not least, 10,000 cigarettes.

Thursday, 23 February. Oh, how happy I am down here at Sanlucar. I live in a sort of peaceful haze of pleasure.

Tuesday, 28 February. We arrived at Epila at 1.30 nicely in time for lunch. The Infanta, Alvaro and Carla were here and were delighted to see us. As this house is so cold we all ate in the drawing room in front of the stove. Everyone told each other all their news at a great rate. After lunch the Infanta had to go to Zaragoza to the hairdresser and Ataulfo on to Lerida. I went too to Zaragoza to inquire about my *equipo* [*with the Infanta*]. We stopped a moment in the Grand Hotel where I saw Gabriel Herbert and went over and talked to her for a moment. Very elegant and well soignée.[17] The news of my *equipo* was nil. So the day came to a peaceful end with rumours in Zaragoza that our troops had entered Madrid. Quite rightly we did not believe it as it is merely excess optimism due to both England and France recognizing Franco today.[18] It is wonderful to know that this is really almost over. I just can't fathom it at all. At lunch time today Ataulfo suddenly turned up in the pink of form, despite having been on a binge all last night with his co-officers drinking champagne and beer to celebrate the fall of Madrid, which has not yet fallen.

Wednesday, 1 March. The news from England tonight was once more all about war preparations in view of the imminent crisis. There is no crisis, but as the Jews have sworn to have a European war this

17 Gabriel Mary Herbert was the daughter of Mary Herbert, widow of Aubrey Herbert. The family was converted to Catholicism by Hilaire Belloc. Gabriel was a devout Catholic, not known in later life for elegant clothes. She left no record of her work as an ambulance driver other than her poetry (privately printed).
18 After vain attempts at a mediated peace which Franco refused, insisting on unconditional surrender, 'The Nationalists have won; the Republicans must surrender without conditions', Britain recognized Franco on 27 February, to Attlee, leader of the Labour Party, 'a gross betrayal of democracy'. Azaña, the President of the Republic, resigned.

spring come what may, I suppose there soon will be.[19] I frankly don't see how it is to be avoided if they are really determined. It will be the end of Europe and of the British Empire, but people are such fools they won't think of that.

Monday, 6 March. Cartagena is evidently still in an undecided position. We have got half the town but the other half is still Red and as our fleet won't go into port to land troops and are thirty kilometres out to sea, the Cartagena people will have to fight it out amongst themselves.

In Madrid Negrín has been slung out of power and fled to Toulouse, while Miaja has taken over and put all the stray Communists under arrest, as he is contemplating surrender.[20] I hope Valencia will rise soon, but they are pretty Red there. Our next advance is supposed to start in about ten days' time, so allowing for the usual delay this ought to be theoretically all over in a month's time or two months at the outside. I am being so lazy here. Anyhow directly the advance starts I will have to be away and working so it does not matter. The only thing to do is to enjoy life while one can and as much as one can.

Tuesday, 7 March. The only news of the war is that in Madrid they are all fighting among themselves. Miaja has ordered all the Communists to shoot their officers and has sent his aviation over Madrid to bomb their headquarters. There is also a certain amount of unrest in Cuenca and various other towns, so it can't last much longer. Perhaps I will never get back to my *equipo* because the war will be over first, but that seems improbable.

Wednesday, 8 March. I have to leave tomorrow. I have finally located my *equipo*, which is down in a town called Don Benito near Merida,

19 This shows how brainwashed Pip had been by German and upper-class Spanish anti-semitism. Pip's mother was half Jewish and proud of it. The remark is quite uncharacteristic of Pip.
20 Negrín's government was considered by Colonel Casado to be dominated by Communists determined to continue a hopeless struggle. On 5 March Casado turned on the Communists and staged a coup against Negrin in the hopes of negotiating satisfactory terms with Franco. The negotiations failed since Franco insisted on unconditional surrender. Casado's forces fought the Madrid Communists, a civil war within the Civil War; it continued till 11 March. The first Nationalist troops entered Madrid on 27 March.

and they say right at the front. I think it is a dismal hole to be sent to. It must be fifteen hours' drive from here. At least it is quite close to Talavera, where the Infanta and Consuelo will be, and to Sanlucar, about five hours from each, probably. It bores me to have to go off there all on my own because I shan't see anyone while I am there because five hours is just too far to do there and back in a day comfortably. The muddle in Madrid continues much the same but the Communists have now more or less given in but there are risings in Cuenca, Murcia, Almeria, Guadalajara and various other places. We have spent all day playing cards, laughing and talking. Our latest craze is playing patiences with wishes on them. Two of my wishes came out, one that the war should end soon, and the other to go to St Moritz next winter.

Friday, 10 March. This wretched village, Don Benito, is about fifty kilometres from Merida and very ugly, moderately destroyed and pockmarked by shell holes and burnt houses and bullet-chipped walls. It is quite big and compact, with dreadful cobbled streets in such disrepair that it is almost impossible to drive through it. I found my way to a hospital where a very painted and crazy Falange nurse accompanied me to the house where my *equipo* lives.

Rumour has it that in a day or two we are to go either down to Panaroya or to Cordoba. Both are dreadful. Cordoba may be a lovely place, but I don't want to be stuck there when Madrid falls. And so far from the Infanta and Consuelo that I shall never hear any of their news or know when they have to leave or what. There is a suggestion that I should go riding tomorrow with Isabel and Victoria on some cart-horses they have found, but I have no pants. Otherwise it would be rather fun. It is so oppressive and dismal being back again. I have to be so unnatural here.

Pip stayed in Estramadura until March. She had no serious hospital work and passed the time riding and visiting friends. She was much alarmed by the prospect of war in Europe.

Monday, 13 March. Read some letters from Bronwen in Kenya which made me laugh a lot. So very English. She liked Mombasa because of the big English-looking trees, Nairobi because of the shrubs like the garden at home, and the general ensemble because there were fluffy white clouds, just like at home! Typical of her. Why does she bother to travel? One from Gaenor was very well written and sophisticated. Very offended that her husband's friends should think her infantile for being the great age of nineteen, and very depressed about war scares.

I got the doctor to take the opportunity to vaccinate me for smallpox, as there is an epidemic in the village we are about to be sent to and I should hate to end this war dead or pockmarked. I think I would prefer dead of the two alternatives, but don't fancy either. The Infanta finally turned up with Consuelo about five.

Wednesday, 15 March. The news on the radio tonight indicates that things have come to a head again in Europe. I could only hear parts as the radio bust as usual, but I gather the Germans have marched into Slovakia and taken it without resistance. There is lots of talk by Chamberlain for peace at all costs and Eden and others for saving our honour even if it means war, but I sincerely hope the danger is blowing over now. God, I hope so.

Thursday, 16 March. We were all comfortably in bed when Carola brought us the news that Germany has definitely taken Slovakia and is now in complete possession. So we argued politics with violence most of the morning. Thank goodness it is over and no one has done anything. I don't trust them an inch yet, but it certainly is a temporary relief. Justo turned up at about eleven and spent the morning finishing his portrait of Vicky while Carola, who has been given leave, packed. She went off to Merida with Parachi at three. Justo turned up again at 3.30 and I sat for him till 6.30. My portrait came out like a very determined Greek god.

Wednesday, 22 March. God, I am in a bad temper tonight. I hate our new place and it is all a muddle. We are now in Pueblonuevo, which we were told was a lovely clean new village. It is a filthy little dump and quite hideous with mines and factories all around.

Once more Vicky and I are sharing a room requisitioned for us in one of the houses in the village. Although we have a bed each this time we are very uncomfortable, as the room is tiny and full of strange and awful little ornaments, so that one can't put anything down anywhere. We had breakfast in Merida with out host, who was a *capitan* doctor and could do nothing but talk of his daughter who was killed in one of Merida's thirty-six air raids. I am sick of people's miseries. Everywhere one goes everyone is moaning over their miseries. We left at ten, and after fixing a puncture and getting covered in dust by convoys of troops, we stopped in Zauaga for lunch. Bustamante and the priest argued the whole time, as usual, but Bustamante was amusing. We went to a bar where they drank beer, then lunch, then another bar for coffee and cognac.

We arrived here about 4 o'clock, since when we have done nothing. Parachi has not arrived, nor has our luggage. We have no house and no food.

Thursday, 23 March. It is hell to have to start this war again when we all thought it was over and finished. I am sick of it and never want to work again in my life. The worst worry is my terror of there being a European war, although things are temporarily quieting down now. It would be ghastly.

Friday, 24 March. Tonight I feel mad. The English news says that representatives of the Red government flew to Burgos today to talk with Franco and that it has been arranged that tomorrow our troops enter Madrid with no resistance on any front, the only condition being that certain members of their government should be allowed to escape abroad.[21] If only it is true! It must be true, it just must be, or I will die of depression. How utterly glorious if it is. Tomorrow in Madrid and the war over and finished. It can't be possible, it is all a lovely dream which will come to nothing and we will drag on in dismal villages either bored stiff or worked to death and watching people die like flies. Filthy! The war must end. I feel so nervous and hysterical I just can't go to bed.

I did not hear any foreign news today as I forgot it was Sunday, but the Spanish news is that on the Cordoba front we have advanced a depth of forty kilometres, taking Pozo Blanco and lots of other villages. We also heard the Red radio, which announced the fact that they had discussed peace with Franco and had promised a theoretical giving up of arms to deliver over their entire air force yesterday, but

21 Two officers, representing Colonel Casado, had flown to Burgos in a last attempt to secure terms for surrender. The negotiations were broken off because the Republican air force had not surrendered.

due to bad weather had been unable to do so and were willing to do so tomorrow.

But Franco answered that he could no longer call off the attack as it was now too late. So the Reds advised their men to give in with a white flag if attacked and pass over to us complete, which is exactly what they have done near Cordoba. In fact it is nearly over now.

6

Madrid
28 March – 31 May 1939

During this period Pip was working with the Infanta in the local hospitals and in the canteen of Barajas aerodrome. She entered Madrid the day after the Nationalist troops occupied it. After the initial euphoria of victory a generalized depression set in. Pip, run down and ill, shared this depression in an acute form. 'There is no doubt', she wrote on 10 April, 'that the war has left us all horribly strung up and hysterical.' This depression was induced by the wretched state of Madrid, full of half-starved sick, the destruction of the houses of Pip's circle, the sorry state of the Francoist supporters who came out of the embassies where they had taken refuge during the war.

At least some of the material damage was quickly repaired. Luis Bolin, who worked for the Francoist propaganda service, noted after the Nationalists entered the city, 'the accumulated filth that the Reds bequeathed to every town... The dust at the Ritz was inches thick'. Yet, by April it was cleaned up for a reception given to the Italian and German aviators and by May Pip was meeting Peter Kemp for drinks there.

Pip's work with the Infanta included visiting the sick and old who had suffered greatly from the food shortage and the lack of medical treatment. Much of Pip's time was spent driving in Madrid and the countryside around for supplies. As in Aragon and Catalonia, her car was virtually requisitioned and at times she felt herself to be a semi-official driver.

The Infanta wrote of Pip's work in Madrid:

It would be difficult even by word of mouth to tell you the admiration I have for Pip's character and work... Here now in Madrid we found the population in a deplorable condition, sights like in an Indian famine.

[204]

We had to visit separately as there was so much work. Pip nursed these people and gave them injections and took food to them. In the evenings she typed reports for the Hospitals all on her own and in perfect Spanish. . .

Where there was no Doctor to hand, she did the diagnosis. . .got the cancer patients into the Cancer Hospital, the tuberculosis patients into the Sanatorium. . .She never made a mistake. . .

Her intelligence and patience have been astounding.

All this without an audience, or a single day off for fun. . .

She is known from one end of Spain to the other. . .never flurried or impatient.

I want you to know all this as in tidy *England you may never have seen her tackle a burden of work single-handed like she has in Madrid.*

Tuesday, 28 March. Madrid has fallen at last! A day no Spaniard will ever forget nor I either. It has been so unbelievable that I don't know how to begin to describe it. At last, at last I am in Madrid, and I doubt if any other English person has entered it for the first time in their lives under similar conditions. I must start right from the beginning of the day, which was much like any other day. We got up at about seven and by nine all went off to our various jobs. The Infanta went to Leganes [*a town twelve kilometres south of Madrid*] to see her other stores, Consuelo went to the convent to unpack and sort the blankets. It was icy cold and of course no one else was about yet, so I set to work shivering and alone. After a bit I was one block of ice. Some Legionarios dropped in at ten with many compliments and the news that we had taken Aranjuez [*the town of the Royal Palace, sixty kilometres south of Madrid*] at nine and they were off to see it. Suddenly, at about 10.30, a girl rushed in like a lunatic shouting that she had just heard over the radio that Madrid had fallen. We stopped in our tracks like statues and she and all the girls rushed out into the street shouting and laughing, leaving Rosario, the other woman and me standing still and waiting in silence. Then in the distance a bell began to ring, then another, the village church, the nuns next door. Every kind of bell tinkling, ringing and clanging. I was so stirred I did not know whether to cry or shout or sing or what. So, of course all I did say was, 'So it is true at last', pick up another blanket and start to

[205]

fold it. Finally we decided that we must tidy things up before going crazy, so solemnly set to work to fold and pile as fast as we could. We had almost finished when Consuelo came dashing in to see if we knew the news. Then there was a heated argument as to what to do. She was all for jumping into the car and going to Madrid, but we decided we had to wait for the Infanta despite the risk of her going without us, as she was away and only one kilometre from Madrid. We were still discussing in the road when her car came flying towards us. Then all became pandemonium. We rushed in different directions, collecting things, furious with impatience. Finally the Infanta set off in her car with an aviator who had come with her, with mine following bringing Consuelo, Rosario, Jesus and me. We had no luggage except Rosario, who had her suitcase, and Jesus a huge sausage. The Infanta had her car full of food, condensed milk, Bovril, biscuits, chocolate, tinned meat, etc. but no luggage either. We went to the aerodrome, where I filled up with petrol while she collected the captain of aviation whose convoy of lorries we were to join. We set off again in the highest of spirits, the Infanta in front in an open grey aviation car with the captain and a lieutenant, then we four bringing up the rear. We were in high spirits and arrived the other side of Carabanchel [*a suburb of Madrid*] singing and laughing. Then to our horror we found the road barred and no cars allowed to pass. The captain got out and produced papers, rang up on the telephone and argued a lot about his column of lorries which had to pass but it was all to no avail, and we had to turn back. We were told all roads were barred as the troops of the occupation had not yet entered. Evidently Madrid gave in even before our forces were ready to enter. We returned to Carabanchel where we drew up on the side of the road to wait. Consuelo was frantic and we were all in a state, with no idea of what was going on. The lorries of the aviators turned up and joined us, too. We had to wait quite a long time. The soldiers gave us some cold fried fish and a little bread, the officers a bottle of wine and a sausage. Finally the Infanta and the captain went off to see if they could get a special pass. Soon after they had gone there was suddenly wild activity. The order had come that the column could pass. Frantic action immediately ensued and all the lorries started to leave, everyone was leaping into their cars, but I said we had to wait for the Infanta. Her chauffeur leapt into the road pale with agitation saying we must not move till she came, so they calmed down again and after touring the cars we sat down to wait. I produced my last bottle of sherry and passed it down the line to cheer them up. We passed it from hand to hand drinking out of the bottle for lack of a glass. It seemed an eternity, but at last the car arrived. The captain said he could not pass us all and everyone had to abandon cars and go in the lorries with the troops. However finally the Infanta and I were allowed to take our cars. At last we set off and this time after slight argument passed the guards and were really on our way. There were many pauses and much running up and down by the fat captain before it was all fixed.

A group of small boys came up beaming with joy. We gave them chocolates whereat they burst into shrieks of pleasure and told us they had lived on lentils so long they had forgotten how anything else tasted. They called the lentils the 'pills of resistance'.[1] We entered Madrid through the famous Ciudad Universitaria along a road built up ten or twelve feet high on either side like a trench. The view of Madrid from there was a waste land. Not a house standing, one mass of ruins.[2] From there on there were enormous numbers of cars and lorries and troops, and we had to crawl along. The people of Madrid were pouring out, shouting and jumping on the running board, begging for food, cigarettes, anything. The Infanta's car which I followed broke down and I had to push it most of the way. What with that and the heat my car boiled over and cracked the radiator, pouring steam in all directions. The fortifications of Madrid were unbelievable. Line after line of barricades of brick with loopholes all along for machine guns. It would have been utterly impossible to have taken Madrid by force except by completely destroying it and with great losses. The enthusiasm was unbelievable, a thing I shall never forget in my life. Flags and shawls and sheets hanging from every window and the streets filled with people shouting themselves hoarse and waving and saluting. We drove all the way in through a delirious crowd. As we had to crawl along they leant in at the windows and patted us on the backs, shook hands, laughed, cried, anything and everything. All the time the aviation were flying over low, zooming over the house tops. We followed the Infanta a long way.

1 Food was scarce in Madrid. The diet of lentils was known as 'Dr Negrín's resistance pills' after the Prime Minister.
2 The University city on the outskirts of Madrid was in the front line after Franco had failed to take Madrid in 1936. As Pip comments, to take the city street by street would have entailed heavy casualties.

She stopped from time to time and the captain leapt out to requisition a car. Finally, as she was taking him to the Jefatura del Aire [*Aviation GHQ*] we parted company as Consuelo and Rosario both wanted to find their relations. We arranged to meet at the Romanian Legation later. That was our first call, as Rosario's brother had been hidden there. But he had gone out, so we went to his flat, but he was not there either. Then to Chile [*the Chilean Legation*] for Consuelo's father, brother and brother-in-law. They were not there. We went to three houses under the Chilean protection. In the last one we were told they might be in a sanatorium. So I left her to telephone while I took Rosario to find her in-laws. We found them in the street and they were all hysterical with excitement. Then back for Consuelo, who had discovered her father and Juan [*the brother-in-law*] were in a pension. When we got there I accompanied her up, but they had gone out, so we decided to go and meet the Infanta. We got to Romania [*the Romanian Legation*] to find she had come and gone. So we went upstairs to wait. There we found an old lady and a young one who had spent all the war there. They were very odd and slightly mad and gave us a cup of tea while we talked of the war. It is dreadful to see the people here. They are all very strange. Either very quiet or very mad. For almost three years they have never been out of the house and lived in constant fear. As the Infanta did not come we went off to look for her. We went to the Estado Major [*General Staff*] of the 6th Division, to her house in Quintana Street, to Helfan's [*the Romanian Ambassador*] house, but could find her nowhere. Her house was shut and looks much of a mess from outside, and they say is utterly destroyed inside, even to tearing up the parquet floors and burning the doors. Twice we went to Romania, but she was not there. However, the third time we found her there talking to the Ambassador in his office and very worried about us, as it was long after dark. We were told Rosario's brother, Ignacio, had fainted in the street and would be back soon. When he turned up it was terrifying how pleased he was. Rosario gasped out his name and they clung to each other crying with joy. We made him sit down and gave him a cigarette, otherwise he would have passed out. He was pale and trembling, with tears streaming down his face. We were all so touched we were gulping like mad. I have gone through so many emotions today for other people that I am limp as a leaf. Then Consuelo and I went off in a little car belonging to the legation to see her family. I accompanied her for moral support. Her father and Juan were living together in a room in a pension and were delighted to see her. We gave them cigarettes and promised to bring more and food tomorrow. The father is a little old dried-up, thin, watery-eyed man. Juan is charming, grey-haired, clean and tidy, and very much a gentleman. They all swapped family news for a long time. It appeared that the brother lived next door. So up we went to see him in the Argentine Legation. He showed us his room, which was the filthiest thing I have ever seen. Everything thick with dirt. After dinner four men turned up to see us, one of whom has worked for Princess Bee for sixteen years. They were hilarious too and we gave them cigarettes and talked and laughed. Everyone is mad with delight at the sight of a cigarette, and we hand them out all round. What luck that I got all mine such a short time ago that I still have some left. As long as I live I shall never forget my first day in Madrid. It has been wonderful, incredibly happy and exciting, and at the same time terribly sad.

Wednesday, 29 March. The Romanian Minister's flat is lovely. He had 200 people in it and the two floors above all through the war. The war is now really over, as all the towns have given in, Almaria and Albacete being the last to surrender. I can't begin to realize it is over. It is too strange and impossible even to think about it. The Infanta is installed in great luxury and has had a hot bath, which made us very jealous as we only have cold water.

She is sad at being separated from us and felt very ill last night, with a high temperature. The first thing we did was to go to the headquarters of the Division 16, to get passes for our cars to enter and leave Madrid. The colonel was very amiable, a small extremely military man, who clicked and bowed to the Infanta in almost German style. The place was full of females dressed in grey and brown striped Moroccan capes. They turned out to be Frentes y Hospitales women of the division, and had been given the military capes as a present by the colonel.

We went off in the two cars to Valdemoro [*thirty kilometres south of Madrid*]. It took us a long time to get out of Madrid as the first road we tried we were stopped as the engineers were about to blow up some mines set up by the Reds, the next was impassable, and the third was so thick with traffic that it took us ages. However, at last we fought our way through. In Valdemoro we found the houses completely empty and deserted, but luckily everything just as we had left it. We shut up the blankets, leaving someone in charge with orders to let no one in, and then went to pack. The only thing missing was my gramophone, which alas one of the companions has removed, so I don't expect I will ever see it again.

We came back through the gardens of the palace [*the Orleans family's Madrid house*], the entrance to which was guarded by the Red machine-gun posts, and trenches actually in the garden. The façade of the palace, having been only some few hundred yards from the trenches, is horribly spoilt, which one does not see from far off at all. We left the Infanta at her house and went to the Legation for lunch.

Suddenly there was a wild shout from below and all the refugees rushed out. Evidently one of the women was the wife of a *guardia civil* who had escaped a year ago. She saw a *guardia* arrive at the door and, thinking it was her husband, rushed out only to discover it was someone else. When she had gone away he told the others that her husband was dead as he had been killed in a house in Barcelona. They all came up again in a terrible state not knowing whether to tell the wife or not.

We went to the Orleans Palace in Madrid. All round was full of shell holes and all its enormous windows and glass galleries were smashed, giving it a very dishevelled and forlorn look, especially from the patio. It is very, very spoilt from outside as all the stone balustrades and everything are broken and twisted and marked by shrapnel. The patio was full of sheep, goats and bullocks, as there was a *tabor* of Moors lodging there. We were shown all round by the two old porters who had managed to stay on. The bottom floor is ruined, due to military occupation. The Infanta's room, all decorated in cream silk with 'B's embroidered all over the walls and furniture covers, was a mess, with one torn armchair and a chipped bedstead. However, the upper floor which is the most important part is almost untouched. We had to go round with torches as the electricity does not work properly and all the windows are sandbagged, which has saved it enormously. It must have been one of the most beautiful palaces in Europe, and I hope will be again one day. It was strange going all round it just as in the dark. The furniture is almost all still there stacked away in some of the rooms and there are still some of the pictures, although most of them have gone and all the tapestries are missing. The worst part is the outside, which is utterly ruined and will take a colossal amount of work to repair. There are two rooms with shell holes in them but luckily not the best rooms.

The staircase is a dream of beauty and unharmed except for two or three shell holes way up in the domed ceiling. I should love to see it all properly, as some of the rooms are wonderful. One entirely made of china, walls, ceiling and everything. It sounds awful but is actually very pretty, the whole room papered with exquisitely hand-embroidered silk. When we finally left the palace the Infanta went to tea with her erstwhile lady-in- waiting, who is now very old, and then to bed, as she was feeling very ill again. We went all round Madrid looking for the headquarters of F y H which we finally found in Hotel Florida. There we sat about gossiping for ages and finally elicited the news that the office would open tomorrow at 10.30.

Just as we were leaving, Prince Ali and Escariot turned up. Evidently a lot of the Red aviation flew over and surrendered itself at Barajas, an aerodrome just outside Madrid, and as there was no one there to cope, Prince Ali was sent for and took possession of the machines and shut all the pilots up. Now his Brigade is given Barajas as its new destination, and he leaves tomorrow to organize moving it over, leaving Escariot in charge of the thirty-five Red machines.

We came back to the Romanian Legation. We were dead tired and the wretched people did not dine till nearly 11 o'clock, which is hell when one has to write a diary and get up early.

Tomorrow we have to start early as the Infanta, Consuelo and I are going to Castillejo [*Princess Bee's farm*] to see how it is.

Thursday, 30 March. We went to the Infanta's country estate via Guadalajara. Between there and Tarrancon (about 100 kilometres) we saw no troops of ours at all, and round about 40,000 Reds. In no other country in the world could one do that, three women and one chauffeur drive alone through an army in flight without mishap. All along the road, some going one way, some the other, in groups of twos and threes, or tens and twelves. They all looked dead tired, pale and exhausted, but quite cheerful. Lots were limping and hardly able to walk. All carrying their rugs and packages on their backs, but no arms at all. I think they are glad to be able to go back to their villages at last, because most of them have no idea what the war was about anyhow. In Salicies we went straight to Camelo's [*the chauffeur*] house accompanied by the guards and followed by the entire population. As so far no troops had entered the village they were all wildly excited to see Camelo. At first they did not recognize the Infanta and asked Camelo rather diffidently who he was driving, not sure whether to arrest him for driving Reds or fête him for bringing Whites. Then they began to recognize the Infanta.

Camelo's mother has rheumatism and is unable to move so could not come to the locked door to let him in when he called. However, he got in by the back and she nearly had hysterics, as she thought it was her son Justin who had disappeared. The Infanta went in too and relations of Camelo's poured in. They all had fits and their shrieks and wails echoed out into the street where we were waiting. Then we left Camelo and went with the mayor to see Castillejo. He has appointed himself mayor, and I think he is very Red and a thief. The Infanta was horrified as her estate was known for its miles of beautiful woods and now there is not one tree there. The bad luck is that it has all been cut recently, as they flew over six months ago and it was still all right. The house too is ruined. Filthy, with no furniture, no doors, no windows, everything broken and the bare rooms filled with straw. The garden the same. The only thing there were her American mules. It was tragic, and she was almost in tears. Amongst the mules she found an old white one who was twenty-one when she left eight years ago and is still living. It was pathetic. She stood a long time looking at it in the dirty old stable, and then said in English, 'Poor old dear, you are about the only person I know that is left here now.' It must have been a lovely house and estate, but is now a ruin.

The mayor had offered us to sleep in his house, as the estate was impossible, but Camelo said he was a Red and on no account was the Infanta to sleep there, so we slept in his house. We lunched there when we arrived and had cocoa for dinner at about seven, so as to go to bed early. His mother is a dear old lady. We all sat round the fire while she and her relations told us the usual stories of what had gone on in the village. If people could see the Infanta, Consuelo and myself all sitting down to lunch together round the kitchen fire in the little cottage with no embarrassment at all, they would not run down royalty the way they do. Camelo's mother had been terribly brave as she had hidden a certain amount of linen from Castillejo and had buried what she could save of the silver in her back yard. If she had been discovered she would have been shot. So I finished the war by digging for buried treasure in the rain by the light of a candle. The whole village stood outside the house all the evening, wanting to see the Infanta, but Camelo as Prime Minister would allow no one in as he said until they were sane and justice had been done she could shake hands with no one as they had all been stealing her things and cutting her trees.

Monday, 3 April. Cripes, what a life this is! I always knew that a few days after this war was over we would all begin to regret it and think of the filthy war which we loathed as 'the good old days'. I have had no time to write this lately, but in the last few days we have all become very bored and depressed. This evening put the lid on it.

But first I must write shortly the last few days. Friday morning we got up at 5.45 at Camelo's house in Salices. It was cold and almost dark, but as we had gone to bed early at least we were not tired. After a nice hot cup of cocoa we set off back to Madrid. Camelo had filled my car with petrol and it must have been filthy, because almost at once it began to run badly until after about half an hour I had to stop as it would go no further. It was pouring with rain and poor Camelo had to get soaked clearing the petrol pump and carburettor which were cluttered up with dirt. It took nearly three quarters of an hour and we had only gone a few more kilometres when it started again and we finished the journey very slowly in jerks, forcing the car on in every way I could think of. By the time I got back I was a nervous wreck and I don't know how I did not kill anyone, as I never knew if the car was going to shoot forward or stop. The rest of the day and all Saturday we went with the Infanta from place to place in the usual tiring and boring way. Canteens, hospitals, emergency stations etc. I met Miss Jackson, head of the Scottish Ambulance, which has been very Red indeed. The Infanta wanted to see her about whether she would go with her on her relief work amongst the population or not. She had two porridge canteens, but one was removed by Auxilio Social.[3] She was furious. An incredible woman, small and square, with a huge bottom. She always dresses in a kilt, thick woollen stockings, brogues, a khaki jacket of military cut with thistles all over it, huge leather gauntlet gloves, a cape also with thistles, and, the crowning glory, a little black Scottish hat edged with tartan and with

3 The Falangist relief organization.

a large silver badge on it. We all laughed ourselves silly afterwards. She had a dreadful discussion with Prince Ali as to whether she was a Red of not.

On Sunday Consuelo and I got up at five and at six set off, picking up the Infanta's agent to Cuenca. We stopped in Salices where we forced the mayor to hand over copies of all the papers about where all things from Castillejo had gone to. It was a dismal day. The car went badly and I had to have it mended in Cuenca. We had two punctures which took us hours to mend, and it was bitterly cold. We neither found the very valuable books nor the silver and jewellery which was supposed to be there, and to finish with, the agent, who had come to look for a Red brother, found he had been shot three days ago, so we arrived at the Infanta's at nine in the evening tired and depressed and hungry. There we found Ataulfo, who had got two days' leave. He was pretty gloomy. He stayed to dinner to our great relief. Today once more we spent a good deal of it going from place to place as usual. We lunched in one of the canteens, where we were joined by various women. All afternoon I spent driving about with Ataulfo and Helfan's daughter. We were rather glum.

Tuesday, 4 April. Ataulfo left this morning very gloomy and bad-tempered saying that nothing would induce him to come back here again and that he did not want to go to Castillejo. He snapped at everything anyone said. The poor Infanta was quite upset. She ended by trying to cheer him and all of us by saying we must all try and go to Sanlucar together. Ataulfo did not answer, so she asked him if he wanted to. He said of course he was going as soon as he got a chance, but he did not know or care if it was all the same to us. Definitely surly. Poor old Ataulfo, he is so upset to see his beloved Madrid the way it is and, like everyone else, having a nervous reaction, now the war is over. When we said goodbye the Infanta begged him to be careful flying and not to think the danger was over because there was no more war. How right she was! Today the best pilot in Spain, Morato, was killed doing an exhibition flight. The second best, Ibarra too, and some five or six others. Everyone is terribly upset about Morato, as he was a brilliant man as well as a brilliant pilot, and the one person people counted on to deal with the future of the Spanish Air Force. Apart from that he was a very great friend of Prince Ali's and his poor wife, whom I have met from time to time, a great friend of the Infanta's, so everyone is miserable about it. After bidding goodbye to Ataulfo, the Infanta and I went at about twelve to Barajas to see the canteen and get Prince Ali to start inquiries about Camelo's brother Santos, who has also disappeared. It was pelting with rain, icy cold and very windy. We sat first in Escariot's and then Prince Ali's office waiting about, admiring the rainswept field. Escariot was frantically telephoning not to let any machines leave for Barajas, but three had already gone, one of which smashed and another still missing. Prince Ali, the Infanta and I lunched in a little alcove off the kitchen where there was just room for the table, a chair for the Infanta and a high stool for me. Prince Ali ate standing up in a corner. Then we went to pack. We spent the afternoon trying to find wine, glasses, cups, *chorizo*, corkscrews and tin openers for the Barajas canteen. We found all except wine, and took it there. Finally at about seven I collected my luggage and all the food stores and moved into our new house. It is a wonderful palace, very comfortable, big, and with all luxuries as it was the Turkish Legation. After dinner Prince Ali and Escariot, who is living here too, went to see Morato lying in state so the Infanta and I stayed talking by the fire. We talked a lot of hospitals, as I have decided I want to do the English end of providing orthopaedic instruments and plastic surgery for the war cripples. It would be very interesting.

Thursday, 6 April. We can't all go on being so depressed and miserable, and as no one seems to be going to cheer us up I have decided I have to do it. Someone must or we will all die of depression. So I am trying to organize an amusing Easter; after all it is the first Easter of peace since 1936 and we ought to celebrate it as we have not yet had time to celebrate the end of the war. We have got paints from Helfan's daughter with which to paint eggs for breakfast; we are going to try and locate the peach brandy and try and get Ataulfo to come. He swore he would on no account return to Madrid. Tonight we tried to ring him up, but could not get through as the telephones are in dreadful disorder.

At three we were back in Barajas. All the girls went off to church and left us in charge of the canteen for a couple of hours. It was lots of fun. The Infanta dealt with the kitchen, Consuelo was the cashier and I was the barmaid. I thoroughly enjoyed it, standing behind the bar serving sandwiches, biscuits, milk, coffee, wine, cognac, washing up the glasses and wiping the bar in true style. I always knew I was a born barmaid. When the others came back we left and went again to the headquarters where we were told nurses were needed for some of the hospitals.

I shall be furious if I am stuck in a hospital again. I am sick of the mere thought of them. We also agitated a lot this morning about various stores. Always the same rows and bothers. Oh my kingdom, never to see a hungry person or a tin of milk or Bovril again. I am so sick of all this fussing and bothering and wearing uniform and never doing anything amusing. And yet I can't bear the thought of leaving this, because it will be so hard to have to start life again. I got lots of letters today, but all pretty old.

Friday, 7 April. Ataulfo arrived. As always we were very delighted to see him. I am feeling so over-tired and wretched that I was delighted someone cheerful had come. Unluckily our good temper was soon spoilt by Consuelo returning with the news that one of the patients has just died of starvation, and the others looked like doing so at any moment. So she went off to the Red Cross for medicines. Various people rang up about innumerable muddles and the Infanta went out to a committee meeting. Consuelo went to the kitchen to prepare lunch. As there was no salt to cook with, Ataulfo and I went in my car to the Romanian Legation to get some. We played cards till four when Mary Angels came round. Then at 4.30 he went to collect his friends and go back to Avila, and we set off to work. He is sad because the only two survivors of his first lot of co-officers were killed in an accident the other day. He really has been terribly lucky, because of the first group there are none left, of the second only one, and of the third and fourth only about half. When he had gone we went on our rounds of hospitals, etc. till I wanted to sit down and scream. Then to drop food and medicine for the sick people. At last, at about seven, home to play cards, the Infanta bemoaning the disorganization, Prince Ali in a furious rage about aviation, and us miserable. Then some people came to pay us a visit. It was all I could do to keep awake, but they were nice and the wife had been a nurse during the whole war, so we talked *equipos*, when the usual subject of her house being ruined, her possessions stolen and her relations killed was over. At last they went and we and Escariot dined. He has been made a major so we drank his health and relapsed back into bad temper and depression. I think if the Infanta does not get away for a rest soon she will have a breakdown. I wish she could finish up her work here so that we could all go to Sanlucar for a rest. But she can't disentangle herself. Anyhow at least she must enjoy Easter – she deserves it.

Saturday, 8 April. Tomorrow is Easter Sunday and maybe the day after I will go to England, but not for good. The Infanta urgently need vitamins, medicines and injections and I have volunteered to get them, so if I go it will be just a flying visit to get the things to Madrid in the shortest possible time. Ataulfo came today as promised.

We were all out when he arrived. After breakfast we sewed on Escariot's new, big stars which was very complicated. Then the Infanta went off with Rosario, and at eleven Consuelo and I went in my car to the emergency station up in one of the suburbs laden with various medicaments they had asked for.

We handed over our things and took charge of a patient, a poor young man with a skin disease and acute anaemia by the look of him, dreadfully thin, pale green with great sunken black eyes. He had been twenty-seven months in prison and looked as if he would die at any moment. It was a dreadful place, full of screaming women and children and all famished. It made me feel quite ill, despite all the filth and misery I have seen, and they all smelt so bad. I shall never get used to it. We took our young man in the car to the Hospital Provincial, a large gloomy building, where we handed him over to the care of two slovenly Red nurses. Then to another emergency station to hand over more things and report having dumped the patient, who has probably infected all my car with his disease. When we got back home Consuelo went off to see her family and I went up alone. I found Ataulfo all alone playing patience, so I went and dealt with the subject of lunch and then kept him company. The Infanta dashed in and dashed out again, God knows where to. We painted eggs for tomorrow, which we have done on and off all day. They are the greatest fun. We had champagne at dinner, which Ataulfo had brought, and brandy afterwards, also brought by him in an attempt to feel gay and festive. It was really quite fun as we were all a little less bad-tempered. I am glad we are cheering up, otherwise Easter would have been too dreary. As it is I think that I have to work in the canteen all morning and visit hospitals all afternoon, but maybe I can worm out of the latter.

I don't mind a bit working if it is necessary but not just fooling around pointlessly.

Ataulfo is very depressed because he wants to go down to Sanlucar, and none of us can persuade the Infanta to go. If she stays here we must stay too, and he does not especially want to go alone, so here we all are. Anyhow, if I go to England for these things I will make her promise that the moment I bring them we go to Sanlucar and then watch me hustle. I can do it in ten days.

Sunday, 9 April. We all wanted to hear Mass in Madrid, as there was to be a Military Mass at the Fuerta de Alcala with a march past, and all the women with big combs and mantillas as they have been for the last three days. I would like to have gone but no such luck. When we arrived at Barajas we started getting things ready and began to serve in the canteen. Then they all went to the Mass, leaving Rosario and me alone in charge, as she had already gone to early Mass and I am not a Catholic. Suddenly soldiers began to pour in and we ran about like lunatics, she in the kitchen and me at the bar, and both trying to deal with the cashier job as well. It was a relief when the others came back. Consuelo settled down as cashier, one girl helped me at the bar and two others in the kitchen. We worked like blacks without a pause to breath till nearly 1 o'clock, when at last the rush stopped and both food and drink had run out almost completely. We were discussing my going to England for vitamins for Madrid when the Romanian First Secretary came to see the Infanta. He offered to go to France to get them within three days so now I need not go, which is quite a relief really. Then Mary Angels and Santa arrived back form Castillejo, bringing the Infanta Easter presents of things they had saved so far of her favourite belongings. A perfectly lovely yellow and red old Spanish embroidered bedspread, too heavenly, and a very valuable museum piece; and the Infanta's own shotgun with her initials and crown on it, very light and very pretty, and some thermos bottles. Santa had stacks to tell of his two days in Castillejo. Some fourteen people have been put in jail for thieving, lots of possessions are reappearing, the farm is running well and will bring in a big harvest this year. In fact it looks as if it will all come out all right in the end. Her joy at seeing things again was unbounded, and we all laughed at Santa's stories of his reception and chasing the criminals.

Monday, 10 April. There is no doubt that the war has left us horribly strung up and hysterical. As usual I woke at about 6.30, as I sleep badly nowadays.

Ataulfo and I went off in his car to see Quintana, the Infanta's house. We stopped on the way in the Romanian Legation to pick up the porter. There we wasted lots of time looking at all the furniture which was rescued from Quintana, and finding a padlock, as the one at Quintana had to be broken to get in, as the key is lost. At last we arrived at the house, forced the padlock and started to explore. It was a dreadful mess and I felt sorry for Ataulfo seeing it like that as he used to adore it and Madrid. At least the damage is not as bad as we expected. Of course the furniture and pictures have all gone, the wall papers and silks are torn off, and a certain amount of general damage is done, all the windows are smashed and the skylight of the hall too, but the doors are all right and the parquet floors, although thick with grime, have not been torn up, nor have the ceiling beams been burnt. Of course the top floor where two shells fell is burnt out and has left a gaping hole in two of the second-floor rooms too. Where the bombs fell the entire two rooms have disappeared. It is really funny. The room below was the library or study and above the bathroom. Now it is all one with an entire bath and complicated douche in the middle of the study floor, miraculously undamaged, and high up on the walls suddenly, a WC and a wash basin, because of course the bathroom floor is completely missing. The whole house is filthy and full of muck and piles of paper and rubbish, amongst which we found a very few funny old photographs. I was even sorrier for the Infanta than I had been for Ataulfo. She says she wants to sell it but Ataulfo is all for repairing it gradually and living there again.

Tuesday, 11 April. We went off with Rosario to Barajas [*the Madrid airfield*], where we worked all morning in the canteen, serving a continual stream of soldiers. All the food ran out and we were in bad tempers anyhow. I passionately longed to hit some chatty, fresh Italians over the head with a bottle, but restrained my impulse. At 1.45 the Infanta turned up to fetch us and we three lunched at home off a small quantity of scrambled eggs. Then Prince Ali turned up and we played cards till four. He brought the news that there is to be a big march past of all the aviation at Barajas on the twenty-fifth, at which Franco is to take the salute and decorate all of them and inspect.

Prince Ali has to arrange it and is immersed in plans of how to fit in all the people, where to line up the planes for inspection, car parks, police, troops, audience, platforms, uniforms, roads, means of approach, times, places and people. There is also a dinner being organized by Prince Ali and Escariot to be given at the Ritz on the 19th for the aviation of the Italians and Germans. Santa's brother is doing decorations, the Infanta designing the menus, Escariot tackling the problem of feeding and serving about 1,000 people, and Prince Ali devising tactful presents and seating arrangements, so that no one should be offended.

Wednesday, 12 April. This morning the Infanta, Consuelo and I went to Leganes with a lorry to collect the stores from the loony bin. As we could not take them all in one go, Consuelo went back there after lunch, while the Infanta rested, and I wrote to Mama, to tell her why I was not coming home yet. At about four I went with the Infanta to Barajas and then to various other places, arranging about food for Barajas, cigarettes, medicines for God knows who and blankets for hospitals. At about seven we went home, followed by a van which was to fetch about 900 yards of material to be made into sheets. Of course it got lost, and finally turned up full of girls.

Thursday, 13 April. Santa appeared at about eleven and explained that the general of the division had forbidden it [*a dinner at the Infanta's house*] at the last moment, saying that there could be no binges before the big march past in Madrid. They are all very disappointed, as they had got everything ready with a band, food, two cooks, waiters and all from Bilbao especially for the occasion. The Infanta went out at 11.30 to collect her ex-lady-in-waiting and visit her house which is to be her future Madrid home. Consuelo and I took my car and went first to the hospital, where we failed to find the person in charge. Then to the Romanian Legation to collect our washing and my gramophone. We waited there about half an hour with the sole result that the gramophone had disappeared, and the washing still drying. Then to the Jefatura de Sanidad where we asked to see the lieutenant-colonel. We were told he was not receiving at that hour, but forced ourselves on him in spite of all protests. We found him a charming, ugly, tall man, closeted with the director of the hospital, a tiny, white-haired, hideous little man, but very sweet.

We asked for a lorry to fetch blankets. They were so overwhelmed that someone had not only promised them blankets, but was actually going to produce them, that they nearly fainted. They said they had no lorry but would try to get one. From there we went to ask if the material had arrived last night, and if they would give us a receipt. Then, armed with the receipt, as it was 1.30, we went home for lunch where we found the Infanta. Our lunch as usual was Bovril and eggs. The afternoon was gorgeously lazy.

After tea Consuelo and I went out in my car laden with powdered milk, sugar, eggs and butter which we took to a General Aguado, who we had been told was ill, and in bad need of food. He turned out to be an amiable old man of eighty-two, very thin and wobbly, having been shut up all during the war. He was simply swimming in his clothes, as he had lost an enormous amount of weight. He showed us all his photographs of his better days, but at last we managed to tear ourselves away from the poor old man, who was pathetically grateful for the food.

Friday, 14 April. At nine, the Infanta, Consuelo and I set off to Valdemoro with a lorry following behind. There we collected about six soldiers and got them to cart out all the sacks of sugar and cases of tinned meat and condensed milk, and load the lorry. The sacks of sugar were all eaten through by swarms of cockroaches we found behind them, so it had to be changed into others. We pottered about a bit looking at the stores of blankets etc., and finally set off back. We dropped the milk in at the emergency station store, where the Infanta was presented, to her disgust, with a paper informing her that she had been elected President of the Emergency Stations, which means still more work, and to her delight she was also given some onions and oranges. We ate onions all the way back in the car.

Saturday, 15 April. I am just too miserable to know where to start tonight. All for such a silly reason too, and yet I mind so much.

The Infanta suddenly suggested we should go to Sevilla for the march past the day after tomorrow. I said we would if she came too. But she said she would not go, excusing herself by saying she was too tired and ill to travel, which she is. So we said we would stay with her. God knows, I would love to go and have fun in Sevilla. One gets so few chances in this life, but I should never forgive myself for deserting the Infanta now she is so tired and unhappy. Prince Ali is foaming and says France refuses to return all the Spanish arms they have, and so Spain refuses to send away the Italians, and that Spain will have to have a row with France, which is the seat of all the trouble. God, what a life! I wish I could go to Sevilla and get so tight I would forget everything. I hate life. Blast it!

Tuesday, 18 April. Dull as ditchwater all day. This morning, while the Infanta went to a committee meeting about the emergency stations and to Barajas, Consuelo and I trotted round in the car, dropped tinned tunny at a canteen, bought, after much argument, a present for the Infanta, ordered flowers, unsuccessfully tried to see the director of a hospital, and finally went to visit a friend of Argillo, who is said to be ill and feeble. He was out, and his two shabby young daughters came in the door of their filthy little flat. They must be pretty Red, because when we asked if anyone was looking after their father, the little one said: 'Oh yes, the socorro Rojo'. The older shut her up hastily and said: 'No, no, it is the commissariat'. Then realizing that also was a faux pas, she began to get in a dreadful tangle explaining.

Wednesday, 19 April. While the Infanta went to another committee meeting this morning, Consuelo and I went off in my car to Valdemoro with six large twelve-litre jars to get wine from the monks. We found one monk looking like a comic waiter. He was frying potatoes and told me he had to get the key of the *bodega* so we would have to wait until the other monk came back from his walk. So we sat in the sun on a bench for half an hour waiting while he went on cooking. Then he appeared with the key, and explained that he had it all the time, but wanted to finish his cooking! I thought monks were not supposed to tell lies.

The *bodega* was charming with large earthenware jars all round. Our monk fooled around for ages unable to find anything with which to get the wine out until his companion arrived. A sweet little fat, round, red-faced man in a blue smock. He got down to it speedily, inserting a rubber tube in the top of the jar and sucking until the wine ran out. When it was all finished, our cheery little monk, after more energetic sucking and spitting, produced some white wine for us to refresh ourselves. He was awfully funny explaining to us how he did not hold with the sort of people who spent all day praying that their life would go well; he personally prayed first thing in the morning, and then went out and chased people around, and got things done. He was so funny explaining that we laughed ourselves silly.

Thursday, 20 April. Today was the birthday of the Infanta, Alvaro and Adolf Hitler. (The latter does not interest me in the least.)

At 8.30 we three went to a cocktail party given by Chicote for Frentes y Hospitales.[4] We stayed for about an hour and a half. It was full of officers and women from the canteens, with a band and also some Galician music. Both bands played continuously at the same time in the same room. One an ordinary tearoom band, the other the Gallegos curiosity of drums, cymbals and the strange Gallegos bagpipes. The noise was colossal. Pilar Franco (the Generalissimo's sister) was hostess. Her daughter, who is teeny, pretty, fat and cheerful, looks sixteen and is married with a child who was born in a Red prison. She has had a dreadful time all through the war in prisons and was a long time in a cell with Paz Goma. Yet she looks the silliest, most uninteresting girl, who has never done anything but amuse herself. Paz and Goma were there, she terribly smart, which filled my uniform-laden soul with envy. Oh, for smart clothes and never to see a uniform again!

Friday, 21 April. After lunch Consuelo went to see her family, and then at four she and I went once more to one of the hospitals to see the director about various details. He then said he was the President of the Institute of Cancer and that, apart for their cancer, his forty patients were dying of starvation. So we told the Infanta, and we all went off to the store house to ask if they could send round some food. So now we have yet another hospital on our hands. As if there weren't enough already.

Saturday, 22 April. We went to the cancer hospital, where we promised food and were shown around. I loathe visiting military hospitals but this was far worse. The patients were of both sexes and too dreadful for words. All dying and pale green and half mad. It was quite dreadful and it gave me the creeps having to talk to them all. I hope I never have

4 Chicote was a smart bar proprietor.

to work in a cancer hospital, or I shall be quite ill. It made a dreadful impression on me, although as a hospital it was quite nice.

I went off to Leganes to buy some bananas and give cigarettes to the lunatics, then to Getafe [*on the outskirts of Madrid*] to find some nuns to whom we were to give food. However, they were the wrong ones and wanted food for small children. So we went to the Carmelites up on the Cerro de los Angeles, who have no food and no water, and delivered it to them. The Mother Superior showed us around. It is completely ruined, and the convent is a mass of ruins surrounded with trenches and barbed wire entanglements. They have found two teeny rooms, one is the chapel, the other a bedroom, with just room for their eight beds. As they are not allowed mattresses and can find no straw, they sleep on cork mats. We got home at six. Prince Ali was upstairs and the Infanta in Barajas. So we had tea and went off to a lovely film full of romance and hysterics. I had not seen one since Barcelona, so thoroughly enjoyed it.

Sunday, 23 April. I am quite weak from laughing. All evening the Infanta and I have been playing the fool imitating people we know. Our conversation became more and more ridiculous. The Infanta is really incredibly funny. I got so into my part after a few hours of it that, in explaining how sad it made me feel that my dear sister has gone on her honeymoon without her maid as chaperone, I really began to cry. We all laughed so much that we nearly died, and me with tears pouring down my nose.

As to the news of the day. Consuelo and I went to Barajas for 10 o'clock Mass. But when we got there we found it had been at 9.30 so had missed it. So we prepared all the things and opened up the canteen and ran it with just the two of us until 11.30, as there had been the usual muddle about cars and the others did not arrive.

We went home to make ourselves respectable. Then we all went to lunch at the Nuevo Club. It is an officers' mess run by the international part of Frentes y Hospitales. It was all very smart and the food was excellent. It was great fun and we all stayed talking for ages. This afternoon we went to visit a man with galloping consumption and took him powdered milk, sugar and Bovril. He was very ill and I think suffering more from anaemia and starvation than consumption, although he is undoubtedly consumptive. He was very surly when we first arrived, propped up in bed, as white as a sheet, very thin, with over-bright eyes and a stubbly beard. However, we cheered him up and promised to bring him a liver medicine and to get him into hospital where he would have more light and air and better treatment. I very much doubt if he can be saved, but one must try. Then we joined the Infanta and got home at about seven, since when we have been playing bridge and laughing. The Infanta has just remembered that it is strawberry time in Sanlucar and we are now madly jealous of Ataulfo eating them all and hope he gets a tickly, nasty rash from them.

Tuesday, 25 April. I have deluded myself into thinking today was going to be an idle day, so of course I have not stopped running around all day. Consuelo and I left at nine for Valdemoro in my car followed by a Red Cross ambulance. There I loaded the ambulance with 900 blankets and made a list of everything there while Consuelo went in search of yeast, but the alleged beer factory turned out to be a malt factory. On the way back we stopped at the municipal slaughter house with rows of fat bullocks hanging up. As always the floor was running in blood. I slipped up and nearly sat in it. When we had unloaded the blankets and got a receipt we went to see our poor consumptive patient to give him the liver. We found him very much worse and about half dead and delirious. I am afraid that despite all our efforts he will die in a week or two, as I think he has septicaemia too. We got home just in time for lunch. After lunch Consuelo and I set off to the beer factory to get yeast. They were very amiable there and filled a biscuit tin we had brought with about five litres. It is revolting stuff and it leaked out in the car leaving a large dollop on the floor looking very compromising. We took it to the Hospital Catolico and handed it over, pouring it into some jars. Then we went to visit another consumptive in a dreadful, sordid, dirty suburb. He was very wobbly and cried all the time we were there. We left him eggs, powdered milk, sugar and Bovril, and have promised to take him injections of calcium. We must try to get him to hospital too. Half Madrid is now consumptive and the doctors are willing to do anything to stop it spreading, so we should be able to manage it. Then to the beer factory where we got out tins filled with yeast and once more to the hospital to hand it over plus a list of the three factories for them to arrange to fetch alternately from each.

Wednesday, 26 April. Poor Consuelo had to get up at seven so as to go to the Hospital Catolico at eight to put injections, as the nurses there are such mutts they can't do it. She was back for breakfast at nine. We visited our consumptives. The bad one is a bit better and the other still weeping. We gave them the medicines they had asked for. Then after searching the whole town, finally found the head office for the anti-tuberculosis, there we saw the doctor re getting our protégées to a hospital. It is no easy matter as out of one million inhabitants of Madrid, 70,000 have consumption and the hospitals are destroyed. It is awful, as they are infecting everyone else. For instance, our bad one has his wife sleeping in the same bed and eating off the same plate, which is a crime. Personally I am terrified even to have to move him in bed.

Thursday, 27 April. Prince Ali and Escariot, as always, left at 9.15. At 11.30 we two [*Consuelo and Pip*] went to the Hospital Catolico, where we were given a list of urgent people to visit. Our first call was out in Vallecas which is the worst *barrio* [*district*] of all as it does not belong to Madrid and has always been quite neglected, and consequently a refuge for all the bad people. We took a long time to find the house as the streets all just meander aimlessly about the countryside. However, at last we arrived. The door was opened by an energetic, ugly, little woman, rather smart for her surroundings. She told us she was the sister of the ill woman and had only just arrived from Cuenca and was horrified at what she had found. And well she might be. We found a married couple of fifty-six and sixty years old in bed, black with dirt and just like skeletons. Their hands and legs were covered with ulcers and blisters, pouring blood, pus and water, tied up in dirty rags. For two months they have lived on orange peel and a few onions they found fermenting in a manure heap. The woman was just able to struggle out of bed to fetch this and water, but unable to cook or get any other food. They were so pathetically pleased to see us and so incredibly brave. We looked at the man's legs to see his ulcers and found just two bones, literally a bone covered with dead, white, shrivelled skin. Even his thigh was so thin I could have encircled it with my finger and thumb. After a great deal of discussion and bribery we managed to persuade the sister to stay a few days and look after them. To wash them, clean the house, change the sheets and cook food. We left them what we had which

[226]

was beans, chick peas, rice, biscuits and cubes to make soup and promised to return tomorrow to dress their hands and legs and buy eggs and milk, and to arrange to get them to a hospital. It is dreadful that people can be allowed to get like that in a so-called civilized country.

Directly after lunch we set off and visited more. A woman in Vallecas in bed very ill with all her legs and arms swollen and full of huge blisters. In a filthy little two-room flat with her mother, husband and four children, all covered in abscesses. She was very bad and must also go to the hospital. The next was a woman with ten children and God knows how many relatives, consumptive and with a bad heart. She also should be got away, and we will have to fix her papers. Then a man who was also terribly pale and thin with his legs full of ulcers, but much more cheerful than the others and obviously with much more resistance. Then an 82-year-old, too weak to move or speak. Hardly worth sending to hospital as she must die in a few days, and the family would rather look after her if we can provide the food.

Then a priest who has gone mad with persecution mania. He lives in fear of anything happening to his sister and brother with whom he lives, and chants to himself without ceasing all day long. Madly nervous and hardly able to speak, singing and stamping and shivering and grinding his teeth. We will have to see if we can find him a loony bin or get his bishop to deal with him. Then to Quatro Caminos [*a garrison town near Madrid*] to an old lady simply weak and a skeleton, with no food and no money to buy any. Then an old schoolmistress the same and stone deaf. To each of the people we gave milk, sugar and eggs and promised to do what we could. Every one of them was in a dreadful state and in horribly sordid little houses, but none so awful as the couple this morning.

Friday, 28 April. Dead tired. I got up at seven and Consuelo very ill, unable to speak, scarlet and panting, coughing and being sick. I could do very little for her as I had no time, but got her some hot coffee and left her with water, aspirin, and all the rest of the paraphernalia. I swallowed a hasty breakfast and at eight set off in a large aviation lorry for Valdemoro. They had sent me two lorries but no men apart from the two chauffeurs and the servant, so loading them took a long time. I watched, counted and arranged what was left, carrying on an argument with the sergeant all the time as to whether there was room for them or not. I finally won by getting them all in. I went out to Vallecas to my old couple. The sister was there to let me in and I found them a bit cleaner and more cheerful. The resistance spirit of the Spaniards is unbelievable. They had eaten a huge plate of baked beans without getting indigestion, and were in high spirits, joking with each other. They were delighted at the news that in a few days an ambulance would come and take them to a smart new hospital. I bought them a dozen eggs, milk and sugar. I started to cure the woman's hands, intending to do her (and his) legs after. But the hands took so long I had to leave the rest till tomorrow. Her hands were a mess, raw, bleeding, with pus, dirty scabs, dead skin etc., so it took me ages to clean them up. Then to the Red Cross for a soothing oil, which I made up with vaseline into a grease for curing the couple tomorrow. I got home at seven exhausted, and talked to Consuelo and relaxed till 9.15, when the Infanta and Prince Ali turned up for dinner. Thank God, tomorrow I need not get up early.

Saturday, 29 April. I went out as usual this morning at twelve after preparing my things and packing my First Aid case and making compresses. I went to visit the two Callecas cases who are both to go to Hospital Catolico tomorrow. The old couple were rather depressed today, but I was delighted to find incredible improvement in the woman's hands, which I have been curing. My pomade, which I had such fun mixing yesterday, was a great success. But I am glad to have them off my hands now.

Sunday, 30 April. I got up in frantic haste and roared off to the hospital. There were only four injections to put, all intravenous, two men who were easy and two women who were devilish. The first had a weak vein, which bled all the time, but I made it first shot; the other had a vein as fine as a hair that wobbled all over her arm and was almost impossible even with my finest needle.

Monday, 1 May. I went to the hospital this morning, getting up at seven. There were about ten intravenous injections to put, some very difficult, but it was one of my good days and I did them all first shot.

I stayed till twelve waiting for my car to come back from Barajas, and helping Consuelo to open and list some of the packing cases of medicines downstairs. At twelve I went off and visited a new person they had asked me to report on at the hospital. She was in a very bad state, a woman of forty-eight looking about seventy, a skeleton with scabs all over her hands and face and the pus running into her eyes, so that she could not open them. Then I went to the old lady of eighty-two where I was told they are being turned out of the house as there is no longer any room, and the Hospital Catolico won't have her. So I said I would do what I could. Then at 1 o'clock I went back to the hospital, where again I met the Infanta with a list of twenty new people to visit, which nearly killed me from the shock. I gave my report saying the woman was definitely in a state to go to hospital. I also found out from one of the nuns the address of a poor-house for the old. So I when went again at four I was able to give the address to the daughter of the old woman. I had also brought food and a job for the other daughter, clearing the Infanta's house in Quintana, so they cheered up. I also visited the consumptive, who seems a little better, another consumptive, a woman who had gone out, an address that did not exist because it was shelled, a typical case of starvation but not bad enough for hospital, and a woman whose tummy has swollen so in the last two weeks that she can hardly move, though it is painless. Now I have a list of thirty-seven visits, which it is not humanly possible to deal with properly. One just has to neglect anyone who is halfway all right, which is heart-rending. There are occasions when I wish I had never come to Spain, and yet it is wonderfully satisfactory work even if one can do so little for the people.

Wednesday, 3 May. Consuelo still voiceless, went to the hospital at eight. I went out at 9.30 with my new companion for visits, Dr Romero. He is small, competent and pleasant to work with. We visited the doubtful cases from 9.30 to 12.30 and from 3 to 6.30. We did twenty visits, of whom two were already dead, two to be sent to the hospital and the rest all assorted, bronchitis, heart, rheumatism, mild avitaminosis, cancer of the stomach, etc. We got on splendidly together. He asks the questions and I am secretary and stand behind with a paper writing it all down. After dinner I copied it all on to the typewriter for our report to the hospital. God, visiting is tiring and depressing and it never ends.

Thursday, 4 May. I am feeling ill, tired and motionless all day and am longing for the moment I can get into bed. I went to pick up the Doctor Romero at 9.30 and to the hospital to give in my report on yesterday's visits. There Consuelo sent my car to fetch yeast, as they had run out as usual. So we sat about without doing anything till it came back at 11.30.

We managed to do six visits before lunch, two were not at home, as they had gone to the hospital, one was dead, one was uninteresting, one was in great pain and probably for the hospital, and the last was dreadful, sixty-eight, quite blind, living entirely alone in a filthy little hovel and covered in sores and dirt. She cooks for herself whatever she can find, despite being blind, and is half dead. After lunch I meant to go out on my own to take food to the ones we have seen who most need it, but I was feeling dreadful and Princess Bee and Consuelo persuaded me to stay in, so we played cards and I typewrote lists, and so on, till bed.

Friday, 5 May. Prince Ali turned up foaming as Kindelán has changed all the plans about the march past and he and the Infanta foamed about canteens, dinners, lunches, bars, drinks, etc. till dinner, without a pause. Oh God, I wish we could all go away. I hate all this so. I was looking dreadful today, my hair lank and dirty, no make-up and a dirty uniform. But I am almost too fed up with life to care. Anyhow, what does it matter? I don't want to see any more horrors. I want to be left in peace with no more work and no more emotions. But I don't think I can see any chance of ever getting rid of either.

Saturday, 6 May. I have had a cracking headache all day and felt very ill most of the time with, I imagine, a temperature, although I did not take it to see. I still feel bad but far less so than earlier on.

At ten I went off on 'visits' with Romero, leaving the Infanta and Ataulfo playing cards. We made eight visits, one of which we could not find, one was out, two were for the hospital and one was an ex-girl friend of Romero's, who is a nurse, and he had not seen for a long time as she had been pursued by the Reds and disappeared. She was terribly ill with anaemia and tuberculosis. He was so overcome that he was quite vague for the rest of the morning. I got home at 12.45 and found the house empty, so had to type out my report. Ataulfo brought two aviators to lunch. Afterwards everyone gradually went off to work. I felt so damn ill I just could not face it as

I felt I would faint at one of the visits. I do hope I am not getting ill again and will feel OK tomorrow again, as this is no time to be ill.

Saturday, 13 May. Since Saturday I have been ill with what must be an attack of 'flu.

Wednesday I was allowed to get up indoors and sit about, also on Thursday but was dreadfully weak and palpitated and felt sick every time I walked from one room to another or ate anything. As it was the day before the march past of aviation it was all a muddle. Everyone dashing in and out almost crying with exhaustion. I did not think I would be well enough to go and Ataulfo said he was not going either and would keep me company. But then the Infanta said she wanted him to go and if I did not he would have an excuse not to, so I heaved a sigh and decided there was nothing in the world I wanted to do more than go. So it was decided that should I be 'wobbly' I should be given an injection and that was that. In the end we all got to be about 2 o'clock after frantic last arrangements. Next morning [*Friday*] the Infanta and Consuelo left at 5.45 for Barajas to serve breakfast to the soldiers. Prince Ali went at 7.30.

I felt tired and ill and went off covered in wings, crosses, arrows, medals, etc.[5] It was a lovely sunny day and Barajas looked splendid with decorations of flags and flowers. Everything newly painted and smart. Franco's guard of Moors in scarlet and white cloaks and white turbans and blue and white uniforms were already stationed on guard in their positions around the stand where he was to take the salute. They stood there in the broiling sun from 9 o'clock till 3 o'clock, without ever moving a muscle.

The place was already full of people when I got there and I stood about watching the people arrive amongst swarms of white-uniformed Frentes y Hospitales women and blue-uniformed Falange females looking like a super school treat. Franco arrived at 11.30 as per schedule and we all saluted while they played the Marcha Real until our arms nearly dropped off. He drove round inspecting the machines which were lined up about six deep in front of the buildings, for as far as one could see. Hundreds of them. Then we took up our positions for serving drinks, Consuelo and I went with the other Barajas regulars to the first-floor balcony to where we were to serve Franco and the generals. He made a speech and then we handed round drinks while

5 Pip had been awarded the Cruz del Merito Militar con Distintivo Rojo.

they all talked until the march past began. Franco is a weeny little man, the size and shape of a tennis ball and looked too funny beside huge lanky Kindelán and even taller, lankier Quiepo de Llano.[6] The place fairly reeked with generals and medals. The march past, which we saw beautifully, was the same as they usually are. The Germans' goose-step made us laugh, the Italians were very few and the Spanish held their own well. Prince Ali marched at the head of his men looking splendid. When it was over at 3 o'clock we went to the canteen and found everyone had broken in and served everything to everyone who had no right to it. So we threw them all out and served water and orangeade and made sandwiches to be sent to the men on duty. Everyone was dying of hunger and thirst and we were there until 7.30. The men were all tight and made rows and shouted until it got so bad we had to shut down and refuse to serve even water. We barricaded ourselves in and they all beat on the doors and bellowed and poked their faces in at the windows begging for water. It was pretty grim and rather funny. We got home at 8 o'clock.

Today when I got up at 8.30 there was no one about, but later the Infanta and Prince Ali turned up for breakfast. I discovered Ataulfo had already gone off to Barajas in my car to find a plane either to Leon or Sevilla. We sat round all day feeling very good-tempered and idle now that the Barajas show is over.

Prince Ali says that Ataulfo is also going to Germany on the 25th. I am glad for him as he wants to really, I think. Now there will only be Princess Bee and I in Sanlucar, which can hardly be considered a binge. Oh dear, I did so want just one binge in Sanlucar and a few days' bathing before saying goodbye to Spain.

Prince Ali gave us some invitations for the aviation cocktail party at the Ritz this evening, so we dressed up as normal people, the first time out of uniform for about three months, picked up three of the Barajas girls and went. It was a huge party with about 1,000 people; two bands, one indoors and the other out in the garden, where there was also a dance floor. I danced once with Goma and spent the rest of the time glumly sitting on a chair watching the others dance.

Monday, 15 May. Escariot took Consuelo and me out to dinner and a variety after, which was quite amusing. I met Peter Kemp

6 Quiepo de Llano was the 'radio general' renowned for his attacks on 'Reds'. He had taken Sevilla for the Nationalists and Andalusia became his private fief.

and have arranged to dine and celebrate with him the day after tomorrow.

Wednesday, 17 May. Today was spirited and full of fun. I breakfasted at eight and went off with Prince Ali to Barajas. He took me up flying in a Savoia 79, as second pilot. It was grand to be up in the air again. We were leading a formation of twenty-five machines, although I could only see the one on my right. Prince Ali let me take over and fly her for about ten minutes, and I was quite surprised to find that after four years without flying I felt quite at home with the controls and despite being a heavy bomber she was as easy to fly and as light as our little old Moth.[7]

Ultano Kindelán with whom I chatted for some time has promised to take me up in his little Miles Hawk tomorrow morning, which has dual control, so I really will be able to fly it. It is heaven to fly again, I love the feeling so. I was up for about three quarters of an hour, ambling about the countryside. Then I washed and tidied and changed out of uniform and went off to the Ritz to meet Peter Kemp. I found him there talking to an Englishman and a Spaniard. The Englishman was oldish, grey-haired, Major Pollard, a spirited man who used to be in the Secret Service. He produced the aeroplane for Franco to fly from the Canaries to Spain to start the revolution.[8] He also dealt with Porfirio Diaz in Mexico and various other revolutions, knows all about efficient tortures, and would use them without a qualm, etc. He accompanied Peter and me to dinner.

Monday, 22 May. They told us that some of the newspapers run by Serrano Suner had said that Franco was to be made king and start a new royal family.[9] How can people be so fantastic, arranging all the titles for his family and the generals. Serrano Suner is probably going to Germany as ambassador, and there is to be a new military government. It is all quite mad and gets worse and worse daily.

7 Pip had qualified as a pilot in England when she was eighteen. Her mother had a pilot's licence and owned a Gypsy Moth.
8 When the Moroccan Garrison rose against the Republic, General Franco was stationed in the Canary Islands. To get him to Morocco, a Monarchist newspaper owner arranged for his London correspondent to hire a Dragon Rapide. Pollard was involved in the whole operation and Franco arrived in Morocco on 19 July.
9 Serrano Suner was Franco's brother-in-law and a prominent Falangist. He was to become Minister of the Interior and Foreign Minister. He was sacked by Franco in 1942.

Friday, 26 May. On Wednesday Consuelo and I went in the after-noon to serve refreshments at a bullfight in the new Plaza. I don't know why Frentes y Hospitales did it, but as we were told we went. We picked up Marie Louise of the Hospital Catolico and all the girls of Barajas. The crush to get in was terrifying. Once we got well into the crowd around the door we were wedged firmly and unable to move. The crowd pushed and we went with them, squashed flat and almost unable to breathe. It was perfectly terrifying, as the impetus of the crowd just swept one on. We swept straight over the guard in the door and carried him with us. Some luckless people were carried up against the wall and were fighting like maniacs, crushed flat and screaming. I thought for one awful moment that I should be pushed there, but luckily I was swept through the door. Shooting through the door was just like being a cork coming out of a champagne bottle. The chaos inside was just as bad as outside, so we never did succeed in getting the refreshments to sell and finally sat on everyone's feet and watched the bullfight. For the first time I enjoyed it. It was definitely good. Ortega, Barera and Buenavida all did beautiful things and the bulls were incredibly strong and tossed the picadors and horses all complete right into the air and trampled on them. The Plaza was packed and must hold some five or six thousand. It was very well arranged with flags and hangings and the Spanish Standard in coloured sands in the ring. We got home exhausted and burnt by the sun at seven. At nine I had to meet Peter at Bacanic. He thought I was going to meet him in the Ritz so arrived an hour late, but I did not mind as I was talking to Frederico Escariot, whom I met there. We drank, we dined and we drove about looking for somewhere to go, till we gave up hope, as no nightclubs were yet open in Madrid.

All yesterday I spent indoors too lazy even to get dressed. Today I spent peacefully tidying up the house, reading, writing and playing the piano. I went to Bacanic at eight to have a drink with Peter. His friend Guido was there too, rather tight and very depressed. Peter says the international news today is very bad and it looks like war. How original of it!

Saturday, 27 May. We started off with the Santa Marias looking for Princess Bee's china. We were taken to the house where it was sup-posed to be and of course found there was nothing there but furni-ture. The cellars and first floor stacked to the ceiling with every kind of furniture piled up any old how. Half the big houses in Madrid are like that nowadays, and the other half are empty. In the hospital I saw all my ex-patients whom I have not seen for nearly a month. The change in them is amazing. My favourite old couple are doing splendidly. He is up in a chair and she, though still in bed, a new woman. She was so overwhelmed with emotion to see me again that she clasped my hand and kissed it all over and told me I must give her my address so that when I went back to England she could write to me. She said her only ambition was to be well enough to get up and cook a large tart for the Infanta and another for me. Too sweet. They really are a couple to encourage one to go on with one's work, despite the lack of enthusiasm of others. Now that Frentes y Hospitales has been dissolved all of a sudden by rude decree and with no warning, there is a lot to do handing everything over and keeping things going, because after all Frentes y Hospitales had some 40,000 girls working in it for one thing and another. And from one moment to another it no longer exists.

Sunday, 28 May. I just managed to be ready at 8.45 for the Mass given for poor Bourdet who killed himself flying three days ago. The church was crammed with people, small, over-decorated, hot, stuffy and smelly. To go up to Communion the people just fought through the crowd as if it were a bullfight, and I was thoroughly relieved when we left. We went home to breakfast and to change out of black into uniform and off to Barajas at eleven. It was the last day of the canteen, so everything was given free to finish up all the stores. It was colossal work as the people poured in, and we served without pause. I had lots of fun manipulating the beer machine which used to be one of my childish ambitions which I certainly never expected to realize. After lunch the Infanta and I went back to Barajas and served all afternoon till we closed down at six with the place cleaned out and the men so full that they could take no more even though it was free. It was certainly a good and worthy ending to the canteen. The Spanish common soldiers are wonderful the way they can drink themselves stupid and still never be rude or coarse or disagreeable. I calculate that we served about 600 litres of beer today and quantities of milk, coffee, orangeade and food.

Tuesday, 30 May. When I got up this morning I was handed a

telegram from Consuelo to say she had booked our passage on a boat sailing on the 5th as there is no other till the 12th, so I had to decide to leave the day after tomorrow for Sanlucar. At about eleven I turned up at Barajas and found Ultano in a shirt and shorts awaiting me. It took some time fiddling with the engine to make the plane function. She looked so tiny and insecure beside the huge Savoias, a sweet little Miles Hawk [*low-wing monoplane with Gypsy Moth engine*] called Dona Sol and painted bright green. We flew for about half an hour. I did all the flying except taking off and landing, and did it pretty badly. I have quite lost the feel though I more or less remember what to do. Anyhow, it was lovely to pilot again and Ultano is going to take me up again tomorrow. I was lent a jacket, helmet and goggles, while Ultano just had a beret and dark glasses. My skirts thoroughly misbehaved. I had to put on a parachute with straps between the legs. Afterwards I sat in the officers' bar and chatted. This afternoon I went shopping and did various odd jobs.

Wednesday, 31 May. My last day in Madrid. I spent the day shopping, going to the hairdresser and having a bath. I set off with Princess Bee and Rosario for the Ritz at 9.15, dressed up to the best of my ability, properly made up for once and with my hair piled on top of my head in a halo of curls. I meant to finish my stay here well. We dined, twenty of us, in a private room. I enjoyed myself a lot. The girls were presented with their bags as presents from Princess Bee, and it lasted till after twelve. Then Princess Bee left and we all drifted out into the lounge and sat about in groups, talking. I saw lots of people I knew. When all the others began to leave I collected Guido and Peter as we had decided to go on a binge, Guido led us to a splendid night club, a bar with lots of private rooms. We took one of the rooms for us three and were brought drinks. It was just an ugly little room with tiled and papered walls, which did not quite reach the ceiling, furnished with one table, four hard chairs and a sideboard. Guido sent for some music and after a bit two men came and spent the evening singing Andalusian songs with a guitar, while we talked and listened to the music, drank and ate cheese and bits of ham. It was great fun as our musicians were quite good, and then all the people in the other rooms would join in the songs, or we in theirs.

So I ended my stay with a typical Spanish evening.

Index